D0418243

The Po
Moder

29 OCT 1998   15 J N 2001

The Policy Process in the Modern State

Third Edition

Michael Hill

PRENTICE HALL
HARVESTER WHEATSHEAF

LONDON NEW YORK TORONTO SYDNEY TOKYO SINGAPORE
MADRID MEXICO CITY MUNICH PARIS

First published 1984
This third edition published 1997 by
Prentice Hall/Harvester Wheatsheaf
Campus 400, Maylands Avenue
Hemel Hempstead
Hertfordshire, HP2 7EZ
A division of
Simon & Schuster International Group

Typeset in 10/12pt Times
by Hands Fotoset, Ratby, Leicester

Printed and bound in Great Britain by
MPG Books Ltd, Bodmin, Cornwall

Library of Congress Cataloging-in-Publication Data

Hill, Michael J. (Michael James), 1937–
    The policy process in the modern state / Michael Hill. – 3rd ed.
        p.   cm.
    Rev. ed. of: The policy process in the modern capitalist state /
Christopher Ham, Michael Hill. 2nd ed. c1993.
    Includes bibliographical references and index.
    ISBN 0-13-269226-0
    1. Policy sciences.   2. Bureaucracy.   I. Ham, Christopher.
Policy process in the modern capitalist state.   II. Title.
H97.H35   1997
320'.6–dc21   96-51506
                                                              CIP

British Library Cataloguing in Publication Data

A catalogue record for this book is available from
the British Library

ISBN 0-13-269226-0 (pbk)

2 3 4 5   01 00 99 98

CONTENTS

PREFACE

This preface must start with an acknowledgement that is much more important than all the others, to Chris Ham who was the co-author of this book's predecessor, *The Policy Process in the Modern Capitalist State*. While this book is more than an update of that book – it has been substantially restructured – it carries forward the approach to the examination of the policy process that Chris and I developed together and uses material from the original.

The basic shape of the book is modelled on the earlier work. After an introduction that explores where this work can be placed in relation to other policy analysis literature, it is divided into chapters on the macro 'theories of the state' that need to be taken into account, followed by consideration of the 'policy process' and then chapters on aspects of 'implementation'. These are not explicitly identified as separate sections, because there are even stronger warnings than before about the dangers of treating the necessary division, for presentational purposes, between policy making and implementation as representing a real distinction in the policy process. Hopefully the disadvantage of shifting from two authors to one, that one person needs to try to keep up with all developments in the field, is counterbalanced by the advantage that there is a more integrated view of the policy process as a whole. The new final chapter is little more than a set of concluding observations; it does not attempt, as its predecessor did, to develop an integrated theoretical approach. The view that alternative theories need to be used as different lenses through which to view a complex and often obscure reality – which Chris used to great effect in his teaching at Bristol (and still does in his health policy text) – seems to me to make any attempt to pull everything together at the end rather inappropriate.

My original collaboration with Chris occurred when we developed a teaching programme on the policy process for the master's course in public policy studies at the School for Advanced Urban Studies at Bristol University in 1979. The original book was published in 1984. In 1993, after I had moved to the University of Newcastle and used the book as the main text for an undergraduate course on policy making and implementation, a revised version was published. Bill Jenkins, reviewing that edition, expressed disappointment at the limited scope of the revisions undertaken at that stage. This very different book, produced only a comparatively short time after that second edition, is a recognition of the justice of that comment.

The author's first major venture into this field was his *Sociology of Public Administration*, published in 1972. Chris Ham and I decided to speak of the 'policy process' rather than of 'public administration' because we rejected the artificial distinction between politics and administration that had dominated much early work on our subject. By the time *The Policy Process in the Modern Capitalist State* was published, there was already a tendency for the expression 'public administration' to be dropped in favour of 'public management'. That development has intensified, particularly in the English-speaking nations. While there are grounds for arguing that this is a change in vocabulary as much as a change in substance, there is no question that market ideas and market models are having an increasing impact on the public policy process. This development is reflected in many ways in this new book.

The fact that the difference between the title of this book and that of the old one consists of the lack of the word 'capitalist' needs no justifying comment. Capitalist economic enterprise has a pervasive impact on the policy process in all modern states. However, an important emergent theme in the analysis of the policy process is that the relationship between state, economy and society takes significantly different forms in different countries. This is explored a little, particularly in Chapters 4 and 5.

Over the years since I started writing about the policy processes, my debts to colleagues and students, both in the institutions in which I have worked and in many other places at home and abroad, have cumulated to the extent that I cannot acknowledge them all. I will confine myself to some of those who have been particularly helpful in the recent past. Wendy Ranade and Bob Hudson have made a particularly important contribution, commenting on draft chapters. In the department at Newcastle I am grateful that colleagues continue to tolerate my book writing at a time when academics are required to turn their hands to

101 tasks. I have found it very helpful to exchange ideas with a new colleague there, John Vail. Continued collaboration with Pieter Degeling from Australia and Peter Hupe from the Netherlands remains important for my thinking on many issues. During the time I have been working on the manuscript two brief academic visits have given me good opportunities to work on the book. Much of the early planning of the manuscript was done during a visit to the People's University in Beijing in 1995 and the final work on the text was completed on a visit to Aalborg University in Denmark in autumn 1996.

Finally, I remain indebted to the support provided by the editorial staff at Prentice Hall/Harvester Wheatsheaf, particularly Clare Grist and Christina Wipf.

CHAPTER 1

STUDYING THE POLICY PROCESS

Synopsis

This chapter starts by setting the book's concern with the study of the policy process in the context of the many approaches to policy analysis. Then the complexity of the meaning of 'policy' is examined. This is followed by exploration of the special features of public policy, related to the rationales offered for public involvement in private life. The study of the policy process is shown to be closely connected to efforts to examine the nature of power in society and to specify the necessary conditions for democratic government. The idea that the public policy process involves 'stages' is related to this concern; it is argued that, while this may lead to a misleadingly systematic approach to the subject, there are clearly advantages in separating different aspects of the process. The chapter ends with a brief comment on methods of studying the policy process, suggesting that it is necessarily often a qualitative and interpretive activity, and commending approaches which deliberately compare the perspectives offered by different theoretical 'lenses'.

Introduction

This book explores the efforts that have been made to understand and explain the public policy process. It is concerned with the way policy is made and implemented. It draws upon theories and case studies from political science and from political and organisational sociology.

The social scientific study of policy has a long history. Not surprisingly, people have sought to apply social science knowledge to problems of government and to influence the activities and decisions of government in a variety of ways. In the widest sense, individuals such as Keynes, the Webbs and even Karl Marx were involved in the study of policy. Even earlier Machiavelli's *The Prince*, published in 1532, may be seen as a contribution to this literature.

An early twentieth-century American president, Woodrow Wilson, had, when he was a professor of political science, made influential pronouncements about this field of activity (1887). From the 1950s onwards there was a rapid growth of activity, particularly in the United States. The political scientist Harold Lasswell made the case for 'the policy sciences' in a variety of publications (1951, 1968, 1970). The policy sciences claimed to offer a new approach to the problems of government. Master's programmes were set up in universities, think tanks were established to advise governments. These initiatives aimed to fuse the rather longer-standing use of economics in policy analysis with new ideas from political science, sociology and organisation theory.

In the 1980s the emphasis shifted in two, in many respects contradictory, directions. On the one hand, there were demands that policy analysis should be more rooted in techniques derived from classical economics and that public management should draw on ideas from private management On the other, there was increasing disillusion with attempts to develop a 'scientific' approach to policy design. There was increased recognition that policy processes are complex, influenced by a variety of external factors which are hard to control and in some respects haphazard. This book is very much in this second tradition.

Some policy analysts are interested in furthering understanding of policy (analysis *of* policy), some are interested in improving the quality of policy (analysis *for* policy), and some are interested in both activities (see Parsons (1995) for an overview of the many approaches). Further, cutting across this are concerns with *ends* and concerns with *means*, with of course in this case a large group of analysts who are concerned about both and not happy about separating them in this way. The typology proposed by Hogwood and Gunn (1981; see also 1984) which draws on an earlier analysis by Gordon *et al.* (1977), points to seven varieties of policy analysis, illustrated in Figure 1.1.

First, there are *studies of policy content*, in which analysts seek to

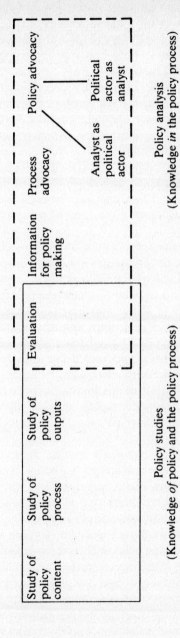

Figure 1.1 Types of study of public policy making (Source: Hogwood and Gunn, 1981)

describe and explain the genesis and development of particular policies. In the United Kingdom, much social policy analysis is of this kind. The analyst interested in policy content usually investigates one or more cases in order to trace how a policy emerged, how it was implemented and what the results were.

Second, there are *studies of the policy process*, in which attention is focused on the stages through which issues pass, and attempts are made to assess the influence of different factors on the development of the issue. Studies of the policy process invariably show some concern with policy content, but in the main they are interested in uncovering the various influences on policy formulation. Studies of the policy process are often concerned with single issues of this kind or with specific policy areas, but they may also focus on the policy process within an organisation or on the influences on policy within a particular community or society.

Third, there are *studies of policy outputs*, which seek to explain why levels of expenditure or service provision vary between countries or local governments. In Dye's terminology, these are studies of policy determination (1976, p. 5), studies which take policies as dependent variables and attempt to understand these policies in terms of social, economic, technological and other factors. Output studies have received much attention in the United States, not least in Dye's own work, but they have been undertaken increasingly in the United Kingdom and other western European countries. A particularly complex area of application of this approach is to be found in the vast literature which attempts to explain national differences in the development of social welfare policies (for a succinct review of this, see Baldwin, 1990, ch. 1).

The fourth category, *evaluation studies*, marks the borderline between analysis *of* policy and analysis *for* policy. Evaluation studies are also sometimes referred to as impact studies as they are concerned to analyse the impact that policies have on the population. Evaluation studies may be either descriptive or prescriptive.

Fifth, there is *information for policy making*, in which data are marshalled in order to assist policy-makers reach decisions. Information for policy may derive from reviews carried out within government as part of a regular monitoring process; or it may be provided by academic policy analysts concerned to apply their knowledge to practical problems.

Sixth, there is *process advocacy*, a variant of analysis for policy in which analysts seek to improve the nature of policy-making systems. Process advocacy is manifested in attempts to improve the machinery of government through the reallocation of functions and tasks, and in efforts to enhance the basis for policy choice through the development of planning systems and new approaches to option appraisal.

Finally, there is *policy advocacy*, the activity which involves the analyst in pressing specific options and ideas in the policy process, either individually or in association with others, perhaps through a pressure group.

This book's concern is with the second of these varieties of policy analysis, though it will from time to time be concerned to explore how this relates to some of the others. The concern to examine how the policy process works was in many respects a minor concern in the period between 1950 and 1980, when policy studies, in their own right, mushroomed so dramatically. If the right policies could be found, and their design difficulties solved, progress would be made with the solution of society's problems. Only a minority – radical analysts on the 'left' who doubted that modern governments really had the will to solve problems, and radical analysts on the 'right' who were sceptical about their capacity to do so – raised doubts and suggested that more attention should be given to the determinants of policy decisions. Clearly the leading figures in the development of policy analysis moved between prescription and description, endeavouring to ground solutions in political and organisational realism. But prescription was dominant in policy studies.

This book's predecessor was, when first published in 1984, a comparatively rare assertion that it was appropriate to concentrate on description, to explore the nature of the policy process to help to ensure that proposals about policy content or about how to change policy should be grounded in the real world in which policy is made. Now that is a much less exceptional stance to take towards the study of policy. Rather, now, the problem may be that a pessimistic realism is so dominant that it is hard to make a case for policy change and for the development of more sophisticated approaches to policy making and implementation. This author's stance is to assert that we must continue to try to understand the policy process – however irrational or uncontrollable it may seem to be – as a crucial first step towards trying to bring it under control.

In examining the policy process – seeing it as a separate but necessary contribution to practical policy analysis and action – we are in the business of trying to develop a knowledge base for the latter. We can perhaps be said to be engaged in trying to create a discipline with a relationship to the wider notions of policy analysis like that between physics and engineering. The problem is that we do this in a pre-Newtonian world in which much knowledge is no more than the compilation of experience on what works and what does not work (drawn up by practical people or those who try to advise them). The earlier aspiration to establish 'policy sciences' was based upon a belief in the capacity of the social sciences to establish a secure body of knowledge – a set of laws of society, perhaps – which few believe in today. Indeed, Kuhn (1962) has even taught us to view the apparently secure status of knowledge in the physical sciences with some scepticism. In the social and political sciences, we recognise how complexity, change and the consciousness of the actors we are studying limit our scope for the establishment of generalisation. We recognise how, particularly in a field like the study of policy, we cannot use experimental methods and we must often use qualitative techniques to study phenomena. Hence, while the study of the policy process is claimed to be the 'purer' discipline upon which the more active contributions to policy analysis need to be based, there is a need not to overwork that distinction. People describe because they want to prescribe. Conversely, people who dedicate themselves directly to prescription will always want to root what they have to say in a realistic appreciation of what 'is', whether derived from academic studies or from their own practical experience.

Meaning of 'policy'

The *Oxford English Dictionary* describes the following as 'the chief living sense' of the word 'policy': 'A course of action adopted and pursued by a government, party, ruler, statesman etc.; any course of action adopted as advantageous or expedient.' We will come back to the 'public' element in this definition. But first it is important to dwell a little on the notion that policy entails something more than simply a decision – that it is a course of action.

That obviously does not get us very far towards identifying a policy. Perhaps we can do no more than adopt the very British pragmatism of Cunningham, a former top British civil servant, who argued that 'Policy is rather like the elephant – you recognise it when you see it but cannot easily define it' (1963, p. 229). A rather similarly vague approach is adopted by Friend and his colleagues, who say that 'policy is essentially a *stance* which, once articulated, contributes to the context within which a succession of future decisions will be made' (1974, p. 40).

However, others have sought to do better than that. Heclo's definition, like the dictionary one set out above, emphasises action: 'A policy may usefully be considered as a course of action or inaction rather than specific decisions or actions' (1972, p. 85). As a variant on this, David Easton notes that 'a policy . . . consists of a web of decisions and actions that allocate . . . values' (1953, p. 130). A further definition is offered by Jenkins, who sees policy as 'a set of interrelated decisions . . . concerning the selection of goals and the means of achieving them within a specified situation . . .' (1978, p. 15). Smith suggests that 'the concept of policy denotes . . . deliberate choice of action or inaction, rather than the effects of interrelating forces': he emphasises 'inaction' as well as action, and reminds us that 'attention should not focus exclusively on decisions which produce change, but must also be sensitive to those which resist change and are difficult to observe because they are not represented in the policy-making process by legislative enactment' (Smith, 1976, p. 13).

The definitional problems posed by the concept of policy suggest that it is difficult to treat it as a very specific and concrete phenomenon. Policy may sometimes be identifiable in terms of a decision, but very often it involves either groups of decisions or what may be seen as little more than an orientation. The attempts at definition also imply that it is hard to identify particular occasions when policy is made. Policy will often continue to evolve within what is conventionally described as the implementation phase rather than the policy-making phase of the policy process.

Let us look a little more at the implications of the fact that policy involves a course of action or a web of decisions rather than one decision. There are several aspects to this. First, a decision network, often of considerable complexity, may be involved in producing action, and a web of decisions taking place over a long period of time and extending far beyond the initial policy-making process may form part of the network.

A second aspect is that, even at the policy-making level, policy is not usually expressed in a single decision. It tends to be defined in terms of a series of decisions which, taken together, comprise a more or less common understanding of what policy is.

Third, policies invariably change over time. Yesterday's statements of intent may not be the same as today's, either because of incremental adjustments to earlier decisions, or because of major changes of direction. Also, experience of implementing a decision may feed back into the decision-making process. This is not to say that policies are always changing, but simply that the policy process is dynamic rather than static and that we need to be aware of shifting definitions of issues.

Fourth, a development of this point is that much policy decision making is concerned, as Hogwood and Gunn (1984) have stressed, with attempting the difficult task of 'policy termination' or determining 'policy succession' (see also Hogwood and Peters, 1983).

Fifth, the corollary of the last two points is the need to recognise that the study of policy has as one of its main concerns the examination of non-decisions. This is what Heclo and Smith are pointing to in their references to inaction. It has been argued that much political activity is concerned with maintaining the status quo and resisting challenges to the existing allocation of values. Analysis of this activity is a necessary part of the examination of the dynamics of the policy process.

Finally, the definitions cited above raise the question of whether policy can be seen as action without decisions. Can it be said that a pattern of actions over a period of time constitutes a policy, even if these actions have not been formally sanctioned by a decision? In this sense, policy may be seen principally as an outcome, which actors may or may not want to claim as a consequence of purposive activity. Writers on policy have increasingly turned their attention to the action of lower-level actors, sometimes called 'street-level bureaucrats' (Lipsky, 1980), in order to gain a better understanding of policy making and imple-mentation. In some circumstances it is suggested that it is at this level in the system that policy is actually made. It would seem to be important to balance a decisional top-down perspective on policy with an action-oriented bottom-up perspective. Actions as well as decisions may therefore be said to be the proper focus of policy analysis. The influence of street-level bureaucrats on policy is explored later in the book.

The view that policies may simply be outcomes of political and bureaucratic processes, as opposed to courses 'of action adopted and pursued', leads on to two important themes for the study of the policy process: (a) the relationship between policy and politics; and (b) the dominance, in much that is said and written about policy, of a view that political action is (or should be) purposive.

A deeper exploration of the *Oxford English Dictionary* reveals that the word 'policy' has an interesting history in English. Among usages of policy which are now obsolete are the notions of policy as a 'prudent, expedient or advantageous procedure' and as a 'device, expedient, contrivance . . . stratagem, trick'. Parsons points out that Shakespeare used policy in various ways:

> Policy encompassed the arts of political illusion and duplicity. Show, outward appearance and illusions were the stuff of which power was made. Shakespeare employed the terms of Machiavellian philosophy . . . Power cannot be sustained purely with force. It needs, in a Machiavellian sense, *policy*: and 'policy sits above conscience', as the bard tells us in *Timon of Athens*. (Parsons, 1995, p. 14)

Some languages, including French and Italian, do not draw a distinction between policy and politics. The purpose of this brief excursion into linguistic history is to emphasise not merely that policy was seen as a simple and expedient, even duplicitous, ingredient in political strategy, but also that this may still be an appropriate way to think of it. We need to ask: what is being said when someone stresses that they have a policy? May they not simply be trying to convince us that they are acting effectively and purposefully? Edelman (1971, 1977, 1988) has devoted considerable attention to the 'symbolic' uses of policy. Further, even if they can convince us, we still need to ask: what are the implications of their policy? Phenomena like proclaimed 'equal opportunities policies' particularly need unpacking in this way.

There is, however, another possibility: that policy claims are rationalisations after the event, to try to convince us that chance events or events that actors did not really control were planned. Lewis (1995) quotes a ninth-century Baghdad wazir who put it like this: 'The basis of government is jugglery. If it works and lasts, it becomes policy.'

It is a particular feature of the modern discourse about policy that it is seen as desirable that politicians should have policies – so that electorates may make choices – and that governments should enact those policies in a systematic way. It was suggested above that the very rise of the study of policy was dominated by that perspective, and that many contributions to policy analysis are motivated by a desire to assist a rational policy-making process. Yet politicians do not necessarily see their roles in this way – power may be more important to them than policy, and power may be used to personal ends rather than to try to solve problems in the way presumed in discussions of policy analysis.

The point, then, about the dominance of a 'rational' model in much modern discourse about policy is that it involves an expectation that the policy process will be an organised and systematic one. Hence in introducing the study of the policy process there is a need to warn readers to be sceptical about writing which takes it for granted that a policy-making process is organised and has specific goals. It may be desirable that it should be like this, but whether it actually is or not must be an issue for research.

Public policy

The dictionary definition of policy quoted above referred to action 'by a government, party, ruler, statesman etc'. But it went on to a more all-encompassing usage which has developed out of this. Individuals sometimes talk of adopting 'policies' and organisations of all kinds regularly do so. This book is about 'public policy'. Is there anything intrinsically different about the definition arising from the fact that it is the state or state organisations which are seen as the owners of the policy? The answer to this is surely 'no' as far as the simple characteristics of policy are concerned, but 'yes' inasmuch as special claims are made about the legitimacy of state policy and its primacy over other policies. This takes us into two difficulties – one about the nature of the state, the other about the special justifications used for the role of the state as a provider of policies.

The basic definition of the state is as a set of institutions with superordinate power over a specific territory. It can be defined both in terms of the institutions which make it up and the functions that these institutions perform. State institutions comprise legislative bodies, including parliamentary assemblies and subordinate law-making institutions; executive bodies, including governmental bureaux and departments of state; and judicial bodies – principally courts of law – with responsibility for enforcing and, through their decisions, developing the law. State institutions are located at various levels – national, regional and local.

There are supra-state institutions which act, to some degree, as superordinate states – the European Union is perhaps the prime example. The very fact that this superordinate power is controversial and is to some degree challenged by the nation-states within the Union offers a nice reminder of the fact that many states have gone through (or are still going through, as in the case of the states emerging from the former Yugoslavia) a process of struggling to achieve a legitimate superordinate role. Institutions vary considerably in the degree of freedom they enjoy from central agencies.

The identification of a complex of institutions as making up the state introduces another complication. This is that the state may operate through institutions which have many features that are regarded as private rather than public. While this has become recognised as a special complexity about modern government, signified increasingly by using the word 'governance' to emphasise that it is more than just the concern of the formal institution called the 'government', it is not really a new issue. In the past, particularly in the early years of state formation, states hired mercenary armies, subcontracted tax collection and delegated law enforcement to local quasi-autonomous barons. In many of the early nation-states, the whole government apparatus was initially no more than an extension of the royal household. In other societies, the establishment of a centralised governmental system was very much a partnership between a sovereign and a religious body.

The modern manifestation of the phenomena discussed in the previous paragraph has been a deliberate shift to the delegation of what had become accepted as governmental functions. What this implies is a contract between government and a 'private' body to operate all or part of a public service. It is often presented as simply a mechanism for policy 'implementation' with policy making still in government hands, but it will be shown later in this book that this policy making/ implementation distinction is not easily drawn. The delegation of a major activity, particularly a monopoly activity, tends to involve some shift of control over policy. A related phenomenon is a public/private partnership where resources are drawn both directly from publicly collected revenues and from private sources; policy control is obviously particularly likely to be shared in these circumstances. Finally, in introducing this subject the word 'private' was deliberately put in inverted commas. Like the concept 'public', this is hard to define when there is a complex partnership between different elements, including state ones. Furthermore, private does not necessarily imply a private profit-making organisation – in this respect, institutions bringing voluntary organi-sations (or even large groups of small shareholders or organisational employees, though this is more contested) into association with the state may be seen as ways of further integrating state and society and increasing democratic participation.

This leads us to the other topic identified above – the issues about the justification of the state as a policy actor. It is necessary to preface this by a reference to types of policy. A widely used policy typology (Lowi, 1972) distinguishes the following:

- Redistributive policy.
- Distributive policy.
- Regulatory policy.
- Constituent policy.

While it is not appropriate to examine the case for this typology here, it serves the useful function of reminding us that, alongside direct activities of taxing and distributing benefits and services, the state regulates private activities and it also engages in the design and redesign of institutions ('constituent policy'). Again here it is clear that policy processes will therefore involve complex interactions between state and non-state actors.

The historical record shows that – subject to minor checks to the process (and various societies may be undergoing one of these at the time of writing) – the state's role as a policy-maker has increased steadily over the past two or three hundred years. The justification for this generally offered – though, of course, authoritarian regimes have sometimes bothered little about trying to justify – has been that, as societies have become more complex, the range of tasks that can be carried out effectively only by a superordinate non-market body has increased. The nation-state has furthermore succeeded in supplanting its rivals for such a task – among which only organised religion offered a temporarily effective challenge. In varying combinations, depending upon its history, the nation-state is both a derivative from other social institutions (called into being to assist them to work better) and an imposition upon them (arising out of successful efforts at domination). Justifications offered for state action rest upon assertions of the former argument; attacks upon the 'intrusive' state are likely to draw upon the latter. The crucial argument, since the evolution of sophisticated economic institutions and still running fiercely today, has concerned the state's claim to override market mechanisms as distributive processes. This claim is, of course, either to regulate or to supplant markets, depending upon the issue at stake.

While this issue takes us deep into matters of philosophy and ideology – about efficiency and justice – that are beyond the scope of this book, it is worthwhile dwelling upon some aspects of the arguments about it in order to highlight what are the characteristics of *public* policy.

Economic theory has tried to identify the circumstances in which market systems will not work satisfactorily. This has contributed to a literature which attempts to define the circumstances in which state (or at least collective) intervention may be justified, for those who believe that market systems are the right ones to settle most social distribution questions (see, for example, Culyer, 1980).

The fact that this literature is principally designed to delineate when state intervention *should* occur, not when it does occur, means that it needs to be used with caution in a discussion of the influences upon actual state actions. However, since it draws attention to problems which capitalism cannot, or cannot easily, solve and since economic theory has been very influential in political ideology, what it has to say is surely suggestive of reasons for public policy development.

A variety of concepts are used in the discussion of this topic, but three are particularly important:

- Externalities.
- Market inefficiencies.
- Monopoly.

Externalities arise when market activities have consequences, either *positive* or *negative*, for people who are not parties to those activities. The clearest negative example is pollution. In the course of producing something, a manufacturer expels waste product up a chimney or into a water course. Neighbours suffer the consequences of this action. Here, then, is a case for state intervention: to prevent a nuisance which its producer has no incentive to prevent, given that any individual sufferer from it is likely to lack the resources to take action alone.

Positive externalities are not, in themselves, a source of problems. However, the difficulty in this case is that the creator of a positive externality is likely to resent the 'free riders' who will benefit from something they do not pay for. If someone builds a sea wall to protect their property from flooding, their neighbours are likely to share that benefit. There may, of course, also be negative consequences somewhere else down the coast (in which case, to anticipate the argument to come, the combination of positive and negative effects further reinforces the case for collective action).

Faced with a high-cost item and the likelihood of 'free riders', an individual is likely to try to secure agreement to collective action (the sharing of the cost among the potential beneficiaries). As far at least as the community surrounding the builder of the hypothetical sea wall is concerned, the wall constitutes what is sometimes called a 'public good'. No one can be prevented from benefiting from it. There are other examples where the benefiting community may be very much larger. Perhaps the largest example is a national, or even international, defence system. If it is true that a nuclear deterrent preserves peace then everyone benefits. The case for a state monopoly of defence (assuming acceptance of that state's legitimacy by its population) is overwhelming. There are similar issues here with regard to policing within a country.

Furthermore, while there have been efforts by states to delegate these tasks – mercenaries were mentioned above – states often then have to deal with severe control problems. Power has been given – in a very strong sense because weapons are involved – to a body of people owing no ultimate allegiance to the state. Mercenaries merely have a contract to receive payment and or spoils in return for their 'work'. It is not surprising to discover that mercenary armies sometimes switched allegiance, particularly when the capacity of the state to deliver on its part of the bargain was in doubt (as it would be if the very action for which the mercenaries had been hired seemed to be failing). Some rather more modern issues also arise about the nature of the 'contract' between the state and implementing actors, in the situations in which the latter seem to have no wider basis for 'allegiance'.

Returning, however, to the notion of externalities: how wide are the implications of positive and negative effects? Do they extend well beyond the examples given so far of environmental protection, law and order, and defence? There are some other examples where the free rider problem can be brought under control – roads, bridges and parks may be privately provided with their use paid for through tolls. Then the argument for public provision lies in questions about the inefficient or inequitable use of resources.

But then the externalities argument can be widened further. For example, to what extent does everyone benefit if their fellow citizens are kept healthy? The 'external' impact of infectious diseases is clear enough, but there are other wider senses in which everyone benefits from living in a healthy community. Then, what about education: are there not similarly benefits arising out of living in an educated nation? Finally, what about 'externalities' relating to income distribution? If the elimination of extreme inequalities makes people with resources safer – from burglary, assault, revolution even – there are surely externalities which derive from income maintenance policies.

Most economic theorists would probably answer 'no' to the last question, and say that this is stretching the concept too far. If they accepted the case, they would probably want to discuss 'trade-offs' with other indirect consequences of state interventions. However, as stressed above, the concern here is not with the philosophical argument, but rather with the fact that there has been a recognition within capitalist economies of a range of justifications for state intervention, often stretching far beyond the obvious examples of 'public goods'. Some economists have added another related concept to the list of special cases – merit goods (Musgrave, 1959) where the collectivity (state) regards it as desirable than people should have something whether they want it or not (in economists' terms this means: are prepared to/can afford to buy it). Education and health services are sometimes put into this category.

But there may be reinforcing reasons for state action. One such reason, which lies very close to economic analysis, involves the extent to which state systems make it easier for employers to socialise costs. Public education and training systems reduce costs for employers, and reduce the disadvantage they encounter when other employers poach those upon whom they have spent training money. Help for the old and sick makes it easier for employers to discard inefficient workers. Unemployment benefits similarly may make the laying off of labour at a time of work shortage a less controversial matter, and may help those out of work to deal with their relocation problems in a more economically efficient way.

Pure economic theory is based upon assumptions of full awareness by all parties of all their options as buyers and sellers. Real world economics concedes that there are many imperfections in the market arising from incomplete knowledge. This suggests that there may be a role for the state in helping to reduce knowledge imperfections. The case for labour market interventions, introducing buyers of labour to sellers of labour, certainly seems to have been based primarily upon this concern. This example is, however, one designed to deal with an essentially short-run problem. There are also long-run problems inasmuch as citizens may find it very difficult to act in the way the economic model presupposes – this is particularly the case when individuals are unwell or disabled. There was some recognition, even by the tough-minded theorists who designed poor law systems, that there might be individuals who could not be expected to behave like 'economic men'.

The issue of monopoly concerns principally the difficulties which competing suppliers might have in entering a market. Ironically, extreme market liberals accept a role for the state in preventing the abuse of monopoly power – the 'night-watchman state' has a duty to restrain those who try to act in restraint of the market. But another issue concerns the variety of situations in which the nature of the activity is such that it is in practice very hard to sustain a competition. The crucial situation here is one in which there is a monopoly or near monopoly supplier and a competing supplier would find the costs of market entry prohibitively high. Examples of this are found in the supply of water, electricity and gas. To a lesser extent they are also found in transport systems (particularly where, like railways, they use fixed plant) and in large institutions like hospitals and schools. There is then an argument for state ownership or regulation to prevent any existing institution from exploiting its position, or perhaps (more controversially) state intervention or subsidy to help create a second supplier.

Economic theory about externalities, incomplete knowledge and monopoly thus provides a series of justifications for public policies – both regulatory and redistributive – of a kind likely to be taken seriously by states in capitalist societies. But there are logical problems about how far to take these arguments. If it is believed that externalities are all pervasive, that incomplete knowledge is the norm and not the exception, and that monopoly tendencies are endemic, then the logical position reached is a state socialist one. But then, as pragmatic socialists have had to come to recognise, there are arguments to weigh on each side – setting the evidence on 'market failure' against what is sometimes called 'state failure', the incapacity of public institutions to function efficiently or equitably (see Self (1993) for a good discussion of this issue).

In the last resort, public policy is whatever the controllers of the state institutions decide to do. Socialist ideology – at least until the fall of communism – was prepared to justify state intervention into almost any area of life. However, politicians in capitalist societies are not necessarily reluctant architects of public policy. Perhaps their main difference from socialist politicians lies in their concern to retain the 'private' element, to keep the state in a regulatory or supportive role. But as politicians they face continual demands that they take action to deal with problems, needs and grievances. For example, ideologues of the right in the United Kingdom and the United States have been only too ready to try to devise public policies to deal with problems they have perceived about family life, sexual behaviour and the consumption of addictive substances. Similarly, governments of many political hues subsidise cultural activities – art, music, literature – which can easily be seen as simple marketed activities with few 'external' effects. Finally, politicians are often quick to rush in to try to respond to special problems highlighted by the media – who demand 'why is the government not doing something?' Two slightly risible UK public policy failures of the Thatcher era concerned attempts to regulate attendance at football matches – as a measure to combat football hooliganism – and an effort to ban 'dangerous dogs'.

This discussion has explored the options for social organisation as involving choices between states and markets. But some of these problems of choice may be exacerbated by an awareness that there are other alternatives which in many ways predate both and which are still in evidence – to allow social behaviour to be governed by shared affiliations and shared norms rather than by formal institutions. Aspects of family and community life are regulated in this way, and we speak of 'culture' as an influence on choice of institutional forms and as a determinant of aspects of behaviour within institutions. Sociological theorists have seen the development of modern society as involving an evolution from these simpler forms of social organisation (community) to formal organisations (associations). Yet they recognise that there have been prices to pay for this development – such as the loss of intimate and immediate face-to-face relationships – and that people will try to resist it. It may be suggested that some of the controversy about both state and market relationships derives from a yearning for satisfactory alternatives to both. Colebatch and Larmour (1993, p. 17) pick up this theme in analysing collective problem solving as involving a choice between not two but three alternatives:

- Bureaucracy – following rules and using hierarchical organisational principles.
- Markets – with private ownership guided by self-interest and with 'incentives' and 'prices' as organising principles.
- Community – practising collective self-restraint and governed by norms and values.

They go on to stress how often these modes are mixed in practice. The analysis in this book is principally concerned with state action using bureaucratic organisational forms. But issues about markets will come up from time to time, not merely as strongly advocated alternatives, but because market organisation is firmly linked with economic power, a key source of influence upon the state. The community alternative will be rather more in the background, a murky and sometimes hard to analyse influence upon administrative culture and bureaucratic behaviour.

On studying the policy process

The discussion in the preceding section about the role of the state indicates that a discussion of the public policy process needs to be grounded in an extensive consideration of the nature of power in the state. The next three chapters will be devoted to this subject. Any consideration of how the process works will tend to involve propositions about who dominates. Omission of this, in statements about the policy process, will tend to have the implication that there are no dominant elements in the state. This is in itself a stance on this much debated subject, congruent with the pluralist perspective that power is very openly and evenly contested. Such a stance has been widely opposed by views which draw upon Marxist theory or élite theory, which see power as very distinctively structured or which suggest that dominance is very much embedded in the nature of the machinery of the state itself.

An important element in the controversy about control over the state concerns the nature of power itself. Dahl has offered a straightforward definition of power which states: 'A has power over B to the extent that he can get B to do something that B would not otherwise do' (Dahl, 1957, p. 203). The problem about this is that it treats the exercise of power as something that is likely to be very visible. Critics of Dahl have pointed out that much power is exercised more covertly and through the subtle cultural processes which influence how people determine their activities and interests (see, in particular, the critique of Dahl in Lukes (1974)).

Attempts have been made to deal with this issue by using other words – authority, influence and domination, for example. Changing the words does not really solve the problem, but it does draw attention to the variety of ways in which power is exercised. Knoke offers a useful approach, using 'influence' to describe what 'occurs when one actor intentionally transmits information to another that alters the latter's actions' (Knoke, 1990, p. 3) and 'domination' where 'one actor controls the behaviour of another actor by offering or withholding some benefit or harm' (p. 4). This helps to get away from a simple model of the way power is exercised, but it does not deal with the problem of deeply structured power, where there is difficulty, as Lukes puts it, in justifying 'our expectation that B would have thought or acted differently' (Lukes, 1974, p. 41). This raises the difficult problem of postulating that B's action or inaction could not have been in his or her interest. We will return to this theme in examining the critics of the pluralist theory of power.

Controversy about the state and about power is closely related to the debate about democracy. Broadly, there is a conflict about the extent to which it is possible to identify – in the society which is under scrutiny (in much of the English language literature it is, of course, the United States or the United Kingdom) – a system of power over the state which can be regarded as reasonably according with some of the criteria for a democracy. While modern political scientists recognise problems about the realisation of any ideal model of democracy, there are differences of view about the scope that any specific system offers for public participation. Sometimes these differences seem like little more than debates about whether the bottle is half full or half empty. However, there has been a strong division between a pluralist camp, taking an optimistic view of American democracy, and a neo-Marxist or élitist camp emphasising, for example, the dominance of the 'military-industrial complex' (Mills, 1956).

A related issue has been the way the whole process of transformation of policy into action should be considered. The theory of representative democracy sees expressions of the popular will as an 'input' into the political system, leading through various processing stages to a policy outcome as an 'output'. An influential nineteenth-century essay stressed the need for a clear distinction, during that process, between politics and administration (Wilson, 1887). Accordingly what may be described as a 'stagist model', influenced by this concern and useful as an heuristic device, but potentially misleading about what actually happens, has tended to dominate discussions of the policy process (Parsons, 1995, pp. 79–81).

Models of policy stages or policy cycles have been developed to assist comprehension of the complexities of the process of decision making. The systems approach outlined by David Easton (1953, 1965a, 1965b) has received considerable prominence. Easton argues that political activity can be analysed in terms of a system containing a number of processes which must remain in balance if the activity is to survive. The paradigm that he employs is the biological system, whose life processes interact with each other and with the environment to produce a changing but none the less stable bodily state. Political systems are like biological systems, argues Easton, and exist in an environment which contains a variety of other systems, including social systems and ecological systems. One of the key processes of political systems is inputs, which take the form of demands and supports. Demands involve actions by individuals and groups seeking authoritative allocations of values from the authorities. Supports comprise actions such as voting, obedience to the law, and the payment of taxes. These feed into the black box of decision making, also known as the conversion process, to produce outputs, the decisions and policies of the authorities. Outputs may be distinguished from outcomes, which are the effects that policies have on citizens. Easton's analysis does not end here, for within the systems framework there is allowance for feedback, through which the outputs of the political system influence future inputs into the system. The whole process is represented in Figure 1.2.

The main merit of systems theory is that it provides a way of conceptualising what are often complex political phenomena. In emphasising processes as opposed to institutions or structures, the approach is also useful in disaggregating the policy process into a number of different stages, each of which becomes amenable to more detailed analysis. For all of these reasons the systems model is of value, and this no doubt helps to account for its prominence in the literature. Yet the model has drawbacks, and understanding of policy and the policy process may be developed further by examining various points of criticism.

First, it would be wrong to accept Easton's conceptualisation of the political system as an accurate description of the way systems work in practice. While Easton's identification of processes is valuable, the neat, logical ordering of these processes in terms of demand initiation, through the conversion process to outputs, rarely occurs so simply in the practical world of policy making. For example, policy-makers themselves may be the source of demands, and although Easton recognises the significance of what he terms 'withinputs', consideration needs to be given to the manner in which individual and group behaviour may be shaped by political leaders. A growing body of work suggests that, far from arising autonomously in the community, political demands may be manufactured by leaders, who thereby create conditions for their own action (Edelman, 1971). Through the manipulation of language and the creation of crises, the authorities may impose their own definitions of problems and help to frame the political agenda. Recognition of these processes is an important corrective to the naive assumptions found in

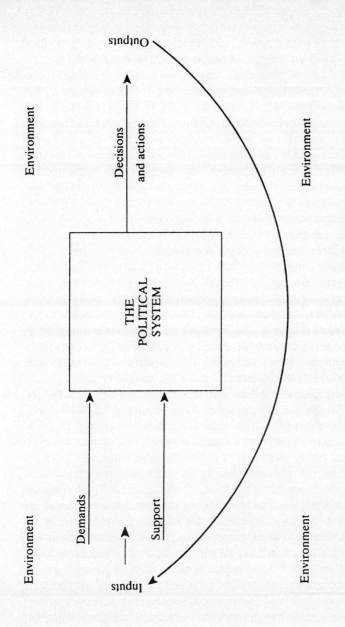

Figure 1.2   A simplified model of a political system (Source: Easton, 1965a)

some applications of systems theory. Edelman's work also draws attention to the way in which policies serve symbolic purposes. That is, policies may often be more effective in giving the impression that government is taking action, and therefore in maintaining political support, than in tackling social problems. As Dye has pointed out, it is a weakness of policy analysis that it concentrates 'primarily upon activities of governments, rather than the rhetoric of governments' (1976, p. 21). As suggested above, students of the policy process should be wary of taking policy-makers too seriously. Policies may be intended to improve social conditions, but examining whether this is the case should be part of the object of enquiry rather than an assumption of research.

A second criticism of the systems framework is that it highlights the central importance of the conversion process, the black box of decision making, but gives it relatively little attention by comparison with the detailed consideration of demands and supports. This indicates the need to draw not only on systems analysis but also on work which has explored the dynamics of decision making. A considerable amount of this book is about penetrating the black box. Included within the political system, as used in general terms here, there is likely to be a great deal of political activity. This may involve inter-organisational politics – between levels of government (central and local) and between different departments at the same level. It may also involve intra-organisational politics, in which the roles of, for example, public servants will be important. These political relationships will be channelled by structures and rules, which will themselves be the subject of continuous political action.

A third criticism which follows from the last point is that the system, and in particular the way processes occur within the 'black box', may itself be the object of political action. There will be various places in this book where we will want to note the importance of what has been called 'meta-policy' making (Dror, 1986; see also Hupe, 1990). This is concerned with setting and changing the systems and structures within which the processes that are concerned with substantive policy outputs occur. Of course, political science gives considerable attention to the big examples of meta-policy making: the determination of constitutions and the battles for political power characteristic of nation building or the disintegration of empires. What may be overlooked, however, is the way in which the relationships between units of government are subject to continual adjustment as powers and duties or financing arrangements are altered. Systematic presentations of the policy process tend to give a game-like appearance to conflicts: the problem is that politics may be about both securing a specific outcome and also changing the 'rules of the game'. Moreover, the latter may be prompted both by an interest in influencing a current outcome and by a concern to influence future outcomes. The systems model tends to treat the system itself as something static and uncontested, or at least only subject to rare fundamental change within the more stable nation-states.

Other writers who do not necessarily share Easton's systems framework have also used the idea of stages in the policy process for the purposes of analysis. For example, Jenkins (1978, p. 17) elaborates the Easton model considerably in recognising complex feedback flows, and identifies the following stages:

- Initiation.
- Information.
- Consideration.
- Decision.
- Implementation.
- Evaluation.
- Termination.

Hogwood and Gunn (1984, p. 4) go further and identify the following:

- Deciding to decide.
- Deciding how to decide.
- Issue definition.
- Forecasting.
- Setting objectives and priorities.
- Options analysis.
- Policy implementation, monitoring and control.
- Evaluation and review.
- Policy maintenance, succession and termination.

Hogwood and Gunn's approach goes beyond a simple identification of stages to suggest actions that they think ought to occur. As such, it offers a version of the 'rational' model of decision making that has been criticised by those who see the whole process as more incremental (Braybrooke and Lindblom, 1963) or even subject to chance events (March and Olsen, 1984). The advantage nevertheless of a stage model, and the preference here is for the simpler one provided by Jenkins, is that it offers a way of chopping up, if only for the purposes of analysis, a complex and elaborate process. It is an approach which is to some extent followed in this book, but in doing so it is emphasised that the following are regarded as fundamentally important:

- Policy processes are in many respects continuous processes of evolution in which a realistic starting point may be far back in history (it is foolish to get into a model of the way policy processes occur which might only apply to a newly annexed desert island where nothing had been done before).
- Inasmuch, however, as it is possible to identify policy 'initiation', it may start anywhere in the system.
- While there are grounds for seeing the stages – as set out in Jenkins' model – as involving the progressive concretisation of policy, this offers no basis for predicting how much will occur at any stage (in other words, while some policies may be formulated in very explicit terms early in the process, others may gradually manifest themselves as they are implemented – this point obviously takes us back to the different definitions of policy set out earlier in the chapter).
- Stages are not insulated from each other and there may be a succession of feedback loops between them – often the same actors are involved at different stages and the policy games they play will be carried on through different parts of the process (this remark is particularly applicable to the policy making/implementation distinction).

Studying policy processes

This is not a social science methodology textbook and there is no reason to suggest that the study of policy processes is any different from any other research enterprise. However, what has been said earlier about the characteristics of the policy process suggests certain problems for research.

First, the object of study is normally a unique sequence of events. This means that there will be little scope for testing earlier research by looking for a situation in which a process is replicated. Policy experiments are rare, and when they occur they are not necessarily set up in ways which make research evaluation easy (Bulmer, 1987; Booth, 1988). The political environments in which they are conducted mean that they are very unlikely to run their course without ongoing adjustments. When they do occur, the very fact that they are atypical limits the lessons that can be drawn from them. Furthermore, the impact of the presence of researchers on the behaviour of the researched will also distort the impressions they give of more ordinary processes.

Policy process studies are likely to be case studies, using qualitative methods. Where quantitative methods are used, they are likely to deal with impact, from which deductions can be made back to process. Perhaps the ideal here is some combination of qualitative observation of process with quantitative work on impact.

One slight exception to the generalisation that quantitative methods cannot be used in the examination of processes is comparative studies which have sought to explain similar activities in different countries (or different local authorities) by reference to contextual variables – demographic data, economic data, information on levels of support for particular political positions, etc. These have played an important role in the evaluation of some of the broad hypotheses about power systems but they leave much unexplained and in particular offer little on what goes on the 'black box' which we have observed as so crucial in the core of the policy process.

Having said that, it must be added that the very use of the expression 'black box' acknowledges that there are activities here which are very hard to observe. This brings us back to the issue of the definition of power. The fact that many power processes are covert – indeed, their very success may depend upon them being so – is acknowledged in many colloquial expressions (the power behind the throne, the kitchen cabinet, the *éminence grise*). Official secrecy is openly used as a justification for restricting access to situations or data necessary to evaluate policy processes. Very much more is just kept secret without any attempt to offer a justification for doing so.

Analysts of policy processes are thus thrown back on methods which must involve inference from the data they can secure. They also find themselves in situations in which – like journalists – they cannot validate their findings by revealing their sources. All social scientists are open to accusations that their theories and ideologies predispose them to particular interpretations of their data. Those who study the policy process are particularly vulnerable to this charge.

One interesting way of trying to deal with this problem is to acknowledge openly the validity of competing frames of reference and then to explore a case study using each as an alternative lens (likely to amplify some parts of the subject and obscure others). Allison (1971) offers a useful approach here. He carried out a study of the Cuban missile crisis of 1962, using three models. First, there is the rational actor model, which sees actions as being formed by purposeful agents with certain goals and objectives. These agents have to choose between alternative courses of action in order to achieve their goals. Alternatives are assumed to have a set of consequences attached, and rational choice consists of selecting that alternative whose consequences rank highest. Second, there is the organisational process model, which sees action not as rational choice, but as the output of organisational behaviour. This behaviour is largely the enactment of established routines in which sequential attention is given to goals, and standard operating procedures are adopted. In contrast, the bureaucratic politics model sees action neither as choice nor as output, but rather as the result of bargaining between groups and individuals in the political system. There are other ways of formulating Allison's alternatives. What we would stress here is the value of the method, which may use various kinds of decision and organisation theory.

A number of other writers have followed Allison's lead, using different models. A particular concern has been to try to evaluate the evidence for an interpretation of a policy process as a fairly open and competitive one (a pluralist-type theory) or as one that is strongly structured or biased in favour of particular actors or interests (broadly a neo-Marxist one). Examples of the use of this sort of approach are found in work on health policy by Ham (1992) and by Harrison *et al.* (1990), and in work on pollution policy by Blowers (1984) and by Hill *et al.* (1989).

These competing theories dominate the study of the policy process. The next part of this book therefore examines them in some depth.

Conclusions

This chapter has stressed that this book deals with the description of the policy process. It will proceed from a discussion of the relevance of competing theories of power (in Chapters 3 to 5) to the examination of various aspects of the policy process. In doing this it will not attempt to offer prescriptions for policy making and implementation. However, it will be seen that it is impossible to maintain a rigid distinction between description and prescription because so many of the authorities on the policy process have combined the two. Descriptions have been offered in order to justify or criticise the way policies are made and implemented.

Some of the most important controversies in policy analysis have been among analysts who differ on what they observe and what they want to observe.

A particularly important aspect of the way in which description and prescription are mixed is that concerns about accountability, managerial or democratic, have been of overriding importance in policy analysis. This is a theme to which the final chapter will return.

One widely quoted proposition from Karl Marx is: 'The philosophers have only *interpreted* the world in various ways; the point, however, is to *change* it' (Marx, 1845, p. 405). Marx was only too clear that he needed to offer a realistic description of the world in order to establish his political programme. The study of policy processes has been dominated by people with concerns to show how power is concentrated, or how politicians may be called to account, or how administrators distort the intentions of their political chiefs, and so on. While this account attempts to achieve a measure of neutrality in this respect, it would be foolish of its writer to pretend that his prescriptive biases will not show through from time to time. And in the last resort Marx is right – the justification for trying to understand is a desire to do things better.

CHAPTER 2

THEORIES OF THE STATE: PLURALISM AND ITS CRITICS

Synopsis

After setting the agenda for the chapter and the two that follow, this chapter explores the nature of pluralist theory. Pluralist theory is seen as deriving from a concern to explain how democracy may still work in a society in which representation is indirect and pressure groups are active. Its critics see its concern with prescribing how power *should* be distributed as leading to weaknesses in analysing how it *is* distributed. This critique is examined and leads the discussion into the scrutiny of approaches to the analysis of the state which stress power concentration – élitist and Marxist theory. The instrumental form of Marxist theory is outlined, leaving consideration of its more structuralist forms to the next chapter.

Introduction

There are probably three simple models of where policies come from, used in everyday discussions and propagated by journalists. These are as follows:

● They emerge from popular demands.
● General forces external to the political system force them on to the agenda (demographic, economic and environmental changes, for example).
● People within the system (the government, in its widest sense) identify needs or problems which need solving.

These three perspectives are represented respectively in the academic models of the state and of the policy process by the following:

- Pluralism.
- Various environmental and evolutionary theories, including structuralist versions and variants of Marxism.
- Theories which stress the power of the state itself and seek to analyse the roles of actors within the institutions of government.

This chapter and the next two concentrate in turn on each of these three approaches. In this chapter we will look at pluralism and at the criticisms that have been advanced against the pluralist perspective. The latter take us into some alternative approaches which, like pluralism, are concerned with identifying the individuals and groups which influence policy inputs. These are élitist theory and those (instrumentalist) versions of Marxism which emphasise the individual links within the 'ruling class'.

The examination of Marxism, however, leads us into Chapter 3. Much Marxist theory is structuralist in nature – dealing with the impact of impersonal technological and economic forces of which individual members of the ruling class are merely 'bearers'. Modern Marxists have modified the original theories in various ways, but you do not need to be a Marxist to subscribe to determinist theories. Modern theories about the pathways of economic development and about globalism have many resemblances to Marxism as far as their implications for the policy process are concerned. Moreover, other theorists have seen other kinds of social change – driven by demography or the environment – as operating in deterministic ways for policy.

Chapter 4 picks up on the way many of the leading theories discussed in Chapters 2 and 3 have treated the state as a passive, neutral entity forced to respond to demands or structural pressures. An alternative view argued in different ways from some of the early élite theories through to modern theories about institutional and constitutional influences has seen the role of the state in a positive way. Few of these theories – except perhaps those of the early 'élitists' – see state actors or state power as all determining. Rather they make connections back to the theories outlined in the other chapters to emphasise the need to deal with interactions between the influences upon the state and the state response. The arguments may perhaps be seen as involving a debate about the strength of the state itself. These issues will therefore be examined in Chapter 4.

Some modern books on theories of the state have given 'public choice' theories separate attention (see, for example, Dunleavy and O'Leary, 1987). This will not be done here. Rather the emphasis in public choice theory on the 'political market place' is seen as placing much of it in the mainstream of pluralist theory. This is where it will first be discussed. But then the second 'leg' of this theory stresses the need to see bureaucratic actors as players in a crucial part of the market place, and accordingly this part of the argument will be taken up in Chapter 4.

Origins of pluralist theory: rescuing the theory of representative democracy

Reference was made in Chapter 1 to the way in which analyses of the nature of the policy process (description) is often very much linked with prescription of how it should work. This mixture lies right at the centre of the debate about pluralism. Defenders of democratic ideals have had to come to terms with the large and complex institutional structures of states. An Athenian ideal of democracy, involving direct participation, has been seen to offer an unworkable model. The alternative has been to see democracy as a representative system. A limited number of people participate in the day-to-day business of government, but they may be the representatives of the people as a whole. The early model for this representation was seen to involve still a relatively personal relationship between the elected politician and the relatively small electorate that elected him (it was always him at that stage of the development of political institutions). With the enlargement of the electorate and the increasing need to organise within the legislature, another institution developed to make the connection between elector and elected more indirect – the political party. Schumpeter (1947) defines democracy as 'that institutional arrangement for arriving at political decisions in which individuals acquire the power to decide by means of a competitive struggle for the people's vote' (p. 269).

But in addition the processes of government increasingly began to involve other groups, organisations of public interests who might try to influence voting decisions at elections or the legislative programmes of political parties. Once established, moreover, these 'pressure groups' were likely to try to influence the policy process at any stage – negotiating the details of legislation, establishing links to influence the implementation process, monitoring policy outcomes and so on. Thus, it is argued that the pressure groups which have grown up alongside the formal institutions of government have come to play an important direct part in representing the views of specific interests.

In the UK context, Beer (1965) notes the development of a collectivist theory of representation legitimising a much greater role for groups than earlier conceptions of representative government. Beer argues that, as governments sought to manage the economy, they were led to bargain with organised groups of producers, in particular worker and employer associations. Governments of both political parties sought the consent and co-operation of these associations, and needed their advice, acquiescence and approval. Similarly, the evolution of the welfare state stimulated action by organised groups of consumers, such as tenants, parents and patients. The desire by governments to retain office led them to consult and bargain with these consumer groups in an attempt to win support and votes.

Beer's thesis has been developed in the work of Richardson and Jordan (1979; see also Jordan and Richardson, 1987), who have argued that the United Kingdom is a 'post-parliamentary democracy' in which policies are developed in negotiation between government agencies and pressure groups organised into policy communities. According to Richardson and Jordan, pressure groups influence public policy from the point at which issues emerge on to the agenda to the stage of implementation.

The pluralist school of thought in political science described and charted these developments, exploring how political parties really worked and the roles played by pressure groups. But many in this school also argued that this was how a modern democracy should work. Theorists like Truman (1958) and Bentley (1967) gloried in the institutional complexity of their society (this was particularly the case in the United States), contrasting it favourably with less open societies where they perceived much group activity to be limited or even suppressed.

Hence pluralism should be seen, in Schwarzmantel's words, 'both as a normative theory and as a way of explaining and analysing the power structure of the liberal-democratic system' (1994, p. 48). Schwarzmantel amplifies this as follows:

> Because pluralism takes as its starting point . . . a modern society in which there are different interests, popular power is realised through group activity, the working of political parties and pressure groups or interest groups, each of which represents one of the many interests into

which a developed society is split. Pluralist perspectives salute and emphasise this diversity of interest, and like liberal theorists they see this variety as a necessary and positive dimension of social life. (p. 50)

Clearly, then, opposition to this work can take two forms. One of these is to argue that this is not a satisfactory model for democracy (it is too indirect or it is impossible to realise the 'general will' through such diversity). This is not the concern of this discussion. The other, which will be, is to argue that pluralism provides a misleadingly optimistic picture of the way power is organised in those societies described as pluralist. This may, of course, then lead back to a critique of the ideal or, as in the case of the work of the socialist pluralist Harold Laski (1925), to a set of proposals for strengthening pluralism by countering the biases in the system (see also Cohen and Rogers (1995) for a modern version of this approach).

Dahl and his followers

Perhaps the most influential exponent of pluralist theory, and certainly a very important one for the study of policy processes, has been Robert Dahl. Dahl (1958) argues that power in many western industrialised societies is widely distributed among different groups. No group is without power to influence decision making, and equally no group is dominant. Any group can ensure that its political preferences and wishes are adopted if it is sufficiently determined. The importance of pluralist theory is demonstrated by the fact that, implicitly if not always explicitly, its assumptions and arguments now pervade much Anglo-American writing and research on politics, government and the state. There are likewise echoes of the same approach in much of the political science literature on continental western Europe and Scandinavia. A particularly interesting national variant of pluralist theory is the analysis of 'pillarisation' in Dutch political life, emphasising the compromises between the three pillars of Calvinism, Catholicism and secular humanism (Lijphart, 1975).

Dahl's major empirical study was an analysis of power in the town of New Haven, reported in his book *Who Governs?* (Dahl, 1961). In asking 'who governs?' in New Haven, Dahl examined a number of more specific questions, including whether inequalities in resources of power were cumulative or non-cumulative, how important decisions were made, and if the pattern of leadership was oligarchic or pluralistic. He concluded that in the period from the 1780s to the 1950s New Haven had gradually changed from oligarchy to pluralism. No one person or group was dominant in New Haven.

What Dahl did in New Haven was to select a number of key political issues and examine who won on those issues. One of the criteria used in identifying key issues was that there should be disagreement among two or more actors about what should be done. An issue was key, in other words, if there was open conflict.Analysis of the handling of three key political issues in the 1950s – urban redevelopment, public education and political nominations – revealed a situation in which power was not concentrated in a single group. Rather, because the resources which contributed to power were widely dispersed in the population, power itself was fragmented between different actors. Different interests were active on different issues, and there was no consistent pattern of success or failure. Indeed, one of the points Dahl notes is that interests opposed on one issue might join together on another. The only actor consistently involved was the mayor, but he was by no means dominant. Only a few people had direct influence over key decisions, but most people had indirect influence through the power of the vote.

Building on the New Haven case study, Dahl and colleagues such as Nelson Polsby (1963) expounded pluralist theory more fully. Their position does not hold that power is equally distributed. Rather, the theory argues that the sources of power are unequally though widely distributed among individuals and groups within society. Although all groups and interests do not have the same degree of influence, even the least powerful are able to make their voices heard at some stage in the decision-making process. No individual or group is completely powerless, and the pluralist explanation of this is that the sources of power – like money, information, expertise and so on – are distributed non-cumulatively and no one source is dominant. Essentially, then, in a pluralist political system power is fragmented and diffused, and the basic picture presented by the pluralists is of a political market place where what a group achieves depends on its resources and its 'decibel rating'.

There is an issue here, to which we will return in Chapter 4, about the way that pluralist theory deals with the role of government agencies. While some writers argue that government is neutral and acts essentially as a referee in the struggle between groups (Latham, 1952), the dominant theme in the work of Dahl is that government agencies are one set of pressure groups among many others. According to the latter interpretation, government both pursues its own preferences and responds to demands coming from outside interests. One point to note about modern pluralist analyses is that the state as such is rarely investigated. As Wolfe notes, over time 'political science became the study, not of the state, but of something at a less rarefied level called government' (1977, p. xii). This point is similarly emphasised in Dearlove and Saunders' work on British politics (Dearlove and Saunders, 1991), where they link it to a comparative complacency about democracy.

The public choice development of the idea of the political market place

The idea of politics as a market place in which leaders compete for votes is taken forward in the work of Downs (1957), who uses economic theory to analyse political behaviour. This development of pluralism has been regarded by some writers as a separate theory, described as 'public choice' theory or the theory of the state particularly identified with the 'New Right' (see Dunleavy and O'Leary, 1987). But it is very much a development of pluralist theory, adding an element of economistic reasoning which sees self-interest as the dominant motive force in political behaviour. In the political market place, parties compete to win power, by responding to the demands of the pressure groups (see Auster and Silver, 1979; Tullock, 1976; Brittan, 1977). There is a very strong pressure upon governments to yield to these demands, and thus to enhance the role of the state as a giver of benefits (using that word in its general sense to embrace jobs, contracts, services and tax concessions as well as direct cash benefits). This is not very effectively restrained by the fact that these benefits have to be paid for, because of the extent to which these costs can be hidden in the short run (by deficit financing) or spread in ways which lead benefits to be more readily perceived than the mechanisms to pay for them. For example, in 1991 in the United Kingdom, a dramatic cut in the impact of an unpopular local tax (the 'poll tax') was funded by a percentage increase in a sales tax rate, which had a slight and gradual impact upon prices paid by consumers. Interest groups seek specific benefits for themselves (business subsidies, welfare services, etc.) whose costs are diffused among taxpayers as a whole (Moe, 1980).

Public choice theorists argue (Tullock, 1976; Brittan, 1977) that, as a result of political responses to plural demands, the state grows in power and importance, in ways which may be damaging to the working of the capitalist economy. They also suggest that these pluralist (or demand-side) pressures for government growth may be reinforced by monopolistic interests on the part of the state suppliers, bureaucrats and professions, in enhancing their 'empires'. At this point, public choice theory does diverge from classical pluralist theory in giving a significant role to the state as an autonomous actor. This is a theme to which we will return in Chapter 4.

Another theme emerging from this school of thought has been the notion that there is a 'government business cycle' in which government expenditure, to satisfy demands and curb unemployment, is pushed up before general elections (Nordhaus, 1975; MacRae, 1977). The consequences of this are problems of inflation and adverse trade balances to be dealt with in the post-election period. Hence, it is argued that political behaviour may contribute to the cyclical problems of the modern capitalist state. While it is comparatively easy to find specific examples of behaviour to support this thesis, it is less plausible as a general hypothesis. The empirical data are not conclusive (see Mosley, 1984), the feasibility of this kind of behaviour depends upon electoral systems, fitting political activities to economic trends is a difficult activity, and there have been attempts to make economic rectitude a political asset (see Dearlove and Saunders, 1991, pp. 66–7).

Other broadly pluralist work: research on the question 'does politics matter?'

There is one body of research which, as far as some of its practitioners are concerned, it may be rather unfair to bracket with pluralism, but which has certainly been influenced by the pluralist approach to political science and can as well be placed in this discussion as anywhere else. This is research which seeks to explain policy outputs. Some of this has been driven by a perspective hostile to pluralism – one that stresses 'environmental' influences on policy outputs (see Chapter 3) – but it is countered by an alternative view that politics is a significant influence on policy outputs. It is the latter concern, together with the fact that research methodologies have been very driven by the positivist approach to the study of politics particularly linked with pluralist theory (see more on this on pp. 37–9), which links this work with the present discussion.

The argument that 'politics' matters – in some countries or contexts – is an assertion that, at least at a very general level, pluralist political competition influences policy. There is now a very large body of studies comparing the policy outputs of local governments. The fact that much of this work has focused on local government can be explained by the fact that at this level a range of broadly similar 'governments' in a similar political system can be compared. The number of variables can be brought under some control and quantitative analysis can be carried out. Studies have suggested that, in many places, policy outputs seem to be affected by differences in party control over administrations. The evidence is complex, and there seems little doubt that 'politics matters' more in European than in American local government, and that the extent to which it matters depends upon the issue at stake (Sharpe and Newton, 1984).

We will see below that one of the most important lines of argument developed by the critics of pluralism is that the unequal distribution of power that even Dahl is prepared to concede is so considerable as to undermine the picture presented. It is therefore of some significance that some studies are able to show that support for political parties of the left influences policy outputs, since it is on this side of the political spectrum that pluralism is seen to be unbalanced.

More ambitious ventures for the 'politics matters' school of thought involve the exploration of differences in policy outputs between countries. In the consideration of bias against the political left, the examination of the extent to which there are policy outputs which influence income inequality, either indirectly through social policy measures or directly through their impact upon economic activity, is obviously relevant. Ironically, if such outputs are to be regarded as evidence of a truly pluralist political system, then the main home of pluralist theory – the United States – does not come out very well by comparison with some of the northern European countries, and particularly Scandinavia, on redistributory policies (Esping-Andersen, 1990) and by comparison with Australia on more direct political influences on pay bargaining (Castles, 1982, 1985).

The problem is that the influences upon policy outputs are very complex. The multinational statistical studies can do little more than indicate directions for more intense policy process analysis. They do not get into what actually happens in the process. Hence, the comparison between the United States and other countries made above perhaps begs the question. Perhaps the less advantaged participate perfectly adequately in the political system of the United States, and are generally satisfied with the inegalitarian status quo. The difficulty lies in judging a system by its outputs. This leads us into an examination of the critics of pluralist theory, who assert that 'The flaw in the pluralist heaven is that the heavenly chorus sings with a strong upperclass accent' (Schattschneider, 1960, p. 35).

The critique of pluralism

The debate about the evidence for the pluralist description of the policy process was initially rooted in an argument about the methodologies used in empirical studies of power in the United States. The discussion here has approached this in a back-to-front way in order to highlight the way pluralist theory dominates discussions about power. Dahl's work can alternatively be seen as a critique of studies which seemed to show that power was very unequally distributed in the United States.

In an article published in 1958, Dahl argues that 'the evidence for a ruling élite, either in the United States or in any specific community, has not yet been properly examined so far as I know' (p. 469). Dahl's article and the criticisms it contains were aimed explicitly at two studies which had claimed to find a ruling élite in the United States. The first study, by Floyd Hunter (1953), examined the distribution of power in Atlanta, Georgia. By analysing the reputation for power of local leaders, Hunter concluded that control rested with a small group of key individuals. The second study, by C. Wright Mills (1956), focused on the United States as a whole, and argued that a power élite drawn from the military, business corporations and state agencies governed American society. In his article, Dahl contends that the research methods used by Hunter and Mills were not sufficiently rigorous to justify their conclusions. In particular, Hunter's approach of examining the 'reputation' for power of local leaders, and Mills' strategy of identifying those in key positions in large-scale organisations, did not meet the test that Dahl proposes should be required of those claiming to find a ruling élite. In Dahl's view, there is a need for researchers interested in the power structure to examine neither power reputation nor organisational position, but rather to focus on actual decisions and to explore whether the preferences of the hypothetical ruling élite are adopted over those of other groups. Only in this way is it possible to test the assertion that a ruling élite exists. As neither Hunter nor Mills had adopted this test, Dahl maintained that the ruling élite model had not been examined properly.

Underpinning Dahl's critique is a definition of power, discussed briefly in Chapter 1, that 'A has power over B to the extent that he can get B to do something that B would not otherwise do' (Dahl, 1957, p. 203). This draws attention to the fact that power involves a relationship between political actors. These actors may be individuals, groups or other human aggregates, and Dahl emphasises that power must be studied in cases where there are differences of preferences between actors. Actors whose preferences prevail in conflicts over key political issues are those who exercise power in a political system. It follows that the student of power needs to analyse concrete decisions involving actors pursuing different preferences. Careful study of these decisions is required before the distribution of power can be described adequately.

This is the method that Dahl used in his own empirical study of New Haven (1961), discussed above. Dahl came under attack from Bachrach and Baratz who, in an article published in 1962, argue that power does not simply involve examining key decisions and actual behaviour. Bachrach and Baratz assert that 'power is also exercised when A devotes his energies to creating or reinforcing social and political values and institutional practices that limit the scope of the political process to public consideration of only those issues which are comparatively innocuous to A' (1962, p. 948). Borrowing a term from Schattschneider, Bachrach and Baratz describe this as 'the mobilisation of bias' (Schattschneider, 1960, p. 71), a process which confines decision making to safe issues. What this suggests is the existence of two faces of power: one operating, as Dahl indicates, at the level of overt conflicts over key issues; the other operating, through a process which Bachrach and Baratz term 'nondecision-making', to suppress conflicts and to prevent them from entering the political process. The implication of Bachrach and Baratz's analysis is that the methodology adopted by researchers such as Dahl is inadequate, or at least partial. A more complete analysis needs to examine what does not happen as well as what does happen, and to unravel the means by which the mobilisation of bias operates to limit the scope of debate.

But what does nondecision-making actually involve? In a second article published in 1963, Bachrach and Baratz define non-decision-making as 'the practice of limiting the scope of actual decision-making to "safe" issues by manipulating the dominant community values, myths, and political institutions and procedures' (p. 632). Bachrach and Baratz argue that a nondecision-making situation can be said to exist 'when the dominant values, the accepted rules of the game, the existing power relations among groups, and the instruments of force, singly or in combination, effectively prevent certain grievances from developing into full-fledged issues which call for decisions' (p. 642). In this respect, Bachrach and Baratz distinguish nondecision-making from negative aspects of decision making, such as deciding not to act and deciding not to decide. In their view, non-decision-making differs from these other phenomena in that, when nondecision-making occurs, issues do not even become matters for decision. That is, issues remain latent and fail to enter the decision-making process because of the impact of the mobilisation of bias.

Bachrach and Baratz emphasise the means by which vested interests are protected by nondecision-making. In their model of the political process, Bachrach and Baratz argue that demand regulation is not a neutral activity, but rather operates to the disadvantage of persons and groups seeking a reallocation of values. These may be expected to be those who are disadvantaged by the status quo.

The pluralists responded to Bachrach and Baratz's critique by claiming that nondecision-making was unresearchable (Merelman, 1968; Wolfinger, 1971). How, they asked, could nondecisions be studied? On what basis could social scientists investigate issues that did not arise and conflicts that did not emerge? Bachrach and Baratz replied by amplifying and to some extent modifying their position. In their book *Power and Poverty*, published in 1970, they maintain that the second face of power operates to keep grievances covert. A nondecision – defined as 'a decision that results in suppression or thwarting of a latent or manifest challenge to the values or interests of the decision-maker' (1970, p. 44) – can be investigated through the identification of covert grievances and the existence of conflicts that do not enter the political arena. If no grievances or conflicts can be discovered, then a consensus exists and nondecision-making has not occurred.

Bachrach and Baratz go on to give a series of examples of the different forms that nondecision-making can take. First, there is the use of force to prevent demands from entering the political process. An example is the terrorisation by whites of civil rights workers in the southern United States. Second, there are various ways in which power can be used to deter the emergence of issues. The co-optation of groups into decision-making procedures is an illustration. Third, rules or procedures may be invoked to deflect unwelcome challenges. Referring issues to committees or commissions for detailed study is one example; labelling demands as unpatriotic or immoral is another. Fourth, existing rules and procedures may be reshaped as a way of blocking challenges.

Bachrach and Baratz also argue that power may be exercised by anticipated reactions. That is, an actor, A, may be deterred from pursuing his or her preferences because he or she anticipates an unfavourable reaction by another actor, B. Anticipated reactions may operate when a community group fails to mobilise because it anticipates an unfavourable response by decision-makers, or when decision-makers themselves do not act because they expect opposition from key political actors. Although these examples involve an exercise of power, Bachrach and Baratz note that this 'is not nondecision-making in the strict sense' (p. 46).

This last point is explored in a study of air-pollution policies in the United States. The study, which was carried out by Matthew Crenson (1971), compares two cities with respect to action taken to control dirty air. The cities, Gary and East Chicago in Indiana, are adjacent steel towns. While East Chicago passed a law controlling air pollution in 1949, Gary did not act until 1962. Crenson explains the differences between the two cities in terms of the existence in East Chicago of many different steel companies and the domination of Gary by a single corporation, US Steel. The delay in legislating in Gary resulted, Crenson suggests, from the power reputation of US Steel. Although it was not politically active, the economic power of US Steel, which was exercised through anticipated reactions, was decisive. Thus, indirect influence was important, with political leaders anticipating that US Steel might move from Gary and adversely affect its prosperity if restrictive legislation were passed. In contrast, in East Chicago the fragmentation of the steel industry meant that it was easier for those seeking to control pollution to secure favourable action.

As Crenson notes, Dahl's empirical work recognises that power may operate in this way, as when Dahl attributes indirect influence to the community in New Haven. Crenson observes: 'if indirect influence can work for ordinary community residents, then there is no reason why it cannot work for US Steel or General Motors or bank presidents or members of families in the Social Register' (p. 108). Crenson maintains that observable action provides an incomplete guide to the distribution of political power. There can be little doubt that Crenson's study lends significant empirical support to the nondecision-making thesis. The comparative method used in the study, and the operation of indirect influence through anticipated reactions, illustrates the way in which the thesis can be tested.

The debate about power was taken a stage further by Lukes (1974), who argued that power must be studied on three dimensions. First, there is the exercise of power which occurs in observable overt conflicts between actors over key issues: the pluralists' approach. Second, there is the exercise of power which occurs in covert conflicts between actors over issues or potential issues: Bachrach and Baratz's method. Third, there is the dimension of power which Lukes adds, involving the exercise of power to shape people's preferences so that neither overt nor covert conflicts exist. In other words, when the third dimension of power operates, there is latent conflict.

Lukes states that latent conflict exists when there would be a conflict of wants or preferences between those exercising power and those subject to it were the latter to become aware of their interests. In this context, the definition of power employed by Lukes is that 'A exercises power over B when A affects B in a manner contrary to B's interests' (p. 27). In Lukes' view, the existence of a consensus does not indicate that power is not being exercised, for as he argues:

> is it not the supreme and most insidious exercise of power to prevent people, to whatever degree, from having grievances by shaping their perceptions, cognitions and preferences in such a way that they accept their role in the existing order of things, either because they can see or imagine no alternative to it, or because they see it as natural and unchangeable, or because they value it as divinely ordained and beneficial? To assume that the absence of grievance equals genuine consensus is simply to rule out the possibility of false or manipulated consensus by definitional fiat. (p. 24)

Lukes' third dimension of power suggests for some a 'deep structure' conditioning policy options (an issue to which we will return in the next chapter). It also draws attention to identifiable actors in the policy process whose indirect influence is difficult to chart, in particular the mass media. These can be studied, for example through the examination of 'social myths, language, and symbols and how they are manipulated in power processes' (Gaventa, 1980, p. 15).

In his elaboration of Lukes' work, Gaventa explores the way in which power is exercised in all three dimensions and stresses the need to see how successful operation on one 'dimension' affects another: 'the total impact of a power relationship is more than the sum of its parts. Power serves to create power. Powerlessness serves to reinforce powerlessness. Power relationships, once established, are self sustaining' (p. 256).

The pluralists rethink?

It is important to note again that all of the more sophisticated exponents of the pluralist position, and in particular Dahl, did not claim that power is likely to be equally distributed. Their theory had two crucial components: one was that the political stage is accessible to all; the other was that the élites who mount that stage do so largely as the representatives of larger groups of people.

Such statements need to be located in times and places; they cannot be taken to be generalisations about everywhere. They might be only applicable to the places which were studied. Indeed, it is not without relevance that Floyd Hunter's study which Dahl set out to refute was carried out in a southern US city in the 1950s, while Dahl's was carried out in a northern city, host to a major university. Bachrach and Baratz's study was conducted in Baltimore, a 'border' city between north and south where the black population have become very much more politically assertive in the years since that research. However, much of the debate was carried out in terms which applied it to the whole United States, and often beyond.

This is not to belittle the important methodological and conceptual issues which figured in this debate, but it is to stress that the degree of concentration of power and the extent of suppression of interests ought to be regarded as empirical questions not simply resolvable by taking sides in the debate. The contributions from Bachrach and Baratz and from Lukes have raised issues about how power should be studied that cannot be disregarded.

It is interesting to note, therefore, a significant shift in position adopted by some of the key protagonists in the debate on the pluralist side. Dahl and Lindblom's 1953 collaboration, *Politics, Economics and Welfare* was revised in 1976 and prefaced with a strong statement on political inequality. Parsons describes it as reflecting on 'many of the failures of policy-making which were becoming evident in the 1970s . . . After Vietnam, Watergate, the "imperial presidency", the growth of urban decay, and social and economic inequality, Dahl and Lindblom confessed to changing their minds on the question of who governs' (Parsons, 1995, p. 253). Lindblom's *Politics and Markets* (1977) also offer powerful evidence on the limitations imposed upon pluralist democracy by the working of business and markets.

However, there are two rather different ways of conceptualising a revised pluralist position, both of which represent compromises between the pluralist perspective and other perspectives, but each rather different in character. One is to reconceptualise pluralism as 'democratic élitism' (Bachrach, 1969), involving a sort of reconciliation between Dahl and the writers like Hunter and Wright Mills whom he originally set out to attack. The other is to take the arguments about the limitations upon pluralism in a much more structuralist direction. The next section addresses the first of these options, leading discussion on towards the stronger statements about power concentration which are associated with Marxism, and thus from that to structuralist issues in the next chapter.

The élitist perspective

The classical élitist position was set out at the end of the nineteenth century by an Italian, Gaetano Mosca:

> Among the constant facts and tendencies that are to be found in all political organisms, one is so obvious that it is apparent to the most casual eye. In all societies – from societies that are very meagrely developed and have barely attained the dawnings of civilisation, down to the most advanced and powerful societies – two classes of people appear – a class that rules and a class that is ruled. The first class, always the less numerous, performs all political functions, monopolises power and enjoys the advantages that power brings, whereas the second, the more numerous class, is directed and controlled by the first, in a manner that is now more or less legal, now more or less arbitrary and violent. (1939, p. 50; original publication in Italian, 1896)

The classical élitist thesis maintains that political élites achieve their position in a number of ways: through revolutionary overthrow, military conquest, the control of water power (a key resource in oriental societies: see Wittfogel, 1963), or the command of economic resources. In the modern state, the position of élites is related to the development of large-scale organisations in many areas of life, with the result that there are different kinds of élite, not just those holding formal political power. Bottomore makes a distinction between the political élite, which is made up of 'those individuals who actually exercise power in a society at any given time' and which 'will include members of the government and of the high administration, military leaders, and, in some cases, politically influential families of an aristocracy or royal house and leaders of powerful economic enterprises', and the political class, comprising the political élite but also leaders of political parties in opposition, trade union leaders, businessmen and politically active intellectuals (1966, pp. 14–15). Defined in this way, the political élite is composed of bureaucratic, military, aristocratic and business élites, while the political class is composed of the political élite together with élites from other areas of social life. What this suggests is that élite power may be based on a variety of sources: the occupation of formal office, wealth, technical expertise, knowledge and so on. To a certain extent, these resources may be cumulative, but power is not solely dependent on any one resource.

In the twentieth century, the growth of large firms, the establishment of trade unions and the development of political parties – all institutions in which effective power is likely to rest with an oligarchic leadership (see further discussion on pp. 78–80) – underlines the significance of organisational control and institutional position as key political resources. Of particular importance in this context was the creation of bureaucratic systems of administration to carry out the increasing responsibilities taken on by the state from the nineteenth century onwards. As Weber (1947) notes, bureaucracies have both positive and negative aspects: positive in that they offer an efficient way of organising administration; and negative because they open up the possibility of power being vested in officials who are accountable neither to the public nor to politicians. The growth of bureaucracies may, in Weber's view, lead to control of the economy by bureaucrats. In this line of argument, élite theory does, contrary to Nordlinger's contention (1981), draw attention to the need to look at the state itself. This aspect of élite theory will be discussed further in Chapter 4.

C. Wright Mills (1956) draws attention to institutional position as a source of power, and suggests that the American political system is dominated by a power élite occupying key positions in government, business corporations and the military. The overlap and connection between the leaders of these institutions helps to create a relatively coherent power élite. Reference has already been made to Mills' book and to the work of Hunter on local power.

The issue which the last section raised was: where does pluralism end and élitism begin? The élitist case is not helped by the fact that many alternative sources of élite power have been suggested. This tends to reinforce the pluralist case, and may be seen as the basis of the theory of 'democratic élitism' mentioned above. Regular elections based on competition between the leaders of political parties, together with participation by pressure group élites in between elections, and interaction between these élites and the bureaucratic élites, are the ways in which democracy operates in the modern state. The fact that different élites operate in different issue areas is a protection against domination by one group. Competition between élites protects democratic government.

There is a problem about sustaining a simple élite theory position inasmuch as there are difficulties in specifying the mechanisms by which power is seized and the techniques used to hold on to it. One, now very unfashionable élite theorist, who worked in Italy around the same time as Mosca, Pareto (1966), offered an answer to that question inasmuch as he saw élite domination as based upon the special qualities possessed by the élite. But even he posited a kind of pluralist process by which the 'circulation of élites' occurs as old élites weaken and new ones arise.

There are, however, two ways in which the questions about the way power is exercised may be answered, and these need further discussion. One, as indicated above, is to bypass the question about how power is acquired but to argue that once that has happened then the institutions of the state offer the means for an élite to perpetuate its power. This perspective is central to Mosca's work. The detailed examination of it will have to await Chapter 4.

The other approach to this question is to emphasise the importance of economic power. Where it does this, élite theory begins to merge with another very important approach to the study of power, Marxist theory, to the extent that some of the key exponents of the position set out above (for example, Wright Mills) are distinguishable from Marxists only by their comparative reluctance to quote Marx in their support. The next section therefore picks up on those aspects of Marxist theory which concentrate on the role of individual actors in the pursuit of power.

Elite theory, in both classical and modern guises, represents an important alternative to pluralism. Yet, while some writers have attempted to reconcile élitism and pluralist democracy, others have used the findings of élitist studies to argue that the power élite is but a ruling class by another name. In other words, it is suggested that institutions may well be run by minority groups, but that these groups come from similar social backgrounds and are therefore exercising power in the interests of a dominant group.

It must be noted that the bridging concept between élitism and Marxism is the idea of a 'ruling class'. However, until recently this class analysis has led to a disregard of the extent to which other forms of social stratification, particularly stratification in terms of gender and ethnicity, may be significant for the distribution of power. Now, within both feminist literature and the analysis of racism, a lively debate has developed about the extent to which these other forms of stratification may operate independently of, or in association with, class divisions, to structure and bias the policy process. This is discussed further in the next chapter.

Instrumental Marxism

In his book *The State in Capitalist Society* (1969), Miliband takes as his starting point not the political process itself, but the form of economic organisation or the mode of production. In advanced western industrialised societies, the capitalist mode of production dominates, giving rise to two major social classes – the bourgeoisie and the proletariat. Miliband's analysis of the distribution of income and wealth, and changes in this distribution over time, demonstrate the continued concentration of wealth in a small section of the population. The question Miliband then asks is whether this economically dominant class exercises decisive political power. In other words, he explores the relationship between economic power and political power.

Taking their cue from Marx, writers like Miliband argue that the state is not a neutral agent, but rather an instrument for class domination. Marx expressed this view in the *Communist Manifesto*, where he wrote that 'The executive of the modern State is but a committee for managing the common affairs of the whole bourgeoisie' (quoted in McLellan, 1971, p. 192). Miliband suggests three reasons why the state is an instrument of bourgeois domination in capitalist society. First, there is the similarity in social background between the bourgeoisie and members of the state élite: that is, those who occupy senior positions in government, the civil service, the military, the judiciary and other state institutions. Second, there is the power that the bourgeoisie is able to exercise as a pressure group through personal contacts and networks, and through the associations representing business and industry. Third, there is the constraint placed on the state by the objective power of capital. Another way of putting this is to say that the freedom of action of state officials is limited, although not eliminated, by their need to assist the process of capital accumulation, which stems from their dependence on a successful economic base for their continued survival in office. In these ways, Miliband contends, the state acts as an instrument which serves the long-term interests of the whole bourgeoisie. As a result, his approach has come to be known as 'instrumentalism'.

Marxism is today seen above all as the ideology which unsuccessfully sustained the collapsed Soviet empire and continues to appear to hold sway in China. But it must be remembered that Marx's original purpose was to analyse the system of economic power dominant within capitalist societies, and to show how that system contained the seeds of its own downfall. The fact that it has not fallen in the way predicted by Marx does not necessarily invalidate the whole of his analysis, particularly those parts relating to the significance of ownership or control of the means of production for power within the state.

However, at the core of the instrumentalist position lies an approach to the analysis of power that has much in common with élitist positions or even with radical versions of the pluralist position (as in the later writings of Lindblom (1977)). Miliband's position, as set out in all but the third of the propositions above, points to ways in which those with economic power exercise political power. And even the last proposition does no more than say that, if it is a taken-for-granted proposition that government is managing a capitalist economy, then attention will be paid to capitalist interests.

But the original theory set out by Karl Marx, though complicated and stated in rather different ways at different times in his life, postulated a theory of history in which the means of production were a dominant and determining force. The 'executive of the modern State' was a committee to manage the 'affairs of the whole bourgeoisie' not because the latter were able to control it, but because it could be nothing else so long as society remained capitalist. In other words, mainstream Marxist theory takes the issues about the determination of policy in a very different direction to the concerns of this chapter, to suggest that a power *structure* determined by the means of production is of dominant importance. Hence we return to explore Marxist theory further in the next chapter.

CHAPTER 3

THEORIES OF THE STATE: STRUCTURALIST PERSPECTIVES

Synopsis

This chapter uses the notion of structural perspectives loosely to embrace a range of theories from structure functionalism through Marxist theory to modern work that stresses economic determinism and the ways in which social divisions – like those involving gender or ethnicity – tend to determine policy choices.

Introduction

Thompson puts as follows the underlying theoretical issue about the relationship between the concerns of this chapter and those of the previous one:

> The problem of the relation between the individual and society, or between action and social structure, lies at the heart of social theory and the philosophy of social science. In the writings of most major theorists . . . this problem is raised and allegedly resolved in one way or another. Such resolutions generally amount to the accentuation of one term at the expense of the other . . . the problem is not so much resolved as dissolved. (1989, p. 56)

Most of the theorists discussed in the previous chapter were largely in the 'action' camp, and it was shown there that some of the critics of pluralism and élitism, particularly the former, have suggested that they neglect issues about the way power is structured. This chapter switches to theories that are very concerned about structure, tending therefore to take the opposite of the two extreme positions described by Thompson.

Structuralist theories which see political action as determined by powerful forces outside human control have a long history in the social sciences. Writers have postulated distinct patterns of human evolution or determinist approaches to history, which have challenged the view that individuals have the capacity to determine their own social and political institutions. Theories of this kind have taken forms which suggest a need to accept the status quo, to regard political choices as predetermined by demographic, social and economic factors. They have also come in 'critical' forms – concerned to analyse what are seen as powerful constraints upon human action which have to be attacked in order to achieve fundamental change. This contrast draws attention to a contradiction lying within much of this theory: that in dealing with the factors which determine social stability in changing societies, it has to try to specify conditions under which change can occur. Its proponents have, particularly in its critical forms, to try to answer questions about the conditions under which actions to effect social change may be appropriate.

Structuralist theory has, in short, to take a stance on the relationship between structure and action. The former determines the latter, yet the latter feeds back to alter the former. All but the most simplistic forms of structural theory – with which we need not bother ourselves because they are so unrealistic – acknowledge some measure of scope for action to secure change. Further distinctions can be made between different kinds of structural theory about the extent to which they are totally determinist. These differences particularly concern the extent to which there are strong evolutionary forces in societies.

Related to this issue of variations in the extent to which theories are determinist is the issue of what is seen as the source of that determinism – demography, technological evolution and economic forces are the key sources. A sort of determinism which lies at the very weakest end of structural theory sees the institutional and ideological configurations which have been established as imposing strong constraints upon future actions.

Hence this chapter will review a variety of theories, arranged roughly in terms of the extent to which they are determinist (starting with those which embody claims about strong forms of determinism). These are as follows:

- Structural functionalism.
- The Marxist form of economic determinism.
- Economic determinism without Marxism.
- Perspectives with a structuralist tinge from analyses of gender and racial domination.

Structural functionalism

This section will be fairly brief. Since this is not a textbook on sociological theory, the roots of this approach will be sketched in very briefly and without supporting references. Structure functionalist theory may be regarded as now fairly dated, offering propositions that few today find credible. Yet it must be mentioned: (a) because of the way in which it poses questions about structural influences that – at least when postulated in a very weak form – still need attention; and (b) because as a theoretical perspective it occupies an important place in relation to the next body of theory to be discussed – Marxism – as a set of propositions which in part support and in part offer a contradiction of that perspective.

Structural functionalism involves a fusion in sociological theory between propositions from early anthropological studies, which suggested how social institutions reinforce each other in ways which support the status quo in allegedly 'static' societies, and propositions from social Darwinism which traced processes of social evolution. Sociologists in this tradition in the United States or western Europe saw their own societies as 'progressing', with their institutions adapting in response to evolving social needs. Where Marxists saw an evolutionary process leading towards social crisis, they saw a progressive adaptation occurring.

What this perspective implied for political choices – and thus for the policy process – was a series of imperatives to which the political system would respond. The evolutionary element in this perspective led some scholars to proclaim that their own societies had reached 'the end of ideology' (Bell, 1960), in which political battles would be muted by a common acceptance of the benefits of the status quo, and less 'developed' societies would evolve along the same progressive path.

Economic development can be seen as a generator of a wide range of social changes (Kerr *et al.*, 1973). In addition to its contribution to the growth of the standard of living, it is a source of urban development. These changes are then held to have influenced patterns of social behaviour, including choices about marriage and family size.

Thus comparative studies have aimed to explain the emergence of public policies – particularly social policy – by correlating their incidence with the phenomena of economic growth, industrialisation, urbanisation and demographic change, linked together in a package of ingredients of 'modernisation' (Hofferbert, 1974; Wilensky, 1975).

Some exponents of the modernisation thesis go on at this point in the argument to consider the demographic effects of industrialisation, urbanisation and high levels of income (for example, Wilensky, 1975). These are lowered birth rates and raised life expectations at the end of life. The second of these, particularly when associated with an earlier fall in the birth rate to limit the size of the prime-age population relative to the elderly, is seen as of importance for social policy expenditure.

Some versions of the modernisation thesis go beyond these issues to try to identify a post-modernist or a post-industrial order with its own distinctive policies. We will find some traces of this approach later in the book when we examine organisational arrangements and find that there are suggestions that we are now in a post-modernist, or more specifically post-Fordist era, in which old bureaucratic and hierarchical models for the organisation of industrial and administrative life are giving way to new forms. Clearly, technological changes – the development of computers and other electronic control devices – facilitate the development of these new forms of organisation. Readers should be suspicious of arguments about these phenomena which come in deterministic forms. It is one thing to say that people are trying new approaches to the organisation of complex activities, aided by new technology, but quite another to dress this up in a technologically determinist form which seems to deny any role for human choice.

The question for all of the discussion in this section is: have we here a set of determinist theories suggesting that public policy developments can be read off from these economic and social developments? Or are these theories merely making the following points?

- There is a general association between economic growth and state growth across the broad band of prosperous nations in the past.
- There may be a certain critical threshold that nations have to pass before significant levels of public services, imposing high costs on the nation, become feasible in developing societies.
- Picking up on the last part of this section, there is a later generation of technological developments which are further transforming some of the record-keeping and surveillance options open to governments.

To go further would be to pay too little attention to the choices made by actors or to variations in response from place to place (Ashford, 1986).

Marxism

Marxism offers a similar perspective on technological and economic growth, with the important difference that it emphasises the malign as opposed to the benign effects of these processes, and argues that they will lead to a crisis which will have a transforming effect upon the character of society.

According to classical Marxist theory, the social structure of a capitalist society is essentially a 'class structure'. The two classes that confront each other in a capitalist society (at least in the last resort) are the bourgeoisie (the owners of the means of production) and the proletariat (who work for the bourgeoisie). Some of Marx's work deals with other classes (see the discussion below), but his logic indicates that they would eventually be sucked into the fundamental class struggle. This struggle would then intensify, as the nature of competitive production forced the bourgeoisie to reduce systematically the rewards going to the proletariat. Such a process of 'immiseration' would eventually lead the increasingly unified proletariat to rise up to overthrow the bourgeoisie. This revolution would lead to the replacement of capitalism by socialism, just as earlier the logic of industrial change had led capitalism to replace feudalism. In other words, at the core of classical Marxist theory there is a set of essentially determinist positions. Our positions in the relations of production determine our long-run political interests. Our fates are set by the working out of that dialectic. Notwithstanding this position, Marx urged the proletariat to organise politically, to work towards the ultimate revolution. In this sense, there is a contradiction at the core of classical Marxism, which has left it open for some to reinterpret the theory in a very much less deterministic way.

The concern here is with the role of the state in the determinist model. As indicated in the preceding chapter, the idea of the state as 'the executive committee of the bourgeoisie' is in this interpretation the only thing it can be. Its role is a supportive and subsidiary one in relation to capitalism. In his determinist 'mood', Marx was not very interested in the role of the state. The problem is that, in his more activist 'mood', he urged the organisations of the proletariat to mobilise to try to take over the state. This engendered an argument within Marxism about the purpose of such activity. Was it just to prepare for, or practise for, or advance the revolution, since the state could neither be transformed nor transform capitalism? Or was there a peaceful road to revolution by way of securing control over the state? It was this alternative which engendered a social democratic form of Marxism which the revolutionary followers of Marx repudiated.

Hence, while generating an elaborate controversy about the state within Marxist ranks (which became increasingly complicated as the role of the state changed in the twentieth century in ways which, for many, did not accord with Marxist predictions), the classical Marxist position is to suggest that the capitalist state's main function is to assist the process of capital accumulation. This means creating conditions in which capitalists are able to promote the production of profit. The state is seen as acting to maintain order and control within society.

Twentieth-century Marxist theory has elaborated these two points in a variety of ways, partly to explain phenomena that Marx had not expected to occur. In specific terms, assisting accumulation means providing physical resources such as roads and industrial sites, while maintaining order is carried out both through repressive mechanisms like the police and through agencies such as schools which perform an important legitimation function. The accumulation process is further assisted through state intervention in the provision of services such as housing and health to groups in the working population. The functions of these services include reducing the cost of labour power to capital and keeping the workforce healthy.

O'Connor (1973) classifies these different forms of state expenditure as social investment, social consumption and social expenses. Social investment increases labour productivity through the provision, for example, of infrastructure and aid to industry; social consumption lowers the cost of reproducing labour power as, for example, in the provision of social insurance; and social expenses serve to maintain social harmony. In practice, nearly all interventions by the state perform more than one of these functions.

O'Connor's analysis suggests that state expenditure serves the interest of monopoly capital, and that the state is run by a class-conscious political directorate acting on behalf of monopoly capitalist class interests. In a similar vein, Gough (1979) makes use of O'Connor's typology to show how the modern welfare state serves the long-term interests of the capitalist class.

Miliband's instrumental Marxist perspective, set out at the end of the previous chapter, is not incompatible with any of this. But Marxists with more structuralist perspectives have criticised the way Miliband deals with the question of the relationship between economic power and political power. Miliband's main protagonist has been Poulantzas, who has maintained that Miliband accepts too readily the concepts and framework of the pluralists. As Poulantzas argues:

> Miliband sometimes allows himself to be unduly influenced by the methodological principles of the adversary. How is this manifested? Very briefly, I would say that it is visible in the difficulties that Miliband has in comprehending social classes and the State as *objective structures*, and their relations as an *objective system of regular connections*, a structure and a system whose agents, 'men', are in the words of Marx, 'bearers' of it – *träger*. (1973, pp. 294–5)

What Poulantzas seeks to demonstrate is that the class background of state officials is not important. The key is the third set of factors in Miliband's analysis, the structural constraints placed on the state by the objective power of capital. It is these constraints, Poulantzas contends, the 'objective relation' between the bourgeoisie and the state, which explain the political supremacy of the economically dominant class. For Poulantzas, then, the state is not a collection of institutions and functions, but a relationship between classes in society. In his later work, Miliband (1977) goes some way towards meeting Poulantzas's criticisms, placing rather more emphasis on structural constraints. However, he in turn criticises Poulantzas, accusing him of determinism. Miliband contends that the structuralist argument 'deprives "agents" of any freedom of choice and manoeuvre and turns them into the "bearers" of objective forces which they are unable to affect' (1977, p. 73). In contrast to the structuralist approach, Miliband wishes to argue that although the state in capitalist societies is a class state, it has some autonomy from the bourgeoisie. This autonomy helps explain why, for instance, the state may carry out reforms in the interests of the proletariat.

This again raises the thorny question of the relationship between economic power and political power. As suggested above, in some of Marx's work there is explicit acknowledgement that the relationship is not simply deterministic, and that the state may enjoy some independence from the bourgeoisie. This is demonstrated by his discussion of Bonapartism in France and Bismarck's rule in Germany, and his analysis of the coming to economic power of the bourgeoisie in England while the landed aristocracy retained political power. Miliband takes up this theme by noting the later growth of fascism in Italy and Germany, and by pointing to different forms of the capitalist state, including bourgeois democracy and authoritarianism. The key to understanding these developments, argues Miliband, is that all capitalist states have relative autonomy from the bourgeoisie (1977, ch. 4). This formulation gives the state a much more significant role and will be explored further in the next chapter.

Like Miliband, Poulantzas uses the concept of relative autonomy to explain the disjunction between economic power and political power. One of the points Poulantzas stresses is that the bourgeoisie, or capital, is divided into different interests, or fractions, and as well as acting in a reformist manner to help the proletariat, the state may also act against the interests of a particular fraction of the bourgeoisie. Thus:

> relative autonomy allows the state to intervene not only in order to arrange compromises vis-à-vis the dominated classes, which, in the long run, are useful for the actual economic interests of the dominant classes or fractions; but also (depending on the concrete conjuncture) to intervene against the long term economic interests of *one or other* fraction of the dominant class: for such compromises and sacrifices are sometimes necessary for the realisation of their political class interests. (1973, p. 285)

It should be noted that the concept of relative autonomy presents a number of problems. In particular, although it provides an adequate description of how the state in capitalist society actually operates, it does not furnish a satisfactory explanation of state activities (Saunders, 1981a). To explain the activities of the capitalist state requires the identification of criteria for locating the limits of dependence by the state on the bourgeoisie and the conditions under which state agencies are able to operate autonomously. Neither Poulantzas nor Miliband is able to deal adequately with this issue.

Hence, two developments in neo-Marxist work tend to undermine its special characteristics as a theory which explains the operation of the state. Once it is acknowledged that capitalists are a divided group, who do not necessarily have interests in common, and that the state has a measure of autonomy, it becomes difficult to predict the outcome of the policy process – that is, the behaviour of the state – by reference to the interests of capital. The question to be addressed here is whether this has the effect of reducing what we can say about the power of capital to a statement, evident to all but the most naive, that state action will tend to support the existing economic order. Such a sentence sums up over a century's intense debate about the feasibility of democratic socialist change in a banal proposition. Yet it must be acknowledged that there are considerable difficulties in distinguishing some of the positions taken by contemporary neo-Marxist writers from those who subscribe to a version of pluralist theory which stresses group inequalities (see further discussion of this 'convergence' in McLennan (1989)).

Despite their differences, both Miliband and Poulantzas see the capitalist state as one of the main means by which class domination is maintained. In this respect, they represent a radically different approach both to the pluralists – who tend to see government as one set of pressure groups among many others – and to the élitists, who argue that the state élite is powerful, but not tied to a particular class within society.

A number of these points are reiterated in the work of Offe, who seeks to provide a general explanation of political activity and the selective attention given to issues in contemporary capitalist societies. Drawing on both Easton's systems analysis and Bachrach and Baratz's nondecision-making thesis, Offe maintains that 'In advanced systems of state-regulated capitalism, political stability can be more reliably ensured through the systematic exclusion and suppression of needs which if articulated would endanger the system' (1976, p. 397). According to Offe, various exclusion rules which are an intrinsic part of the institutions and structures of capitalism operate to select certain issues for attention and omit others. The former include the application or threat of acts of repression by the police, armed forces and judiciary, while the latter include formal and informal limits as to what matters can be dealt with by the state. These mechanisms act as 'a system of filters' (1974, p. 39), narrowing the scope of political events and screening out non-capitalist demands. Offe contends that the difficulty in researching these mechanisms, and in demonstrating a consistent pattern of bias in the filtering which occurs, results from the fact that the capitalist state has to deny its class character and claim neutrality as a condition of its survival. Nevertheless, he argues that the state does intervene to support capitalist interests, and in this sense there is a systematic bias in what the state does. At the same time, Offe considers that autonomous action is increasingly a feature of state intervention under conditions of late capitalism.

This discussion has ranged widely over a theoretical discourse in which determinism figures, but where some writers have been prepared to back off a little to acknowledge forms of 'relative autonomy'. Meanwhile the point here is that Marxist theory tends to take a stance which treats state action as to a considerable extent constrained and determined by economic institutions. There are many studies of policy processes which use a neo-Marxist framework to explain policy determination or to define limits to political action (see, for example, Ginsburg (1992) on social policy, Ball *et al.* (1988) on housing, and Ball (1990) on education studies).

Economic determinism without Marxism

There has recently been some stemming of the flow of overtly Marxist-inspired studies. This may perhaps be attributed to the fall of the Soviet system, and the tendency of writers to proclaim 'we are all capitalists now'. But it must be pointed out that for a long while it has been accepted that a western form of neo-Marxist analysis has developed which offers an account of the way capitalist societies function without any reference to the characteristics of the communist societies being necessary for the validity of the accounts. Further, many had argued that the so-called socialist revolutions were premature – they did not occur in mature capitalist societies. Finally, most western Marxist intellectuals had abandoned any allegiance to organised communism well before its fall; they had been provoked by Stalin's atrocities, by the Hitler/Stalin pact at the beginning of the Second World War and by the invasion of Hungary in particular. Many therefore regarded Soviet communism as a cruel distortion of the Marxist dream.

Nevertheless perspectives can be identified on economic determinism which either diverge so far from classical Marxism that it is inappropriate to call them Marxist or involve propositions about the dominance of economic considerations in the policy process of a kind that have no foundations in Marxist theory.

First, there is a perspective which suggests that there is built into the politics of any but the poorest societies a set of concerns about the need for advances in the standard of living which politicians will disregard at their peril. Related to this – particularly since the collapse of communism – is a view that only capitalist economic institutions can provide those advances. This perspective is obviously advanced in philosophical works which celebrate capitalist economic institutions (Hayek, 1944, 1960), and is more generally taken for granted in much contemporary political analysis. The pronouncement by the Chinese leader Deng Xiaoping – to justify his flirtations with capitalism – that it does not matter what colour the cat is so long as it can catch mice (Shambaugh, 1995, p. 88) perhaps sums up this post-Marxist consensus.

It is interesting to note how implicit economic determinism crops up in the ranks of thinkers from all parts of the ideological spectrum. Arguably there is a thread of thinking from the 'right' which is very like Marxist structuralism, but without any theory of change or revolution. This is a view that there has been a process of evolution to the ideal economic order (capitalism) and the ideal political order (representative democracy), and that here the kind of 'directional History' embodied in the theories of Hegel and Marx comes to an end (Fukuyama, 1992). Such a perspective suggests that:

> All countries undergoing economic modernization must increasingly resemble one another: they must unify nationally on the basis of a centralized state, urbanize, replace traditional forms of social organization like tribe, sect and family with economically rational ones based on function and efficiency, and provide for the universal education of their citizens . . . the logic of modern natural science would seem to dictate a universal evolution in the direction of capitalism. (pp. xiv–xv)

Fukuyama explores this theme with a caution not evident in this quotation, but he does in many respects advance a 1990s version of Bell's earlier 'end of ideology' thesis (see p. 50).

More pragmatic versions of this perspective involve taken-for-granted assumptions about the need to limit public expenditure or taxation – with its implicit consequences for other policies – in the interests of the maintenance of the capitalist economy. Clearly there is here a kind of structuralist perspective – specifying a distinct limit to the extent to which politicians can disregard economic forces. Or are these just guidelines for the wise politician?

Second, and rather closer to Marxism, is globalist theory, which sees a sequence of worldwide economic developments as of determining importance for contemporary policy making. Globalist theory has developed on a massive scale, and in the process has branched in many directions. It embodies various themes – the development of global financial markets, the cross-national diffusion of technology, the emergence of transnational or global corporations (and the increasing economic pressure upon large corporations to 'think globally') and the emergence of global cultural flows. All these trends offer challenges to state autonomy and stimulate new political formations beyond the nation-state. More cautious statements on this topic stress the extent to which this is in some respects a gradual change, acknowledge that complex supra-national economic developments have a long history, and recognise that the speed of modern communications heightens awareness of the phenomenon.

There are variants of globalism which are close to classical Marxism, in that they see the processes described by Marx as now taking place on a world scale (Wallerstein, 1979; Cox, 1987). This is a view that is not particularly new: it was set out originally by Lenin. It suggests that there is a complicated working through of the postulated conflict between capitalists and proletariat across the world, postponing the eventual crisis and raising difficult tactical problems for international Marxists, who have to face difficulties in getting the proletariat to think globally rather than to accept nationalist interpretations of exploitation.

Within Marxist thinking there are distinctions to be found between those who see capitalism as an increasingly international phenomenon and those who argue that companies are rather more supra-national than global (that is, that they spread out from a national base) and that their power is not necessarily an external imposition upon nation-states, but something established within them (see Panitch, 1994). As Panitch puts it in a rhetorical question: 'Is it really to international finance that governments in London or Ottawa are accountable when they prepare their budgets? Or are they accountable to the City of London or to Bay Street?' (p. 74).

Alternatively, globalist theory may accept that capitalist economic relationships are increasingly organised on a world scale, but not set out this view in Marxist terms. The question that emerges for this discussion is then to what extent a globalist position is really a determinist one. Is globalist theory saying that there are a series of structural developments about which politicians can do little? Or is it merely saying that the issues about the power of economic interests – which even pluralist writers like Lindblom have come to accept as critical for the policy process – need to be analysed in supra-national terms? In other words, this is not so much a determinist point of view as one which emphasises *either* that national policy-makers must increasingly be able to deal with interests organised outside their country *or* that effective policy processes need to be supra-national too (Hirst and Thompson, 1992). The latter position may lead to a pessimistic stance on the feasibility of achieving solutions to political problems in the face of institutional complexity, but it is not ultimately a determinist stance.

This is certainly the position reached by many analysts of issues about pollution policy (see, for example, Hurrell and Kingsbury, 1992), energy policy (see Yergin, 1991) and monetary policy (Walter, 1993).

Perspectives with a structuralist tinge from analyses of gender and racial domination

Some of the structuralist arguments originating from feminism link very closely with Marxist theory. Gender divisions in society are seen as further ways in which the proletariat are divided and controlled. The growth of a female workforce which is poorly paid and insecure is seen as a particularly insidious development in the 'reserve army of labour' which keeps the proletariat cheap and weak (Barrett, 1980; Hartmann, 1979).

Other feminist theory focuses rather more upon male domination of economic and political institutions *per se*, not seeing it in the Marxist context of class divisions (Millett, 1970; Delphy, 1984). Inasmuch as this perspective is structuralist in nature, it opens up a very important issue with ramifications beyond the relations between the genders. What is involved is an argument that there is a range of institutions – the family, the church, the economy, the state – which are linked together in a structure that has a powerfully determining impact upon what gets on the agenda. We are back here with Lukes' third face of power. This structure influences culture, discourse and behaviour, defining the political agenda. As such it defines out many female concerns.

Schwarzmantel makes a direct parallel with Marxism using the concept of 'deep structure':

> Both feminism and Marxism take a common stance, in that both are concerned to reveal . . . a 'deep structure' or power dimension which exists in the liberal-democratic state and the society that surrounds it, and in other forms of state and society as well. The power dimension is in both cases seen as a 'fault line' or basic division which is to some extent hidden from view. (1994, p. 115)

Rhetorics of equality are seen as masking real inequalities of power. An ideology of male domination is seen as embodied in a division between the 'public' sphere and the 'private' sphere. The public sphere for a long time excluded women, while at the same time regarding issues in the private sphere as outside the realm of the political. This had the effect of keeping issues about domineering behaviour by men within the household off the agenda.

Schwarzmantel perhaps takes the parallels between feminist theory and Marxist theory too far. What the general feminist position brings into the discussion is a good example of how policy processes have been structured with the effect that they support the status quo and suppress certain issues, in the way described by Lukes. They take us into a very much looser and more general approach to the way in which policy processes are structured.

Before considering this, it is important to recognise that the arguments deployed here apply also to ethnic divisions. The equivalent of radical feminism's development of Marxist theory is a body of work that stresses the way ethnic divisions function to keep the proletariat divided (Solomos *et al.*, 1982). The term 'ethnicity' needs to be interpreted widely here – going far beyond recognised biological differences (which are in any case ambiguous and contestable) to comprise national, linguistic, cultural and religious divisions which create or are used to create divisions of an 'ethnic' kind. In this case there is a connection back, too, to the issues about globalism. There are economic differences associated with divisions between countries, where the 'national interest' is invoked both to attack and to defend inequalities. The world 'division of labour' has ethnic dimensions. Migration has further complicated this by contributing to the reproduction of these divisions within countries (Cohen, 1987).

Just as there is a conflict within feminist theory between those who link gender and class issues and those who focus primarily on gender, so in the analysis of ethnic divisions there are those whose analyses are embedded in Marxist theory and those who see that perspective as too limiting for a satisfactory analysis of the exploitation of ethnic groups (Rex, 1986).

In the analysis of ethnic divisions, as in the exploration of gender divisions, there is a need to analyse structural constraints upon political action in historical terms, examining both the establishment of institutions which privileged some and disadvantaged others and the development of ideologies which set out to justify inequalities. In the case of ethnicity, the establishment of cohesive nation-states involved the deployment of rules to define who did and who did not belong, and ideologies to justify those rules.

In this section, as in the previous one, it is open to question whether the phenomena being explored should be described as 'structural'. What is being described are divisions within societies, which are maintained and reinforced in various ways. It is implicit in feminist theory and in attacks upon ethnic divisions that there is a politics of challenge to these divisions. Where the structuralism comes in is in regarding challenging such divisions as a difficult political task. It is a task, moreover, where policy processes have to involve not just changing distributive or regulatory rules, but also challenging the ideologies that have underpinned those rules.

Conclusions

This discussion of structural determinants of policy processes has moved from theories which seem to be strongly determinist – structural functionalism and classical Marxism – to perspectives that many would not call structuralist at all, since they merely spell out factors which are likely to have a strong influence on political choices. Parsons (1995, pp. 608–9) argues that some of these may simply be incorporated into accepted constraints: 'The distinction between politics and economy and society . . . needs to be revised to take account of the argument that the world of "facts" and social and economic forces is not simply "out there".' He goes on: 'it may well be that external environments are better understood as mirrors or projections of the values, beliefs and assumptions which frame the internal policy-making process'.

This is, however, perhaps to make too little of some powerful forces at work. The case for a discussion of structuralist theory lies not primarily in a need to outline what are in many respects rather overdeterministic theories, but in a need to stress that there is running through any policy process a series of strong biases or influences on action. This may be described as an influential 'deep structure' (Schwarzmantel, 1994) or in terms of Lukes' 'third face of power' (see p. 41). Social change – in which the policy process plays an important part – involves a dynamic in which structure influences action and is at the same time altered by that action.

It has been shown that structural perspectives do not necessarily put 'class interests' and 'economic forces' as the only kinds of determining agents. Implicit in the concept of structure is a system which gives dominance to a range of powerful groups (see Degeling and Colebatch, 1984). Such groups will include professional and bureaucratic élites; males; specific ethnic, religious, linguistic groups, and so on. This dominance is given structural form by customary practices and modes of organisation. It may well be built into language, and manifested symbolically in a variety of ways.

Structures are not fixed and immutable. They vary in their strength. In giving attention here to formalised political institutions, it must not be forgotten that they vary considerably in strength and in the extent to which they are formalised. A distinction may perhaps be drawn between structures and institutions, where the latter are see as 'regularized practices *structured* by rules and resources "deeply layered in time and space"' (Thompson, 1989, p. 61). They are changed by action, and some actions may be specifically directed at trying to change structure. The prevailing order is continually being renegotiated. This is clearly not an easy process, but in addressing the determinants of decision making, it is one which must not be entirely disregarded (this sort of approach to the relationship between structure and action is explored in the sociological writings of Giddens (1976, 1984)).

This discussion of structure has left out a rather less deterministic theory, very much in this tradition, about the way in which existing institutions (from constitutions to 'standard operating procedures') influence the policy process. This is the concern of the next chapter.

CHAPTER 4

THE STATE AND THE POLICY PROCESS

Synopsis

This chapter explores a variety of theories which emphasise the need to see the state – as a whole or as clusters of actors – as an active element in the policy process. They build upon, supplement and to some extent contradict the pluralist, élitist and structuralist theories which treat the state as a relatively passive entitity. Approaches given particular attention are corporatist theory, emphases upon the roles of policy networks and policy communities, the economic theory of bureaucracy, explorations of the characteristics of bureaucrats, and institutional and constitutional analysis. The chapter ends with a brief section drawing upon comparative ideas which try to delineate the respective characteristics of strong and weak states.

Introduction

In Chapter 1 the institutions of the state itself were described as being treated as a 'black box' in some of the attempts to model the policy process. It has been suggested that, during the period in which academic political science developed rapidly in the United States and the United Kingdom between the 1950s and 1970s, there was a tendency to neglect the study of state institutions (Nordlinger, 1981; March and Olsen, 1984). The claim that there was a need for work 'bringing the state back in' (Evans *et al.*, 1985) rather exaggerated the earlier neglect. State functionaries, including the military, figured as key concerns in élite theory. Yet it was true that classical Marxist theory tended to see the state simply as a supporting player for the capitalist system, and that early pluralist theory largely treated it as a neutral institution which groups in society would compete to control.

March and Olsen contrast institutional theory with pluralist theory as follows:

> There are two conventional stories of democratic politics. The first story sees politics as a market for trades in which individual and group interests are pursued by rational actors. It emphasises the negotiation of coalition and 'voluntary' exchanges. The second story is an institutional one. It characterizes politics in a more integrative fashion, emphasizing the creation of identities and institutions as well as their structuring effects on political life. (1996, p. 248)

Their model, at least as expounded in their 1996 essay, sees a need for a fusing of the two approaches – the latter framing the former, but being open to change under various circumstances.

The various ways in which efforts have been made to explore within the 'black box' of state institutions are often linked to the earlier theories which writers are trying to amplify. A number of direct links back can be made to the issues discussed in the preceding two chapters, which it is hoped will be helpful in elucidating how the state can be brought more fully into the analysis. These are set out schematically in Table 4.1.

Table 4.1 Theoretical developments giving more attention to the state

Original theory	Development	Later developments
Pluralism	Corporatist theory	Networks and policy communities
Public choice pluralism	Economic theory of bureaucracy	Bureau shaping
Elitism	Wider exploration of characteristics of bureaucrats	Concern with the 'core executive'
Instrumental Marxism	Marxist corporatism	
Structural Marxism	Theorising the 'autonomous state'	
Structure/action theory	Institutional analysis	Analysis of constitutional constraints

Table 4.1 inevitably exaggerates the links between approaches: for example, there is little evidence that the historically minded political scientists who developed institutional analyses were very interested in the sociological theory on the relationship between structure and action. It also, in some cases, imposes a time sequence view of developments when there was not really one: for example, the economic theory of bureaucracy was probably, from the outset, a feature of public choice theory. However, its aim is to illustrate connections between the ideas to be discussed below and those examined earlier.

The following discussion will explore the ideas outlined in summary form in Table 4.1, apart from the Marxist theory of the 'autonomous state' which was examined in the previous chapter because of its essential connections with Marxist structuralism.

Corporatist theory (or corporatism)

Schmitter describes corporatism as a system of interest representation. He defines the ideal type of corporatism as:

> a system of interest representation in which the constituent units are organised into a limited number of singular, compulsory, non-competitive, hierarchically ordered and functionally differentiated categories, recognised or licensed (if not created) by the state and granted a deliberate representational monopoly within their respective categories in exchange for observing certain controls on their selection of leaders and articulation of demands and supports. (1974, pp. 93–4)

In Schmitter's analysis there are two forms of corporatism: state and societal. State corporatism is authoritarian and anti-liberal. The label is applied to the political systems of fascist Italy and Nazi Germany. In contrast, societal corporatism originated in the decay of pluralism in western European and north American political systems. Schmitter hypothesises that, in the latter systems, changes in the institutions of capitalism, including concentration of ownership and competition between national economies, triggered the development of corporatism. The need to secure the conditions for capital accumulation forced the state to intervene more directly and to bargain with political associations. The emerging societal corporatism came to replace pluralism as the predominant form of interest representation.

Much of the English language literature on corporatism has explored the concept's applicability to the United States and the United Kingdom. Its use to encapsulate the policy process in some of the continental European countries – and particularly Scandinavia, Austria and the Netherlands – has been rather more taken for granted. For example, writing about the last named country, Kickert and van Vucht say:

> The threat of labour revolt and rising socialism was countered at the end of the 19th century by the creation of 'corporatism': the institutionalisation of socio-economic cooperation between ... organised capital, organised labour and government. Based on this ... the Netherlands developed into an extreme example of the modern non-statist concept of *neo-corporatism*. This concept emphasises the interest representation by a number of internally coherent and well organised interest groups which are recognised by the state and have privileged or even monopolised access to it. (1995, p. 13)

This emphasis upon an organised and legally recognised system certainly highlights a difference from the rather uncertain evolution of the 'Anglo-Saxon' systems in this direction. Speaking primarily of these, Winkler (1976) argues that the state in capitalist society has come to adopt a more directive and interventionist stance as a result of a slowing down of the process of capital accumulation. Winkler points to industrial concentration, international competition and declining profitability in the UK economy as examples of significant changes in the economic system which prompted the shift towards corporatism. In his writings, Winkler stresses the economic aspects of corporatism, seeing it as a system of private ownership of the means of production combined with public control. According to Winkler, examples of corporate involvement by the state in the United Kingdom are provided by the development of policies on prices and incomes and the attempt during the 1970s to develop planning agreements with industry. These policies were worked out by the state in collaboration with business and trade union élites. Winkler does not specify precisely the role of the state in a corporate economy, nor does he discuss in detail the sources of state power. However, what seems clear is that, according to this view, the state is not controlled by any particular economic class or group, but plays an independent and dominant role in its relationship with labour and capital.

The political history of corporatism in the United Kingdom has been outlined most fully by Middlemas (1979, 1986). He argues that a process of corporate bias originated in UK politics in the period 1916 to 1926 when trade unions and employers' associations were brought into a close relationship with the state for the first time. As a consequence, these groups came to share the state's power, and changed from mere interest groups to become part of the extended state. Effectively, argues Middlemas, unions and employers' groups became 'governing institutions' (1979, p. 372), so closely were they incorporated into the governmental system. By incorporation, Middlemas means the inclusion of major interest groups in the governing process and not their subordination. The effect of incorporation is to maintain harmony and avoid conflict by allowing these groups to share power.

The impact of Margaret Thatcher in the 1980s led some British writers to dismiss UK applications of corporatist theory as merely a description of a passing phase (see, for example, Gamble, 1994). During this period the trade unions were dismissed from the 'triangular' relationship, and at times even the role of business seemed to be downgraded. But this evidence surely only discredits those who proclaimed, borrowing Marxist historicism, that we entered, in the 1970s, the 'age of corporatism'. Corporatism remained in other countries, and could return in the UK, as a way in which the state may 'manage' its relations with key economic actors.

In the United States, the relevance of the corporatist thesis has been questioned by observers such as Salisbury (1979), who have argued that Schmitter's model of societal corporatism does not fit the American experience. A different stance is taken by Milward and Francisco (1983), who note important trends towards corporatism in the United States. According to them, corporatist interest intermediation occurs around policy sectors based on government programmes. In these sectors, state agencies support and rely on pressure groups in the process of policy formulation. The result is not a fully developed corporate state, but rather 'corporatism in a disaggregated form'. In Milward and Francisco's view, neither federalism nor the separation of powers has precluded the development of corporatist policies, because corporatism is based on policy sectors which cut across both territorial boundaries and different parts of government.

It is apparent that corporatism is viewed in different ways by different writers. Theorists such as Winkler define corporatism mainly as an economic system to be compared with syndicalism, socialism and capitalism. In contrast, Schmitter, Middlemas, and Milward and Francisco discuss corporatism as a political system or sub-system. Reviewing different approaches to the use of the concept of corporatism,

Panitch (1980) argues for a limited definition. In his view, corporatism is not a total economic system, as Winkler argues, but rather a specific and partial political phenomenon. More concretely, corporatism is a political structure within advanced capitalism which 'integrates organised socio-economic producer groups through a system of representation and co-operative mutual interaction at the leadership level and mobilisation and social control at the mass level' (p. 173).

Those who see corporatism as a total system take up a position that is perhaps closer to Marxism than to pluralism, particularly if they see it not as a tripartite division of power among capital, labour and the state, but as an accommodation between capital and the state. It is for this reason that there is an entry in Table 4.1 on 'Marxist corporatism'. It is most appropriate to go on to this here.

It has been shown in the earlier chapters that a key element in neo-Marxist theory is a recognition of the role of the state as helping to deal with the crises of late capitalism (see, in particular, O'Connor, 1973; Gough, 1979). Wolfe (1977) sees corporatism developing as one response to this crisis. Noting the tension between the demands of accumulation and the need for legitimation within capitalism, Wolfe argues that political alternatives have been exhausted and that one response to government overload is a corporatist organisation of the state. In Wolfe's analysis this could involve, among other things, the economy being under the domination of monopolies making private investment decisions; the state planning apparatus working closely with these monopolies to further their investment decisions; representatives from trade unions acting as consultants to planning agencies; and the institution of price and wage controls.

The corporatist thesis has been criticised by Marxists for failing to develop an adequate theory of the state. Thus, Westergaard argues that in Winkler's analysis the state 'figures in a curiously disembodied form' and 'its ability to put the powers which it has acquired to uses of its own is only asserted, not demonstrated' (1977, p. 177). Westergaard goes on to maintain that the principles which guide corporatism are merely those of capitalism, and that corporatism is not a distinctive economic system. For his part, Winkler does not argue that corporatism favours redistribution or equality; nor does he quarrel with the view that the state acts to restore private profitability and to enhance capital accumulation. Where Winkler and other writers in the corporatist tradition take issue with the Marxists is in their analysis of the role of the state and its autonomy. The corporatist thesis is that the state has moved from a position of supporting the process of capital accumulation to directing that process. In making this shift, new patterns of relationships have developed between the state and the major economic interest groups, and the state, although constrained by these interests, has autonomy deriving from its command of legal, organisational and other resources. It is this autonomy which enables the state to act in the interests of capital, labour and other interests as appropriate.

For some writers, corporatism is seen as the best way of managing the conflict between the needs of the economy and the demands of consumers, highlighted as a problem for democracy by public choice theory (see Mishra, 1984). This brings us back to the more cautious formulations of corporatist theory discussed above. They talk about a variety of looser links between interest groups and the state. These formulations have generated a rather different way of conceptualising relationships between interest groups and the state. Grant (1989) has summed up the fate of UK corporatist theory, under the impact of political change and academic elaboration:

> By the time they had developed a conceptual apparatus to analyze the phenomenon, and had managed to organize large-scale research projects, the object of study was already dwindling in importance. The corporatist debate did, however, help to stimulate a new wave of theoretical and empirical work on pressure groups promoting a re-examination of pluralist theory, and thereby encouraging the development of new forms of pluralist analysis such as the idea of policy communities. (p. 36)

This leads us into the next section.

Policy networks and policy communities

As suggested above, the elaboration of ideas about corporatism led theory in some important new directions. Corporatist theory has indicated that there is a need to pay attention to the ways in which powerful interest or pressure groups outside the state and groups within the state relate to each other. But while it tends to seek, in a rather generalised way, to develop a single model embracing the 'parties' to this relationship into three over-arching groups – capital, labour and the state – other pluralist work has certainly suggested that the first two should not be regarded as united. The same point could be made about the state. Indeed, analysts of government have recognised that there are many difficulties in getting departments to act corporately. Many policy issues are fiercely contested between departments in relatively unitary systems of government, between central and local governments and between the many different elements in complex systems like that of the United States. These issues are further explored in Chapter 7.

Surely, therefore, it has been suggested, rather than seeing systems of corporatism, might there not be a variety of separate linking systems between interests within government and those outside? One such formulation postulates the existence of a variety of 'iron triangles' embracing the state and both sides of industry, and operating in specific industrial sectors and not necessarily across the economy as a whole (Jordan, 1986; Thurber, 1991; Salisbury, 1979).

A related alternative formulation, using the concept of corporatism, comes from Dunleavy (1981), who argues that it is possible to identify systems of 'ideological corporatism' (p. 7) in operation in policy communities. These systems derive from 'the acceptance or dominance of an effectively unified view of the world across different sectors and institutions' (p. 7). In many cases the unified view of the world emanates from a profession – the medical model is a good example – and provides 'ideological cohesion' (p. 7). Dunleavy goes further to suggest that:

> underlying apparent instances of policy shaped by professional influences it is possible on occasion to show that structural parameters and dynamics shaped by production relations and movements of private capital play a key role in shifts of welfare state policy. But I doubt if fairly specific policy changes can ever be reduced to explanation in such terms alone. (p. 15)

Both of these formulations suggest relatively strong links between actors – *iron* triangles, policy *communities*. Others have borrowed from transaction theory and from the sociological study of inter-organisational relationships to suggest that, where powerful institutions need to relate to each other over a period, they develop a variety of ways of doing business which assume a measure of stability (see Knoke, 1990). Furthermore, it should not be assumed that these relationships are simply one-way. Pluralist theory can be seen as stressing the amount of competition among groups to try to influence the state. Marxist theory goes to the other extreme of regarding the state as the 'creature' of capitalism. An alternative view is that both sides need each other – the pressure groups need to influence policy, the institutions of the state need support from powerful groups outside it. The exchanges may even be more explicit than that – when the two sides need to trade knowledge, expertise and influence over other actors. Hence, another contribution to the understanding of these relationships comes from the application of exchange theory (see Rhodes, 1981). State institutions and non-state institutions can be seen as linked by both reciprocal connections and more complex network relationships.

Smith thus argues that:

> The notion of policy networks is a way of coming to terms with the traditionally stark state/civil society dichotomy . . . State actors are also actors in civil society, they live in society and have constant contact with groups which represent societal interests. Therefore the interests of state actors develop along with the interests of the group actors and the degree of autonomy that exists depends on the nature of policy networks. (Smith, 1993, p. 67)

Smith explores the relationship between the two concepts outlined in the above discussion: 'policy networks' (the expression 'issue networks' is also used in this literature) and 'policy communities'. These are closely related ideas, between which there is no need to make a choice while formulating a policy theory drawing upon them. Communities are stronger versions of networks. Clearly, therefore, networks may cohere into communities and communities may disintegrate into networks. There may be some issues where communities are more likely than networks and vice versa. There may also be some institutional situations where one pattern is more likely than the other and so on.

Smith's analysis has been developed from the work of Jordan and Richardson (1987), which tends to use the expression 'policy communities' for a range of relationships of varying stability, and that of Rhodes (1988), which identifies networks of varying cohesiveness. Marsh and Rhodes (1992a) then build on this to characterise *policy communities* as follows:

- Having comparatively limited memberships, often with economic or professional interests, sometimes consciously excluding others.
- Sharing values and interacting frequently.
- Exchanging resources, with group leaders able to regulate this.
- Having a relative balance of power among members.

By contrast, *issue networks* are more likely to have the following characteristics:

- Large and diverse.
- Fluctuating levels of contacts and lower levels of agreement.
- Varying resources and an inability to regulate their use on a collective basis.
- Unequal power.

What is particularly important about this work – distinguishing networks and communities from simple pluralist clusters of organisations – is the emphasis upon the state interest in fostering them. Smith (1993), drawing on Jordan and Richardson (1987) identifies, for the UK case, four reasons for this:

- They facilitate a consultative style of government.
- They reduce policy conflict and make it possible to depoliticise issues.
- They make policy making predictable.
- They relate well to the departmental organisation of government.

An example of this is the grouping associated with the development of UK agricultural policy after the Second World War, involving close consultation between the government department responsible, the associations representing farmers' and landowners' interests, and the major suppliers of fertilisers and pesticides. This grouping has been seen as working in a concerted way, resisting influences from consumer interests and anti-pollution lobbies, and presenting itself as the manager of the countryside in opposition to other government departments as well as to outside pressure groups (Lowe, 1986). Between the 1940s and the 1970s, this could be described as a typical policy community; more recently it has weakened and has had to consult more widely, and it is now perhaps more appropriately described as a policy network.

Both concepts – and particularly policy communities – postulate a stable pattern of interest organisation, but there are some important issues about how such systems change over time. Smith (1993, pp. 91–8) suggests there is a need to recognise that, notwithstanding a considerable stability, change may be engendered by external relationships, general economic and social change, new technology, internal divisions within networks, and challenges between networks and within communities. In the case of agriculture outlined above, this change has come about because of the United Kingdom's membership of the European Community, together with the growth of a rural population with no commitment to agriculture (people working in or retired from the towns) and other events that have put consumerist and environmental issues on the political agenda.

There is a problem about policy community and policy network theory rather similar to that with the weaker versions of corporatist theory: that it offers a description of how policy decision processes are organised, but not any explanation of why they are organised in this way. This body of theory perhaps only refers to a tendency – a way relationships between the state and interest groups may be regulated. Drawing upon empirical studies, it is suggestive of the way in which relationships between the state and interest groups are likely to be regulated in a comparatively stable political system. Smith's book (1993) explored parallels between the United Kingdom and the United States, suggesting characteristics of the system of government in the latter that make networks more likely than communities, but still a great deal depends upon the policy sector. Studies in other societies suggest the existence of similar phenomena (see, for example, Kickert and van Vught (1995) on the Netherlands).

This emphasis upon networks and communities offers an important corrective to accounts of the political system and the operation of the state which treat them as homogeneous and unified entities. It also offers a of challenge to the 'stagist' approach to the policy process inasmuch as it emphasises how networks and communities function in a relatively integrated way from agenda-setting processes through policy making to implementation. There will be a variety of places in the next two chapters where readers will be reminded of this insight.

Economic theory of bureaucracy

We move on now, from a very cautiously advanced, research-based body of work about the relationships between the state and interest groups, to a much more abstract, deductive theoretical approach to emphasising the way interests *within* the state influence the policy process.

The public choice theory which was discussed in Chapter 2 as a form of pluralist theory sees political competition to win support as an activity that can be analysed like economic 'market' behaviour. This is a 'demand-side' theory about state behaviour. It is reinforced by a 'supply-side' argument which is concerned with the consequences of the fact that public bureaucracies tend to be monopoly providers of goods and services. This perspective then draws upon economic theory on monopoly which stresses the absence of constraints upon costs when these can be passed on to consumers, and the extent to which in the absence of market limitations a monopolist will tend to oversupply commodities. It is argued, therefore, that bureaucrats will tend, like monopolists, to enlarge their enterprises and to use resources extravagantly (Niskanen, 1971; Tullock, 1967; Buchanan and Tullock, 1962). Thus Tullock argues: 'As a general rule, a bureaucrat will find that his possibilities for promotion increase, his power, influence and public respect improve, and even the physical conditions of his office improve, if the bureaucracy in which he works expands' (1976, p. 29).

This theory has an intuitive plausibility, but comparatively little empirical evidence has been produced to support it. Self argues that 'these descriptions of the political process can be seen to be . . . overdrawn and exaggerated' (1993, p. 58). Earlier in the same book, Self describes the work of the key theorist on this topic, Niskanen, as 'logically and mathematically elegant . . . [but] empirically wrong in almost all its facts' (pp. 33–4). Self goes on to make the following five critical points:

1. The salary of a bureau chief is **not** closely related to the size of his bureau . . .
2. Bureaus are not necessarily monopolistic . . .
3. Political controllers are not so starved of information as Niskanen claims. . .
4. In any case bureau chiefs are . . . subject to the control of super bureaucrats . . .
5. It is impossible to say that bureaus produce an excessive output if there is no objective way of valuing the output. (p. 34)

It is not necessarily the case that bureaucratic success is measured by bureau enlargement. Brian Smith (1988, p. 167) points out how some of the most powerful and highly paid roles in civil services, in central finance departments for example, are in small organisations. Self has observed that 'Bureaucratic self-interest takes many different forms, depending on the different career patterns and normative constraints found in different public services' (Smith, 1988, p. 167, paraphrasing Self, 1985). Indeed, the political attack on big government has led to situations in which civil servants have been rewarded for their skills at cutting budgets, privatising public services and so on.

The use of such an economic model to theorise about public bureaucracy does, however, help us to analyse such organisations. It has led to a diligent search for situations in which 'perverse incentives' may be built into the day-to-day work of public organisations (see, for example, an influential examination of this issue in relation to the UK National Health Service in Enthoven (1985)).

The model has also provoked a radical counterblast, cast in its own terms. Where market considerations apply, organisations are likely to try to externalise costs. Without the constraints imposed by markets, bureaucracies may also, Dunleavy has suggested (Dunleavy, 1985, 1986, 1991), internalise costs. Examples of this include: exemplary employment practices (in relation to wages, equal opportunities, employee welfare, etc.), responsiveness to clients' needs and interests (appeals procedures, opportunities for participation on policy issues, etc.) and indeed general openness to political intervention. Demands that bureaucracies operate as if they were private firms therefore challenge directly a variety of 'benefits' (that is, the costs which have been internalised), therefore, that have often been taken for granted as characteristics of the public service. Privatisation of such organisations, Dunleavy (1986) argues, may both undermine the provision of these benefits and create situations in which there are incentives to externalise costs (pollution, income maintenance needs arising out of low-wage policies, health consequences of employment practices, etc.).

Dunleavy accepts that bureaucrats will tend to engage in self-interested activities which are directed towards maximising their own welfare; but he shows that whether or not this will involve maximising the size of their organisation will depend upon the task of the organisation, the external (including political) pressures upon it and their own roles within the organisation. He describes their strategies as 'bureau shaping'. He sums up his position as follows:

> Rational bureaucrats therefore concentrate on developing bureau-shaping strategies designed to bring their agency into line with an ideal configuration conferring high status and agreeable work tasks, within a budgetary constraint contingent on the existing and potential shape of the agency's activities. (Dunleavy, 1991, p. 209)

Hence public choice theory has *both* provided a set of arguments to support an attack on public bureaucracy *and* stimulated thinking about how we analyse organisational outputs. The attack on the public sector has taken the forms of both outright privatisation and efforts to create competition between or within bureaucracies (see Olson (1965, 1982) for the development of a rationale for this). Nevertheless, in both this theory and Dunleavy's alternative to it, it must be noted that the emphasis, as in classical economic theory, is upon what will be expected from an individual acting upon 'rational' self-interest. There remains a need to test whether actual behaviour is determined in this way. Thelen and Steinmo argue:

> people don't stop at every choice they make in their lives and think to themselves, 'Now what will maximise my self-interest?' Instead, most of us, most of the time, follow societally defined rules, even when so doing may not be directly in our self-interest. (1992, p. 8)

It will be shown in Chapter 7 that much research on organisations has raised doubts about the use of a simple model of 'self-interest' to explain behaviour.

The irony is that, inasmuch as public choice theory has been taken seriously, it has had a certain self-fulfilling effect. Strategies to control bureaucrats and professionals which assume that self-interest is the crucial motivating force in their lives tend to reinforce that phenomenon (through incentive structures) and to undermine altruistic behaviour by controls which send the message that the official is not regarded as trustworthy. Self (1993) puts a related point, with particular reference to the use of insecurity as a device to control bureaucrats:

> The problem of moral hazard, according to the theory, is that the bureaucrat will always tend to substitute his own personal wishes . . . However a short-term contractual relationship may well increase this danger . . . An official on limited contract will have less commitment to the public service and may be more disposed to use his position to establish useful contacts and opportunities in the public sector. (p. 166)

One can go further than that, seeing dangers both in strategies likely to be used to enhance job openings in the future and tactics to protect the current job.

We will return to aspects of this theme later in the book. What is clear is that the debate provoked by this aspect of public choice theory – on all sides – certainly does not treat bureaucrats as passive instruments who have policies imposed upon them. It has this in common with the theories derived from 'élitism' examined in the next section.

Exploration of the characteristics of bureaucrats

It has already been stressed that it is inappropriate to see élite theory as weak on the role of the state. Before going on to modern work which links with the élitist tradition or tests élitist hypotheses, it is necessary to look at what some of the earlier theorists in this tradition said about the state and its personnel.

In many respects, élite theory's origins (particularly the work of Mosca) lie in an attack upon Marxist dismissal of the potential of the state as an autonomous source of power. This attack acquired greater potency when allegedly proletarian states were set up, and the theory of the 'dictatorship of the proletariat' was used to justify autocracy (Lenin, 1917). Another critic of Marx, who cannot necessarily be described as an élitist, Max Weber, supplied significant supporting arguments for élitist work on the state with his careful examination of bureaucracy and his exploration of the relationship between bureaucracy and democracy. Weber's work on bureaucracy will be elaborated further in Chapter 7.

Part of Weber's thesis about the growing power of bureaucratic officials was illustrated with reference to one specific political area by Roberto Michels. In his book *Political Parties* (1915), Michels sets out to show that power in democratic mass parties becomes concentrated in a few hands. A key part of his argument is that full-time officials in socialist parties and trade unions are in a very strong position as 'professionals' relative to the 'amateurs' who may challenge them from the ranks of their supporters. A logical extension of this argument is to point out that permanent civil servants are in a similarly strong position relative to politicians. Moreover, Michels argues that radical and socialist politicians tend to become conservative, compromised by the bourgeois comfort of their own positions. They enjoy a situation in which they are at least partially accepted by the established order which they were elected to challenge, and inevitably many of them identify with one-time 'class enemies' rather than with their own mass supporters. In such cases they are ill-equipped to offer an effective challenge to civil servants who do not share their political commitments.

The primary target for Michels' attack was the democratic socialists, aspiring to achieve peaceful social change through control of the state by a mass political party, but his argument does hint indirectly at the problems that face the proletariat in controlling their own political apparatus in the Marxist post-revolutionary situation. Mosca (1939), on the other hand, is concerned to show much more directly that a socialist state will inevitably centralise power, and that mass democratic institutions are unable to control those at the centre of the political system. His argument implies either that permanent bureaucrats will enjoy a powerful position relative to politicians or that politicians will become, in effect, bureaucrats rather than servants of the people. While the actual institutional structure may vary, the ultimate tendency will be for politicians and bureaucrats to become indistinguishable, and as far as democracy is concerned, it will matter little whether what has happened has been the 'bureaucratisation of the politicians' or the 'politicisation of the bureaucrats'. To avoid this it is necessary to prevent the monopolisation of political power. The development of a powerful central bureaucracy must be checked by other independent institutions providing a source of countervailing power. What this seems to involve, in particular, is the continued existence of economic power outside the control of the state. Mosca is one of the first theorists, therefore, to argue that pluralism must be sustained to protect democracy from bureaucrats.

Mosca's theory was taken up in the 1930s by Burnham, who is best known for his argument that managers are replacing owners as the dominant group in capitalist society. But Burnham (1942) also widens his argument to suggest that members of the 'managerial class' that he claims to identify are beginning to dominate the state bureaucracy in all advanced industrial societies. He argues that the extension of state activities has helped to accelerate this trend, by widely extending the power of administrative bureaux. Burnham's position probably represents an extreme view about bureaucratic inevitability. He pays little attention to the possibility that bureaucracies may differ in kind and may be dominated by different kinds of people. As Gerth and Mills (1963) argue:

> much of the cogency that Burnham's thesis has is due to the simple fact that the form of organisation all over the world is, perhaps increasingly, bureaucratic. But the ends to which these structures will be used, who will be at their tops, how they might be overthrown, and what movements will grow up into such structures – these are not considered; they are swallowed in the consideration of the *form* of organisation, the demiurge of history, the 'managerial world current'. (p. 65)

While Burnham is little read today, the burden of Mosca's attack on bureaucratic power has been taken up by the public choice theorists, who were discussed in the previous section.

C. Wright Mills, though a critic of Burnham, was equally concerned about the power of bureaucracy. He claims:

> Great and rational organisations – in brief, bureaucracies – have indeed increased, but the substantive reason of the individual at large has not. Caught in the limited milieux of their everyday lives, ordinary men often cannot reason about the great structures – rational and irrational – of which their milieux are subordinate parts. Accordingly they often carry out series of apparently rational actions without any ideas of the ends they serve, and there is increasing suspicion that those at the top as well – like Tolstoy's generals – only pretend they know. (1963, pp. 237–8)

Mills argued that, paradoxically, these juggernauts, which are currently being run 'without reflection' by 'cheerful robots', can be brought under control. He thus asserted:

> In the polarised world of our time, international as well as national means of history-making are being centralised. Is it not thus clear that the scope and the chance for conscious human agency in history-making are just now uniquely available? Elites of power in charge of these means do now make history – to be sure under circumstances not of their own choosing – but compared to other men and other epochs these circumstances do not appear to be overwhelming. (1963, p. 244)

Mills' argument focuses upon the fact that centralised decisions are taken in bureaucratised systems of government, and it is his view, therefore, that there are key decision points which are open to influence. The conclusion this suggests is that, before rushing to any of the available macro-sociological conclusions about the role and control of bureaucracy in modern society, it is necessary to study precisely how decisions are taken, and to what extent there are really key positions of power. It is also necessary to ask questions about the kinds of people in powerful roles, about who is able to influence them, and about who benefits from their decisions. This takes the argument from high-level theorising down to some quite detailed questions about the exercise of power. As Lipset argues: 'The justified concern with the dangers of oligarchic or bureaucratic domination has . . . led many persons to ignore the fact that it does make a difference to society which set of bureaucrats controls its destiny' (1950, p. 271).

This points to the need to examine the characteristics and affiliations of public officials. We have already noted Miliband's view that the social origins of officials place them firmly in the capitalist camp. Rather different positions are taken by Kingsley (1944) and by Lipset (1950). Kingsley shows that the British civil service was transformed from an aristocratic into a bourgeois organisation during that period in the nineteenth century when the commercial middle class were becoming politically dominant. The British bureaucracy was thus made representative of the dominant political class, but not, of course, of the people as a whole. To work effectively the democratic state requires a 'representative bureaucracy', Kingsley argues, thus taking up the theme, developed also by Friedrich (1940), that the power of the civil service is such that formal constitutional controls upon its activities are insufficient. Kingsley sees the recruitment of the civil service from all sectors of the population as one means of ensuring that it is a 'responsible bureaucracy'. This issue has traditionally been explored very much in class terms (for a more recent comparative exploration of this issue along the same lines, see Aberbach *et al.* (1981)). This has meant a disregard of the equally important issues about gender and about ethnic, regional or religious origins or background.

Lipset's treatment of this issue can be found in his study of the Saskatchewan socialist party, the Co-operative Commonwealth Federation, where he analyses the difficulties the party found in implementing its policies once it acquired power. Lipset supplements Kingsley's argument about the social backgrounds of civil servants by pointing out that previous experience of serving more conservative governments will also have an impact upon the behaviour of civil servants called upon to implement markedly different policies. With reference to Saskatchewan he says:

> Trained in the traditions of a laissez-faire government and belonging to conservative social groups, the civil service contributes significantly to the social inertia which blunts the changes a new radical government can make. Delay in initiating reform means that the new government becomes absorbed in the process of operating the old institutions. The longer a new government delays in making changes, the more responsible it becomes for the old practices and the harder it is to make the changes it originally desired to institute. (Lipset 1950, p. 272)

This approach to the problem is much more clearly in the pluralist tradition. It does not treat civil service impartiality as an unalterable fact, but nor does it take the conspiratorial view that portrays civil servants as persons naturally committed to undermining a government of the left. Civil servants are recruited from certain kinds of social background, given certain kinds of training, and become accustomed to working for certain kinds of people and dealing with certain kinds of problem; any new group of political masters who want to turn their attentions to new issues and problems are bound to find that they cannot easily reorient the civil servants. Indeed, it is interesting that, while in the United Kingdom in the 1980s the higher civil service remained as biased in its social origins as ever (despite efforts to change this in the late 1960s), some representatives of the comparatively 'radical right' Conservative government which came to power in 1979 did precisely hint at this kind of concern. There has subsequently been some controversy about the extent to which Mrs Thatcher directly intervened in appointments to deal with this 'problem' (see Young (1989) for this claim, and Hennessy (1989) for arguments to the contrary).

The 'Whitehall model' (allegedly firmly established in the United Kingdom) is one in which public servants enter the service of the state early in their adult lives and are expected to serve varying political regimes impartially in return for career security. Campbell and Wilson argue:

> politicians in few countries place as much faith in bureaucrats as do the British. The British system contrasts not only with the patronage system at the top of the executive branch in the United States but also with the continental European practice (as in Germany) of placing senior civil servants in temporary retirement if a governing party loses power . . . the dependence of elected politicians on the non-partisan, permanent civil service was the core of the system that has been exported to other countries and admired by many non-British scholars. (1995, p. 293)

Earlier writers on the UK civil service (for example, Chapman, 1970) suggested that civil servants in the United Kingdom have strong reservations about party politics while at the same time possessing commitments to particular policies. The implication is that these officials find changes in their political masters easy to adjust to, so long as they do not involve violent ideological shifts. Officials can operate most easily in a situation of political consensus. Where consensus does not exist, however, their role may become one of trying to create it. Graham Wallas (1948) sums this up most neatly:

> The real 'Second Chamber', the real 'constitutional check' in England, is provided, not by the House of Lords or the Monarchy, but by the existence of a permanent Civil Service, appointed on a system independent of the opinion or desires of any politician and holding office during good behaviour. (p. 262)

This approach sees bureaucrats as a comparatively independent element in the political system. However, a number of observers of the scene have suggested that this picture of UK bureaucracy may be increasingly inaccurate. Interestingly, it is two American observers of the UK civil service, Campbell and Wilson, who bring out this argument most powerfully. The transformation they chart goes much further than simply a series of Thatcherite interventions to advance those who are 'one of us'. They argue that the traditional Whitehall model has been destroyed in several ways:

- The breaking of the monopoly of the civil service as advisers to ministers.
- The development of a system to help the prime minister contest civil service advice (a central 'policy unit').
- Most importantly, 'whole generations of bureaucrats and politicians have been socialised since the 1970s into very different professional norms . . . enthusiasm for government policies has been rewarded more than honest criticism' (Campbell and Wilson, 1995, p. 296).
- '[T]he erosion of the belief that the civil service is an established profession, like all professions delineated from society as a whole by clear boundaries' (p. 297).

Campbell and Wilson chart some similar developments in other systems close to the 'Whitehall model' in Australia, New Zealand and Canada. In Australia, however, Pusey has raised a rather different issue: that in a situation of conflict of values – over alternative ways of managing the economy –there has been a systematic effort to ensure that 'economic rationalisers' have advanced to dominate the civil service (Pusey, 1991). An ambiguity in Pusey's analysis concerns the extent to which this has been tacitly encouraged by elected politicians, on the Labour side as much as the Liberal.

Peters (1995) explores comparatively various models of the civil service career. An alternative to the Whitehall model is the American pattern at the top of the federal government service:

the revolving door, or the 'government of strangers' described by Heclo. In this system there is a great deal of movement between the public and private sectors, with most people staying in government only a few years . . . The majority of these 'in and outers' would be in political appointments made by the President and his cabinet. (Peters, 1995, p. 102; also quoting Heclo, 1978)

Another pattern involves a regular shift of career civil servants to employment in the private sector, as in France and Japan. Yet another is like the Whitehall model in respect of the permanence of civil service status, but this is not regarded as incompatible with a move elsewhere – even into a political role (as again in France and also in Germany and the Netherlands).

While the main focus of arguments about the values and allegiances of public servants concerns the top bureaucratic echelons, similar issues are raised by some writers about lower-level officials, about professional staff and about local government. In the whole of this debate there are dangers in treating public servants as a unitary group or class. But we should also not lose sight of the fact that there will be differences of interests, experience and culture within a vast state bureaucracy, and in particular differences between the personnel of different departments (see Hennessy, 1989, especially ch. 10). There are also groups of state employees to whom we have given little attention – such as the military, the police and the security services staff – who are radically different from most career administrators. Since it is maintained in this book that the policy process is important at all levels, these points too raise some important issues. We will return to some of them later in the book.

This section has examined a range of work which treats the characteristics and allegiances of state employees as of great importance for the study of the way the state works. It stresses the power of bureaucrats, seeing them as a potentially unified élite. In Chapters 7 to 9 this perspective will be contrasted with others which stress how organisations may be weak and divided. In Table 4.1 a 'later developments' column was included in relation to this theory – exploration of the role of the 'core executive'. This is a speculative and contentious addition. Rhodes has identified the core executive as a topic for exploration in relation to the UK system of government. He sees this theme as an extension of his own theory about networks and policy communities, and as developing Dunleavy's work on 'bureau shaping' (Rhodes, 1995).

However, the recognition that the UK system facilitates a high concentration of power involves in some respects an élite model – of the kind highlighted by Wright Mills. Furthermore, Campbell and Wilson's (1995) analysis of the development of the Whitehall model of government, quoted above, gives further sustenance to this theme. Finally, in the book of essays in which Rhodes explores the concept of the core executive, an essay by Thompson about decision making on exchange rates argues that 'the policy community approach was always at its least plausible in relation to strategic economic issues' (Thompson, 1995, p. 269). This theme, that in the United Kingdom – and perhaps in some other highly centralised countries – there is a 'high politics' which is very much an élite preserve, will be explored further later in the book. Clearly, the interest in the analysis of the core executive need not be seen as propagating an élite theory of politics inasmuch as that executive is democratically accountable. But is it?

Institutional and constitutional analysis

This section is concerned with the impact of the institutions, and the constitutional structure, of the state upon the policy process. As is the case with policy network theory, a key influence upon the institutional approach to the study of the policy process has been the importation of ideas from organisational sociology. This has been going on for a long while. Selznick's classic study of the Tennessee Valley Authority was published in 1949. Theorists like Barnard (1938) and Simon (in particular in his *Administrative Behaviour*, 1957) stressed the need to see policy decision making in its organisational context. Selznick (1996) has reasonably been critical of the clear line that modern institutionalists have tried to draw between their work and his, but then academics have to try to claim originality!

Another feature of the development of institutional analysis has been the recognition of the need to employ historical analysis, to trace the evolution of policy over a long period of time. Some of the key theorists have described themselves as 'historical institutionalists'. They see themselves as drawing inspiration from 'a long line of theorists in political science, economics and sociology including Polanyi, Veblen and Weber' (Thelen and Steinmo, 1992, p. 3)

March and Olsen explain their view of the importance of the institutional approach as follows:

> Political democracy depends not only on economic and social conditions but also on the design of political institutions. The bureaucratic agency, the legislative committee, and the appellate court are arenas for contending social forces, but they are also collections of standard operating procedures and structures that define and defend interests. They are political actors in their own right. (1984, p. 738)

Hall makes a rather similar point in stressing the ways policy actors' behaviour is shaped:

> Institutional factors play two fundamental roles in this model. On the one hand, the organisation of policy-making affects the degree of power that any one set of actors has over the policy outcomes . . . On the other hand, organisational position also influences an actor's definition of his own interests, by establishing his institutional responsibilities and relationships to other actors. In this way, organisational factors affect both the degree of pressure an actor can bring to bear on policy and the likely direction of that pressure. (Hall, 1986, p. 19)

Hall's approach involves stressing institutional influences outside the formal institutions of government. He asserts, contrasting his work with that of others – including March and Olsen – that he 'ranges more widely to consider the role of institutions located within society and the economy' (p. 20). His study of economic policy making in the United Kingdom and France pays considerable attention to the ways in which economic interests are formally represented in the political process. His perspective is therefore very close to that of the writers on policy communities discussed above.

The quotations above tend to project a static view of the institutional approach. They suggest that an examination of a policy process needs to be seen as occurring in organised contexts where there are established norms, values, relationships, power structures and 'standard operating procedures'. But much of the work in this tradition is also concerned to look at how those structures were formed and to elucidate the extent to which they impose explicit constraints and the circumstances in which they are subject to change. As March and Olsen say: 'while institutions structure politics, they ordinarily do not determine political behaviour precisely' (1996, p. 252). Hence the examination of this approach in this chapter rather than the previous one.

Skocpol (1995) and her associates (Weir *et al.*, 1988) have used the institutional approach to good effect to explain the evolution of social policy in the United States. Their analysis explores policy change or its absence over a long period. In the United States in the nineteenth century, democratic political institutions (only for white males, of course) predated the elaboration of public administration. This created a situation in which patronage practices were the main form of response to political demands, as opposed to distributive policies using a state bureaucracy. For example, pension provisions for civil war veterans were extended as political favours way beyond their original intentions. Political institutions were functioning to deliver benefits to some, but to limit the scope for more fundamental state-driven reform.

In the context of a federal constitution requiring complex alliances to secure social reform, policy change was difficult to achieve. Many promising movements for reform failed to put together winning coalitions. This remained the situation until an economic crisis in the 1930s enabled the 'New Deal' leaders to put together a coalition of the northern urban working class with the whites of the rural and racist south, which could initiate new policies and offer a brief challenge to the older interpretation of the constitution. But the changes achieved were limited because the president still had to carry a resistant legislature.

The legacy of the policy changes in the 1930s continued into the post-war period, and into the period when emergent black groups had some success in challenging the status quo and the constitution. But such social policy legislation as had been achieved in the 1930s had added the northern white working class, who had gained through the development of social insurance pensions, to the coalition against more radical reform. A policy change at one point in time created institutions which would serve as a barrier to change at a later point. As March and Olsen say: 'Programs adopted as a simple political compromise by a legislature become endowed with separate meaning and force by having an agency established to deal with them' (1984, p. 739, drawing here upon Skocpol and Finegold, 1982). This analysis is taking a general point, which is quite often made, about the barriers to political change imposed by the US constitution, and expanding it into an analysis of both barriers to and opportunities for policy change in a context in which one set of changes then sets the structure for future events (or non-decisions).

Immergut (1993) has carried out a somewhat similar analysis on a comparative basis, exploring the evolution of health policy in Switzerland, France and Sweden. She writes of a policy game being played within a set of rules. In her study, other events, over a turbulent period in European history, had an influence on the 'rules'. These had an impact, in different ways in each country, upon 'veto' points where those opposed to change (principally the medical profession) could be successful and 'access' points where change agents could succeed.

Immergut's approach has been developed interestingly by Hwang (1995) in a study of health reform in Taiwan. A generalised commitment to state health policy originating in the republican constitution developed on the mainland of China in the 1920s, and a series of limited *ad hoc* social insurance developments in the period between 1950 and 1980 to help to engender social support for the authoritarian regime, set a framework for the rapid moves towards a national health insurance scheme as Taiwan democratised in the late 1980s and early 1990s.

The institutional approach, if applied satisfactorily, needs to handle the relationship between structure and action, and not just to emphasise institutional constraints. For example, it is only too easy to treat the US constitution as a straitjacket which effectively makes it impossible to get some issues on the agenda. An examination of the history of efforts to secure a universal health insurance scheme in that country encourages this view (see Skocpol, 1995, ch. 9). Yet the US constitution has been amended many times and, perhaps even more importantly for the policy process, it has been subject to reinterpretation in ways that in the 1930s widened the scope for federal action and in the 1960s opened the door to the civil rights movement. Political activity is not just a game played within rules, it also often involves efforts to renegotiate the rules. The revision or reinterpretation of the rules ('meta-policy making') is important. In a study of the development of Swedish labour market policy, which examines the way trade union interests were built into the policy process, Rothstein suggests that: 'In some, albeit probably rare, historical cases, people actually create the very institutional circumstances under which their own as well as others' future behavior will take place' (1992, p. 52).

The other point, which Skocpol's work particularly emphasises, is the way successful action generates new constraints (rules or structures). But constraints are not necessarily either structures or rules. Hall's work (1986) has concerned the rise and fall of Keynesian economic dominance in government, seeing constraints not so much in structures as in dominant ideologies, and charting how these change over time. He shows how a Keynesian orthodoxy became established in the key policy-making institutions that framed all policy choices. A shift to policy options outside that framework first required an ideological shift, facilitated in the case of the United Kingdom by the victory of a government disposed to encourage it.

March and Olsen draw attention to the work of Bachrach and Baratz discussed in Chapter 2, and by implication also to Lukes' work in arguing that so-called 'rules' embody implicit exclusion assumptions:

Constitutions, laws, contracts, and customary rules of politics make many potential actions or considerations illegitimate or unnoticed; some alternatives are excluded from the agenda before politics begins . . ., but these constraints are not imposed full blown by an external social system; they develop within the context of political institutions. (1984, p. 740)

A related point is made by Thelen and Steinmo, who argue that the use of class differences in explaining political behaviour needs to be supplemented by exploring 'the extent to which it is reinforced through state and societal institutions – party competition, union structures, and the like' (1992, p. 11).

Clearly this institutional approach to the study of the policy process involves interpretation. It does not suggest that outcomes can be easily 'read off' from constitutional or institutional contexts. Immergut sets out her games analogy as follows: 'Institutions do not allow one to predict policy outcomes. But by establishing the rules of the game, they enable one to predict the ways in which policy conflicts will be played out' (1992, p. 63). There is a suggestion here that institutional analysis may need to lay so strong an emphasis upon specific configurations of institutional situations and actors that all it can offer is an account of past events, from which little generalisation is possible. In other words, the example from Hall's work quoted above may involve no more than quoting, with the benefit of hindsight, all the things that reinforced the Keynesian orthodoxy at one point in time and then undermined it later. This is the direction in which some of the things March and Olsen had to say about the institutional approach seem to be leading:

the new institutionalism is probably better viewed as a search for alternative ideas that simplify the subtleties of empirical wisdom in a theoretically useful way.

The institutionalism we have considered is neither a theory nor a coherent critique of one. It is simply an argument that the organisation of political life makes a difference. (1984, p. 747)

There are two parts to this problem. One is that institutional theory brackets together a very wide range of potential constraints from constitutions and laws, through institutional self-interest and standard operating procedures to ideologies. To some extent this mixing of the formal and the informal is justifiable: sociologists have rightly warned us against treating constraints built into rule books as if they are necessarily firmer than custom and practice, particularly when the latter have penetrated into our language. But in analysing policy constraints we do need to make some distinctions in order to explore what breach of them may involve. We will return to this issue at various points later in this book – notably in Chapter 7, where Selznick's contrast between 'organisations' and 'institutions' is quoted (p. 165), and in Chapter 8, where Feldman is quoted as comparing formal limits with a wall and social context limits with a rushing stream (p. 193).

The second problem concerns the identification of the conditions under which change occurs. These may be conceptualised in terms of 'access points' (Immergut, 1993) or 'punctuated equilibrium' (Krasner, 1988) or 'critical junctions' (Collier and Collier, 1991) or 'performance crises' (March and Olsen, 1989). There is clearly a methodological difficulty here – these can be readily identified with the benefit of hindsight, but can they be recognised in advance?

Thelen and Steinmo recognise this, saying – specifically about the model of 'punctuated equilibrium' – that the problem is 'that institutions explain everything until they explain nothing' (1992, p. 15). They go on to argue that their concept of 'institutional dynamism' addresses the problem by identifying situations 'in which we can observe variability in the impact of institutions over time but within countries' (p. 16). The problem remains, however, that work from this school involves the interpretation of case studies where the reader is invited to share the writer's understanding of events.

Going even further down this problematical path, March and Olsen have given us, from their work with Cohen, a memorable expression to typify an extreme version of the institutional approach: 'the garbage can model'. They say, almost as if distancing themselves from their own idea:

> In the form most commonly discussed in the literature, the garbage-can model assumes that problems, solutions, decision makers, and choice opportunities are independent, exogenous streams flowing through a system (Cohen *et al.*, 1972). They come together in a manner determined by their arrival times. Thus, solutions are linked to problems primarily by their simultaneity, relatively few problems are solved, and choices are made for the most part either before any problems are connected to them (oversight) or after the problems have abandoned one choice to associate themselves with another (flight). (March and Olsen, 1984, p. 746; see also March and Olsen, 1989)

There is a problem that, once any attempt to generalise is left behind in this way, the student of the policy process is being required to take a position like a purist atheoretical historian, determined to let the facts speak for themselves without any principles to help organise attention or lessons to draw from the study. Or is he or she being urged to look to psychology to offer some organising principles? Certainly there has been a whole range of policy analysis literature which suggests the need to draw upon psychology. There is obviously no objection to this. The problem is that, except in some forms of social psychology which are very closely linked to organisational sociology in endeavouring to explain how structures influence attitudes and thus actions, much of this literature does no more than tell us that individual attitudes, emotions etc. will influence decisions. Parsons makes this point well about Ken Young's essay (1977) on the 'assumptive worlds' of policy actors: 'The problem is . . . how can we students of public policy actually study this "assumptive world"? . . . Surface, observable forms of politics   are somewhat straightforward as compared with "values", "beliefs", "assumptions", and the "subconscious" aspects of policy-making' (Parsons, 1995, p. 379). There is obviously a need to be sensitive to unique juxtapositions of events and the unique responses of individual actors, but if we are sitting in the 'garbage can' watching the latter deal with the former, we can do little but describe what happens on each unique occasion.

Clearly the extreme positions described in the last few paragraphs are not typical of the institutional school, but they do remind us how much institutional analysis of the policy process is an intuitive art. Institutionalist writers offer a critique of other approaches to policy analysis. For example, Immergut portrays her work as 'a break with "correlational" thinking' (1992, p. 57), argues that it goes beyond the static perspectives of interest group theory (p. 66) and asserts that 'the view that institutions are somehow congealed social structure is not especially helpful' (p. 85). But do institutionalist writers actually replace or supplement other theoretical approaches?

The remark above about 'intuitive art' is perhaps applicable to all policy process studies. Certainly the drift of argument in this chapter and the two that precede it has been that all the bolder generalisations about the policy process should be received with some scepticism. The concerns with policy networks and communities, with the careful study of the characteristics, situations and attitudes of public policy-makers and with institutional configurations and constraints discussed in this chapter offer looser and less dogmatic approaches to the study of our subject. These ideas will be applied throughout the rest of this book, in varying combinations.

Strong and weak states

Before leaving this discussion of the role of the state in relation to the policy process, it is appropriate to note that distinctions are made by some writers between 'strong' and 'weak' states. This is obviously pertinent to the above remarks above institutional theory, since this work is very concerned with differences in the effects of different state structures. It is also relevant to the discussions of corporatism and of policy communities, where there are again explicit or implicit comparative observations around about differences between the United Kingdom and the United States and about the role of the 'corporatist' state in some continental European countries.

Dyson's (1980) analysis of the differences between the way the state is conceptualised involves describing the United Kingdom and the United States as 'stateless'. This is a rather deliberate exaggeration – to describe societies in which the state is large and costly in this way violates common sense. His object is to emphasise both an absence of ideologies which ascribe a special role for the state in society, and to show that a fragmented view of the state is dominant in the way institutions work. In this book the formulation 'strong' and 'weak' states is preferred to 'state' and 'stateless societies'.

Analysis of the state in the Anglo-American tradition, according to Dyson (1980, particularly p. 217) leads to a narrow concern with the working of institutions, cutting any critical discussion off from the mainstream concerns about the relationships between politics and society. Accordingly there has been a tendency, particularly in the United Kingdom, to see 'public administration' as a rather pragmatic descriptive topic, a poor relation of mainstream political science as research developed on elections, political parties and Parliament. This tendency was also perhaps related to a view that the process after basic policy setting was rather unimportant – the straightforward translating of policy into action. This is a view to which much of the rest of this book offers a challenge.

Dyson argues that the concept of state, inasmuch as it means more than an actor in international relations, involves: 'a legal conception which attributes a distinct personality to a particular institution or complex of institutions'; 'a political conception which establishes the unique character of . . . the exercise of public power'; and 'a sociological conception which refers both to an institution endowed with a remarkable coercive power and to a special type of communal bond capable of generating sentiments of affection and disaffection' (1980, p. 206). These characteristics are then more evident in some societies than others.

Dyson describes strong states as resting upon a tradition which involves 'a widespread sense of the legitimacy of public action . . . and . . . a willingness to define "public power" as distinctive and to exercise it authoritatively' (p. 256). Such states do not necessarily have bigger governments – his proposition is about how power is exercised. Weak states, by contrast:

> are characterised by the strength of pluralism, representation and the debating tradition in the political culture; an instrumental view of government and a pragmatic conception of politics . . .; a pervasive informality in politics . . .; a preference for 'social' models of the constitution or economic analyses of politics which emphasize the role of élites rather than institutions. (p. 52)

It is interesting to note how the strong state idea is used by Pusey about a society which might be expected to be very much in the Anglo-American camp. Pusey sees Australia as a 'nation building state' or alternatively as 'born modern', in that from an early stage in its existence the state took upon itself the role of steering economic development and protecting the interests of its working people. Crucial to this view of Australia is the importance of the establishment of protective trade barriers and a minimum wage policy (and also, of course, less to its credit 'the white Australia policy') at the beginning of the twentieth century (Macintyre, 1985).

The Australian case is the subject of controversy – while it is seen by Esping-Andersen (1990) as a typical 'liberal' state, Australian analysts have alternatively argued that its distinctive stance of egalitarian economic management makes it rather different from the United Kingdom and the United States (Castles, 1985; Castles and Mitchell, 1992). Pusey's similar typification of Australia must, however, be recognised as contained within an attack on the extent to which 'economic rationalists' within the Australian government are shifting it into the liberal camp.

The examination of the case of Australia draws attention to other societies where a very positive role for the state has been adopted – Japan, South Korea and Taiwan, for example. While the Japanese case may have parallels with the shift from absolutism traced by Dyson in Europe (see, for example, Harrop, 1992), South Korea and Taiwan are examples of societies where states have accepted a crucial modernising role from the outset (inasmuch as these states assumed their modern forms only in the 1940s). The east Asian model of state-led development has, of course, attracted widespread attention (Lau, 1986; Sandhu and Wheatley, 1990). It is interesting that all three states mentioned here were in a sense American 'protectorates' in the post-war period. While there were distinctive efforts to implant 'pluralist' political ideas in these societies, the initial defensive need for the 'strong state' was evident. Confucian doctrines about the state and the roles of its servants seem also to have had some influence on the subsequent translation of these into strong economic roles.

The weak states are those, as Dyson's definition makes clear, in which bargaining between interests is clearly seen as legitimate. The strong states manifest powerful views of the public interest which do not of themselves rule out bargaining (indeed, where they do this is a crucial aspect of a drift into authoritarianism, according to Dyson's analysis). Corporatism is seen by Dyson (1980, p. 70) as a crucial aspect of the process of accommodation between the strong state and strong interest groups (particularly in the Netherlands and Austria), involving the latter fully in the policy process, but expecting in return some regard for the over-arching state interest (see also the quotation from Kickert and van Vucht on p. 67).

In the weak states, administrators are seen as crucially subordinate. They are expected either to play neutral roles, responding to demands, or to be clearly identified (as political appointees or people co-opted for their links to interest groups) as on a particular 'side' in arguments.

In the strong state, permanent administrators have been accepted as much more likely to be involved in policy processes very fully and from very early on. Implicit in this is the acceptance that they are committed to the state interest. The alternative models for the roles of civil servants in France and Germany were explored earlier. Both accept a very central role for them in the policy process, and both have been the subject of some concern. In the French case, the debate has been about 'technocracy' (Meynaud, 1965). In the German case, the argument has entered into the wider international literature through Max Weber's anxieties about the relationship between bureaucracy and democracy (Gerth and Mills, 1948, pp. 77–128).

There are dangers in using the concepts of 'strong' and 'weak' states. Atkinson and Coleman (1989) have pointed out that their application needs to be modified by taking into account the extent to which there is centralisation, and then – inasmuch as there is not – recognising the variations there may be between policy sectors. Their analysis of state strength also goes on to remind us that, if the concept is used, there needs to be some consideration of the strength of the elements in society that the state is striving to influence and regulate. Strength is a relative concept – a so-called 'strong state' may not look so strong when it is dealing with a unified and well-organised group of economic actors. Howlett and Ramesh go on from that point to argue 'there is no reason to believe that strong states will necessarily make policies that serve the interests of society as a whole, rather than those of self-serving groups' (1995, p. 60). In other words, do not allow usage of the concept of the 'strong state' to leading to a begging of the question about the respective power of the state and other groups involved in the policy process.

In fact there are grounds for applying the concept of the weak state only to the United States among the states considered here – as a policy-making system in which parties are weak and interests are strong, set in a constitution which makes a very complex bargaining process essential for policy change.

The case of the United Kingdom is more curious. A Canadian, applying state theory to a comparison between her country and the United States, suggests that:

> political structures that adhere to a parliamentary system of government, have a propensity for party discipline and executive dominance, a tradition of a permanent, low profile, independent and experienced civil service, and a long history of interventionist social policy, produce a potentially strong and autonomous state in relation to social institutions. (Boase, 1996, p. 290)

That description seems to fit the United Kingdom well. Since the arrival on the scene of the Labour Party, and the related shift away from 'economic liberalism' by the Liberals at the beginning of the twentieth century, the UK policy-making scene has been dominated by strong programmatic stances by the political parties. The electoral and parliamentary institutions have tended to polarise political debate into distinctive 'left' and 'right' positions. Furthermore, one side in that polarity – the left – has tended to need to strengthen the state in order to realise its goals.

Hence, there is a need to be cautious about the typification of the United Kingdom as a 'weak state'. The title of Gamble's analysis of 'the politics of Thatcherism', *The Free Economy and the Strong State* (1994) encapsulates the crucial point here. As Gamble suggests: 'The idea . . . involves a paradox. The state is to be simultaneously rolled back and rolled forward' (p. 36). It can perhaps be said that state strength has been used to weaken the state, at least in relation to the industrial sector. Hall makes the same kind of point in a rather different way – emphasising ideology – in his exploration of Thatcherite economic policy, where he cites this as evidence of the way 'A coherent and technically plausible set of ideas, commanding the support of some body of experts, can confer a degree of independence on the state' (1986, p. 128). There was in these events, in effect, a weakening of the state by the state; a paradoxical development only possible because of the incapacity of many interest groups to block determined state action.

The further general point here is that the importance of party politics in the UK system makes the role of the state an area of controversy in a way it is not in the United States.

The peculiar impact of the dominance of a single party in the United Kingdom, throughout much of the recent past, has been highlighted in Dunleavy's analysis of 'policy disasters'. It is suggested that 'five main factors seem to be involved in generating policy disasters: scale aggregation, overly speedy legislation and policy making, political hyperactivism, the arrogance of Whitehall, and ineffective core executive checks and balances' (Dunleavy, 1995, p. 59). The first two and the last are essentially institutional factors – unitary government, a simple law-making process ('the fastest law in the west', Dunleavy says, taking this expression from a comment on the government of a smaller similar case, New Zealand) and very centralised power. 'Political hyperactivism' can be seen as a characteristic of the contemporary ideological climate, while Dunleavy's fourth point emphasises the way in which 'political responsiveness and policy activism' (p. 62) are at a premium in the top civil service.

This rather complex comparative analysis could be considerably extended. It has been appended to this chapter on the role of the state to bring out some of the ways in which quite complex social, cultural and institutional analysis is needed to explore the role of the state in the policy process. It requires a fusion of institutional theory with an awareness of the characteristics of core élites and a recognition of the roles of policy networks and communities. The next chapter, particularly its second half, picks up some of these issues.

CHAPTER 5

POLICY MAKING

Synopsis

Chapter 1 pointed out that many discussions of the policy process analyse it as a series of stages. It also suggested that this approach has been widely criticised, and acknowledged that there are dangers implicit in such an approach. It argued nevertheless that a book which is trying to explore a large and complex process needs to divide that process up in some way. The most obvious way to make that division is to give separate attention to policy making and implementation. This is what is being done here, while attempting to ensure that readers do not lose sight of the links or interactions between these two processes.

Various writers have tried to analyse how policy is made, influenced by a desire to prescribe the *best* way to do it. This chapter will start with this vein in the literature, exploring the arguments about the so-called rational model of decision making and the incrementalist alternative. This will be followed by some examination of the roles of the main participants in policy processes – party politicians, interest groups and administrators. While these are analysed as separate topics, there is an important link between them. An influential group of prescriptions about how policy should be made will be shown to encounter problems because of their disregard of the extent which policy making is a *political* process. But then a political process, particularly in a democratic context, is one in which some actors are seen to have a more legitimate policy-making role than others. Hence, there is a potential conflict between the best way to make policy and the claims of particular actors – politicians – to have particular rights to make policy. This issue has been summed up by Lindblom and Woodhouse in terms of the question: 'How can government be organized to locate power and wisdom in the same place?' (1993, p. 23). They set out to offer an answer. This chapter will not do that, but rather explore the issues which need to be taken into account in trying to do it.

Decision-making theory and policy making: introduction

The controversy about the way policy decisions should be made has been a dispute between an approach which is distinctly prescriptive – rational decision-making theory – and alternatives of a more pragmatic kind, which suggest that most decision making is 'incrementalist', and that this offers the most effective way to reach accommodations between interests. The following discussion will briefly outline the argument between proponents of the rational model and the incrementalists, and examine some compromise positions between them. It will then go on to argue that neither theory really addresses the issues about the impact of ideological influences on policy.

The rational model

Herbert Simon's *Administrative Behaviour* (1957) constitutes an important early contribution to thinking about decision making. In his view, a theory of administration has to be concerned with 'the processes of decision as well as with the processes of action' (p. 1), and to this end Simon attempts to specify exactly what is involved in decision making.

Beginning with a definition of a decision as a choice between alternatives, Simon states that rational choice involves selecting alternatives 'which are conducive to the achievement of goals or objectives within organisations', and that this is of fundamental importance in giving meaning to administrative behaviour. Rational decision making involves the selection of the alternative which will maximise the decision-maker's values, the selection being made following a comprehensive analysis of alternatives and their consequences.

There is a danger of oversimplifying the positions of the contributors to the debate about rationality. Simon's position is by no means that of advocacy of a simplistic, politics- and pressure-free model of decision making. Nor is he unaware of the complexity of the ideal of 'rationality'.

Simon acknowledges difficulties with the rational approach. The first is: whose values and objectives are to be used in the decision-making process? Clearly, organisations are not homogeneous entities, and the values of the organisation as a whole may differ from those of individuals within the organisation. Simon's response to this point is to argue that 'a decision is "organisationally" rational if it is oriented to the organisation's goals; it is "personally" rational if it is oriented to the individual's goals' (pp. 76–7).

This leads on to a second difficulty with Simon's approach: namely, that it may not make sense to refer to the goals of an organisation. A similar problem arises here as in the discussion of policy (see Chapter 1): that general statements of intention within organisations are implemented by individuals and groups who often have discretion in interpreting these statements. Goals in public organisations are 'policies', and are likely to be the continuing subjects of dispute and modification. If, furthermore, as is argued in the next chapter, policy is to some extent made, or at least reformulated, as it is implemented, then it may be less useful to refer to an organisation's goals than to the goals of the individuals and groups who make up the organisation.

The third major difficulty with Simon's model of rationality is that, in practice, decision making rarely proceeds in such a logical, comprehensive and purposive manner. Among the reasons for this are that it is almost impossible to consider all alternatives during the process of decision; knowledge of the consequences of the various alternatives is necessarily incomplete; and evaluating these consequences involves considerable uncertainties. But it is precisely because of these limits to human rationality, maintains Simon, that administrative theory is needed.

What Simon is arguing then is the need to explore ways of enhancing organisational rationality. There is a fourth difficulty in achieving this: namely, how to separate facts and values, and means and ends, in the decision-making process. The ideal rational model postulates the prior specification of ends and the identification of means of reaching these ends. Simon notes a number of problems with the means–ends schema, including that of separating facts and values. As he argues, the means of achieving ends are not devoid of values, and a way of coping with this has to be found in decision making. Simon's proposed solution is 'A theory of decisions in terms of alternative behaviour possibilities and their consequences' (p. 66), in which 'The task of decision involves three steps: (1) the listing of all the alternative strategies; (2) the determination of all the consequences that follow upon each of these strategies; (3) the comparative evaluation of these sets of consequences' (p. 67). Rationality has a place in this model, in that 'The task of rational decision is to select that one of the strategies which is followed by the preferred set of consequences' (p. 67).

It follows that the means–ends rational model is, as Simon always intended, an idealised view of decision making in organisations. Simon recognises this, and he notes various ways in which actual behaviour departs from the theory. Accordingly, Simon elaborates the idea of 'bounded rationality', in the preface to the second edition of his work (p. xxiv), to describe decision-making in practice. Bounded rationality involves the decision-maker choosing an alternative intended not to maximise his or her values, but to be satisfactory or good enough. The term 'satisficing' describes this process, and bounded rationality enables the administrator faced with a decision to simplify by not examining all possible alternatives. Rather, rules of thumb are adopted, and as a result important options and consequences may be ignored.

Through all this, as identified in relation to Simon's first and second areas of difficulty, policy decision making is an interactive process, involving individuals with often conflicting interests and goals. There is a tendency for Simon to offer rules for *the* decision-maker – in the singular – when what is involved is a complex collective process. This is where the incrementalist theorists offer a superior model.

Incrementalism

If Simon is a complex thinker whose views tend to be oversimplified, this is even more true of the leading exponent of the incrementalist view, Charles Lindblom. His work is particularly confusing because he has revised his position several times. Lindblom is critical of the rational-comprehensive method of decision making. In its place, he sets out an approach termed 'successive limited comparisons', starting from the existing situation and involving the changing of policy incrementally.

In describing decision making by successive limited comparisons,

Lindblom reiterates many of Simon's reservations about the rational model. Braybrooke and Lindblom (1963) note eight failures of adaptation of the rational-comprehensive model or, as they call it in this context, 'the synoptic ideal'. They argue that it is not adapted to the following:

1. Limited human problem-solving capacities.
2. Situations where there is inadequacy of information.
3. The costliness of analysis.
4. Failures in constructing a satisfactory evaluative method.
5. The closeness of observed relationships between fact and value in policy making.
6. The openness of the system of variables with which it contends.
7. The analyst's need for strategic sequences of analytical moves.
8. The diverse forms in which policy problems actually arise.

Consequently, decision making in practice proceeds by successive limited comparisons. This achieves simplification not only through limiting the number of alternatives considered to those that differ in small degrees from existing policies, but also by ignoring consequences of possible policies. Further, deciding through successive limited comparisons involves simultaneous analysis of facts and values, and means and ends. As Lindblom states, 'one chooses among values and among policies at one and the same time' (1959, p. 82). That is, instead of specifying objectives and then assessing what policies would fulfil these objectives, the decision-maker reaches decisions by comparing specific policies and the extent to which these policies will result in the attainment of objectives.

This theme has been taken up very forcefully by Gregory (1989), who takes issue with a restatement of the 'rationalism' case by Goodin (1982), and questions the value of adopting an 'ideal' approach which flies in the face of political realities.

Lindblom argues that incrementalism is both a good description of how policies are actually made, and a model for how decisions should be made. Prescriptively, one of the claimed advantages of muddling through is that serious mistakes can be avoided if only incremental changes are made. By testing the water, the decision-maker can assess the wisdom of the moves he or she is undertaking and can decide whether to make further progress or to change direction.

This is developed at some length by Lindblom and his collaborators.

In *A Strategy of Decision* (1963), he and David Braybrooke describe in detail the strategy of disjointed incrementalism, which is a refinement of the successive limited comparisons method. Disjointed incrementalism involves examining policies which differ from each other incrementally, and which differ incrementally from the status quo. Analysis is not comprehensive, but is limited to comparisons of marginal differences in expected consequences. Using disjointed incrementalism, the decision-maker keeps on returning to problems, and attempts to ameliorate these problems rather than to achieve some ideal future state. What is more, decision-makers adjust objectives to available means instead of striving for a fixed set of objectives. Braybrooke and Lindblom note that disjointed incrementalism is characteristic of the United States, where 'policy-making proceeds through a series of approximations. A policy is directed at a problem; it is tried, altered, tried in its altered form, altered again, and so forth' (p. 73).

This theme of co-ordination is taken up in Lindblom's *The Intelligence of Democracy* (1965). The problem addressed in that book is how to achieve co-ordination between people in the absence of a central co-ordinator. 'Partisan mutual adjustment' is the concept that Lindblom develops to describe how co-ordination can be achieved in such a situation. Partisan mutual adjustment is the process by which independent decision-makers co-ordinate their behaviour. It involves adaptive adjustments, 'in which a decision-maker simply adapts to decisions around him', and manipulated adjustments, 'in which he seeks to enlist a response desired from the other decision-maker' (1965, p. 33). Each of these forms of adjustment is further divided into a variety of more specific behaviours, including negotiation and bargaining. In a later article, Lindblom (1979) notes that, although there is no necessary connection between partisan mutual adjustment and political change by small steps, in practice the two are usually closely linked. This has been shown by Harrison *et al.* (1990, pp. 8–13) to be a weakness in Lindblom's argument, since a sequence of essentially incremental changes may well occur in a context in which certain parties are dominating and therefore 'mutual adjustment' is not occurring. This, they contend, has been characteristic of change in UK health policy, where medical interests have dominated.

Later, Lindblom altered his position, moving away from the rather optimistic pluralism of his earlier work. In *Politics and Markets* (1977), Lindblom accepts that pluralism is biased in favour of certain groups, particularly businesses and corporations. Yet he resists the argument that centralised planning would be a preferable means of making decisions. Rather Lindblom argues that the veto powers so prevalent in the US political system, and which prevent even incremental change occurring in some policy areas, need to be challenged through a restructuring of 'mutual adjustment'. Specifically, he proposes that the role of planners in the policy-making process should be to help to give 'absentees' a voice. The overall aim should be 'greatly improved strategic policy-making, both analytical and inter-active' (1977, p. 346). This case is argued through fully in his work with Woodhouse (1993), where Lindblom reasserts his critique of 'bureaucratic intelligence' and speaks of 'the potential intelligence of democracy', which can be realised if the 'impairments' of the political process are remedied through measures to increase the influence of ordinary groups of citizens as opposed to the influence of business élites.

Lindblom also accepts, in his later work, that partisan mutual adjustment is only active on ordinary questions of policy. Certain grand issues such as the existence of private enterprise and private property, and the distribution of income and wealth, are not resolved through adjustment. Rather, because of 'a high degree of homogeneity of opinion' (1979, p. 523), grand issues are not included on the agenda. Lindblom adds that this homogeneity of opinion is heavily indoctrinated, and in *Politics and Markets* he explores the operation of ideology. Lindblom's argument is that in any stable society there is a unifying set of beliefs which are communicated to the population through the church, the media, the schools and other mechanisms (1977, ch. 15). These beliefs appear to be spontaneous because they are so much taken for granted, but they favour and to some extent emanate from dominant social groups.

There is thus an interesting shift in Lindblom's position, from one in which bargaining is seen as both inevitable and desirable, to one in which ideology is seen to play a role, but essentially as a limited influence upon the range of actors and the range of options going into the bargaining process.

Alternative perspectives on decision making

In the light of the carefully qualified position taken by Simon and the many modifications that Lindblom has been prepared to make to his earliest statements of the incrementalist position, there might be thought to be little middle ground between them. But this has not stopped scholars trying to occupy that ground. Key examples of this are found in the work of Dror (1964) and Etzioni (1967). For Dror, Lindblom's favoured strategy of muddling through more skilfully acts 'as an ideological reinforcement of the pro-inertia and anti-innovation forces' (p. 153). According to Dror, this strategy is acceptable only if existing policies are in the main satisfactory, there is a high degree of continuity in the nature of problems and there is a high degree of continuity in the means available for dealing with problems. These criteria may be met when there is a large measure of social stability, and Dror argues that incrementalism may be appropriate in many policy areas in the United States. But where the conditions do not prevail, and where a society is seeking to bring about significant social changes, then incrementalism will not be appropriate.

The alternative to muddling through, suggests Dror, is not the rational-comprehensive model, but a normative optimum model which is able to 'combine realism and idealism' (p. 157). In broad outline, such a model involves attempts to increase both the rational and extra-rational elements in decision making. The extra-rational elements comprise the use of judgements, creative invention, brainstorming and other approaches. The rational elements involve not a comprehensive examination of alternatives and their consequences, and the complete clarification of values and objectives, but a selective review of options and some explication of goals. What this implies is a decision-making method somewhere between the rational-comprehensive and incremental methods. Thus, while Dror is prepared to accept the validity of incrementalism as a descriptive theory, he argues for an optimal method as a means of strengthening and improving decision making. One of the features of the method is the stress placed on meta-policy making: that is, 'policy-making on how to make policy' (1968, p. 160). In Dror's analysis, there is a need to invest resources in designing procedures for making policies in order to produce better decisions.

Etzioni accepts the force of the argument that a series of small steps could produce significant change, but adds that 'there is nothing in this approach to guide the accumulation; the steps may be circular – leading back to where they started, or dispersed – leading in many directions at once but leading nowhere' (1967, p. 387). In place of incrementalism, Etzioni outlines the mixed scanning model of decision making, a model he suggests is both a good description of how decisions are made in a number of fields and a strategy which can guide decision making.

Mixed scanning rests on the distinction between fundamental decisions and incremental or bit decisions. Etzioni suggests that fundamental decisions, such as the declaration of war and the initiation of the space programme, are recognised by the incrementalists, but are not given sufficient emphasis. In Etzioni's view, fundamental decisions are important because they 'set basic directions' (p. 388) and provide the context for incremental decisions. Mixed scanning is an appropriate method for arriving at fundamental decisions because it enables a range of alternatives to be explored. Essentially, mixed scanning involves the decision-maker undertaking a broad review of the field of decision without engaging in the detailed exploration of options suggested by the rational model. This broad review enables longer-run alternatives to be examined and leads to fundamental decisions.

The importance of mixed scanning and of Dror's optimal model is mainly that they are attempts to meet widely held reservations about incrementalism as a prescriptive approach.

Lindblom, in his later writings, appears to be in sympathy with the need for different kinds of contributions to decision-making processes. This much is indicated by his advocacy of 'methods that liberate us from the synoptic and incremental methods of analysis' (1979, p. 522). Ultimately, this amounts to an argument for strategic analysis on appropriate issues to be joined by various forms of creative problem solving. It is in this direction that a new form of rationality may emerge.

This search for compromise very much involves efforts to separate fundamental or important or strategic decisions from more routine ones. Is this feasible? As Smith and May note, 'fundamental decisions in one context are incremental in another and vice versa' (1980, p. 153). Etzioni's example of declaration of war seems an obvious enough fundamental decision, yet wars have emerged from a succession of incremental decisions, made with a minimum of open debate (Vietnam!). Another example cited by Lindblom is the nuclear energy programme. Here the evidence is that nations drifted into this, developing scientific research in secret because of nuclear power's close links with defence, only gradually realising the dangers involved in the nuclear energy programme and then tending to play these down in order not to cause public alarm.

At this point we thus encounter three new problems. The first of these is that – as in the examples above – processes of policy evolution may be incremental yet, since not involving 'partisan mutual adjustment', still not participative in the pluralist sense. This position rests upon a view about the unequal distribution of power, which has been shown to be taken into account in the Lindblom's later work.

The second involves an emphasis upon the importance of institutional constraints. This picks up on March and Olsen's work, discussed in the preceding chapter. Such constraints make both 'rational' policy planning and 'partisan mutual adjustment' difficult. March and Olsen argue that 'Insofar as political actors act by making choices, they act within definitions of alternatives, consequences, preferences (interests), and strategic options that are strongly affected by the institutional context in which the actors find themselves' (1996, p. 251). We also saw that in some of their work March and Olsen seem to go even further in seeing the way policies emerge as like the way rubbish accumulates in a 'garbage can' (see p. 90). Kingdon (1984) has similarly written of 'policy streams' and the concept of 'primeval soup', used by writers on the early stages of natural evolution, as something from which 'policy entrepreneurs' draw in an opportunist way. He sees three independent streams – problem recognition, policy proposals and political events – which must come together for policy making, but regards their joining as essentially unpredictable. Theories of this kind continue to provoke work, rather like that of Dror and Etzioni, to try to rescue rationality from the 'garbage can' by fusing it with a realistic appreciation of the politics of decision making (see, for example, the work of Sabatier and Jenkins-Smith (1993), discussed briefly later).

The third point is that the most significant attack upon the instrumentalist position comes not from the advocates of closed administrator-dominated 'rational' decision processes, but from those whose ideological commitments lead them to demand bold steps. A very old ideological argument, influential in the 1950s and 1960s, led to a peculiar distortion of the arguments about incrementalism. Incremental decision making was seen as a characteristic of pluralistic societies, while comprehensive planning was seen as a feature of totalitarian societies (Popper, 1966). The suggestion above that private decision making may be just as incremental as public decision making is reinforced by the now increasing evidence that the so-called planning of the communist societies was often a very haphazard process. We now see that those societies seldom engaged in holistic planning, despite their claims and rhetoric; rather they tended to lock themselves into bureaucratic allocation systems which were hard to change.

Furthermore, when there were great leaps forward in policy, these were ideologically driven, not the product of the kinds of planning process described by Simon (see, for example, various analyses of the Great Leap Forward and the Cultural Revolution in China, e.g. Brugger and Reglar, 1994, ch. 1). While today dramatic policy changes motivated by socialist ideology have become rare, if not extinct, on the other political wing, ideologues of the 'liberal' right seem prepared to disregard Popper's endorsement of the desirability of 'piecemeal social engineering' in their endeavours to eliminate the collectivist state or to enforce their concept of the ideal family. In other words, the clearest recent examples of policy-makers disregarding the warnings of the incrementalist school come from ideologically driven politicians of the right, committed like Margaret Thatcher to eliminating 'socialism' in the institutions of the central and local state and restoring 'Victorian values'. 'Policy disasters' (see p. 96) have emerged from the recent hyperactivism of the UK right.

The rationalism/incrementalism debate is beside the point when it is party political commitment or ideology rather than either rational planning or 'partisan mutual adjustment' which drives the policy debate. The following scenario is surely by no means unlikely:

- A problem exists to which it is difficult for government to develop an effective response – its causes are unknown, or beyond the reach of government action, or are phenomena with which the government is reluctant to deal (for example, economic influences upon crime).
- Nevertheless the key policy actors want to be seen to be 'in control' or at least doing something (have made claims that they can manage the economy, combat crime, solve international conflicts).
- In addition, some of the actors are driven by strong ideologies (particularly important as far as politicians are concerned).
- The result is a series of actions presented as problem solving, but which may equally be the thrashing around of a system which needs to be seen as active, but does not really know what to do (in these circumstances it is important not to be deceived by the rational action language that politicians are likely to use).

These issues will be explore further by shifting from this literature about policy decision making to some of the questions about who makes policy.

Who makes policy?

Policy making is a process which involves elected politicians, appointed civil servants and representatives of pressure groups who are able to get in on the action. The purer forms of rational decision-making theory seem to want civil servants to be dominant. One of the strengths of the incrementalist critique is that it attacks this perspective as unrealistic and not necessarily productive of better decisions.

In the study of policy processes, there has been a long-standing concern to define appropriate roles for the various protagonists. Simon's 'rational model' envisages politicians making the value choices, forming 'premises' for the more detailed decision processes to be carried out by officials. In doing this he was echoing the influential early work of Wilson (1887), which tried to delineate the respective territories of 'politics' and 'administration'. Wilson's dichotomy may be seen as to some extent an attempt to draw a distinction between the 'policy process' and 'implementation', whereas Simon more realistically recognises that the early – policy-framing – stages of the policy process inevitably involve more than politicians' input.

Wilson's dichotomy has been widely attacked, not so much for its prescriptive aspirations, as for its impact upon the way policy processes are described. It is seen as a 'hindrance to accurate scholarship' (Skok, 1995). It is important to observe how often politicians or administrators are involved in the policy process on the 'wrong' side of the boundary in Wilson's dichotomy. In fact, permanent officials are almost universally involved in the preparation of policy, while politicians' need to be responsive to the problems faced by their electors leads them often to take an intense interest in the implementation process. The next chapter returns to the latter theme, while this chapter will now proceed to explore the former.

A typology for the analysis of the role of the participants in the policy process

The discussion of the relevance of theories of the state in the previous three chapters has directly indicated that policy-making processes are likely to involve the following:

- Efforts to influence and bargain about policies by a variety of interest groups (even those who reject pluralist theory acknowledge roles of this kind played by élites or economic interest groups).
- Activities by 'insiders' within the state, both elected and appointed.

In addition, what that discussion did not focus on directly – though it is there indirectly both in the consideration of political parties in pluralist politics and in Marxist and élitist theory – is the role of party political commitments or programmes in the policy process. Policies are made in a context in which there are contested value systems – inevitably strongly linked to competing interests – which are articulated to varying degrees by political parties. Some policies are directly portrayed as efforts to enforce changes compatible with a specific ideological goal (in particular, the curbing or advancement of market systems of distribution, the strengthening of the nation or the curbing of ethnic or gender biases in society). Many more policies are advanced in ideological ways – projected in terms of what they will do to increase freedom, protect the family or increase equality – even if their links to these ideals are fragile. Ideology – or more loosely the specification of policy goals by (or within) political parties, whether used symbolically or not, plays an important part in the rhetoric of policy making – being seen as giving direction and purpose to the activity. These inputs into the policy process will be given the label 'party political' in the discussion below, but reference will also be made to their ideological foundations.

The three threads in the policy process identified above are drawn out in Table 5.1, and will be followed through in the rest of the chapter.

It is always risky to advance a typology – opening oneself up to criticism for oversimplifying the world and disregarding the extent to which types are mixed in reality. This typology is advanced in the recognition that most actual policy processes embody aspects of all three process types and that events do not necessarily occur in the order or with the participants that this typology suggests. However, the justification for this typology will, it is hoped, emerge from the discussion below. In short, its object is to highlight some distinctive aspects of some parts of many policy processes.

Two general ideas are embodied in this typology. One is that there

Table 5.1 Threads in the policy process

	Party political	Bargaining	Administrative
Kinds of issue	Perceived to have major distributive consequences	Affecting powerful interests	Nearly all
Key actors	Political parties	Pressure groups	Civil servants
Stage – space	Public	Public and private	Private
Key stage – time	Early	Middle	End

are different types of policy. While the most influential work on this subject was done by Lowi (1972) (see the account of this on pp. 11–12), a rather simpler approach seems more appropriate here. A distinction is drawn between issues perceived to have major redistributive consequences (in terms of either resources or power), which may include Lowi's 'regulatory' and 'constituent' policies, and may provoke general political mobilisation on each side and those which have a narrower and more specific impact upon some groups of citizens. It is recognised that it may not be so much the types of policy *per se* which are important, but rather the ways people are affected and the numbers and kinds of people affected. Wilson (1973), for example, has distinguished 'concentrated' and 'dispersed' costs and benefits, and Hogwood (1987) has suggested that policies vary in the extent to which their benefits can be distinguished.

The other element in the typology is the use of theatrical metaphors (Goffman, 1971), seeing people as 'actors' and recognising that there are significant processes occurring 'offstage' (away from public scrutiny or participation).

In addition, some attention is given to the extent to which the process may be seen as going through a number of stages (acts, in dramatic terminology). This may be seen as reintroducing the 'stagist' approach to the policy process in another way. However, the aim is to recognise that there are sequences of activities and that there are differences in the kinds of actor involved (even if clear distinctions between political and administrative roles cannot be made). Differences between political institutions, political cultures and policy sectors will be seen as relevant to the way in which these roles are mixed in different situations.

One other distinction between policy processes which might have been built into the model concerns the extent to which there is a relationship between a so-called new policy and both its predecessors and those policies it will be alongside. A theme which is explored further in the next chapter, when we look at implementation, concerns the fact that what may be called 'policy space' is generally crowded. Policies supersede, supplement or even conflict with other policies. They seldom involve innovation in an area where government has hitherto been inactive. Hogwood and Peters (1983) have suggested that policy processes are likely to involve one of the following, other than simply 'innovation':

- Policy succession – involving replacement but with strong elements of continuity.
- Policy maintenance – adaptation or adjustment of policy.
- Policy termination – when a decision to stop something must also be seen as deliberate policy change.

This distinction is introduced here because it obviously complicates the interactions to be discussed below. Existing policies that are the subject of change are likely to have political and pressure group support (and opposition) and involve administrative participation. The same will be true of other policies in the 'space' which an innovation is expected to enter. These will have an impact on the way the policy-making, and the implementation, process is played out.

Party political processes

There is an interesting tendency for journalists to exaggerate the political aspects of the policy process and for political scientists to play them down. The latter is partly a recognition of the complexity of the policy-making process – the long transforming process from initial goals to final outcome, a process in which the party political input inevitably becomes watered down. The model used here acknowledges the importance of this, but it is suggested that the party political or ideological element in the policy process should not be given too little attention.

Ideology is clearly important in the formulation of political party stances on policy. Pluralist political science has been particularly prone to play it down – perhaps because of its discomfort about the indirect concept of democracy it works with, perhaps because of its relative unimportance in the competition between American political parties. Ideology has been seen as something associated with extremist political movements – fascism and communism – in which a political claim to embody the 'general will' is used to suppress the expression of particularist interests. In the cold war period after the defeat of fascism in Europe (Bell, 1960) and in the era since the fall of the Soviet empire (Fukuyama, 1992), some writers have been prepared to proclaim the end of ideology – meaning the replacement of broad ideological conflicts by the very specific politics of competing interests.

The 'end of ideology' perspective has been widely criticised for deliberately ignoring the extent to which there is an explicit ideological consensus among political élites and decision-formers, masking or suppressing alternative views. A consensual party politics – about individual 'spoils' – involves a disregard of the continuance of broad divisions in society – big differentials in income, wealth and power – around which political mobilisation would be appropriate. Much of the argument about ideological forms of politics centres upon socialist or social democratic politics. The fiercest condemnation of the end of ideology school of thought comes from socialists who still see very good reasons for mobilising around redistributive causes. They are opposed by those who, as suggested in Chapter 3, adopt an almost structurally deterministic view about the inevitability of the capitalistic economic system and the resource distribution consequences of market systems.

However, it is a curious characteristic of much of the politics of the last quarter of the twentieth century that the strongest injection of ideology into politics has come from the advocates of market systems – the 'New Right' or the exponents of 'market liberalism'. These people have argued that politicians who have the best interests of society at heart should stand out against the pluralist forces which dominate day-to-day policy processes (see pp. 96 and 108). In the United Kingdom since 1975, therefore, a considerable amount of policy analysis has concerned itself with the character of the new ideology (Hall and Jacques, 1985; Self, 1993; Gamble, 1994) and with the extent of its impact on policy outcomes (Marsh and Rhodes, 1992b). While some of this has suggested that there has been a tendency to exaggerate the impact of 'Thatcherism', it surely does not underestimate its significance as a new ideological injection into the policy process. That it seldom achieved its initially proclaimed goals is simply to acknowledge the complexity of the policy process. Much the same can now be said as we view the 'wreckage' of the highly ideologically driven and 'undemocratic' policy processes which occurred in the Soviet Union.

The other delusion of the 'end of ideology' school of thought was a tendency to regard other general bases for political mobilisation – race, nationality, religion, gender – as unimportant in developed and prosperous societies. This delusion was, of course, linked to disregard of economic inequalities, since there are strong links between these other foundations for ideological politics and material disadvantages. Nevertheless some of the fiercest political conflicts in the modern world are about participation in political and other institutions, or even the formation of new political units, in situations in which the distributional consequences of change are unclear. The conflict in Northern Ireland, while it has its roots in the original British conquest and subsequent Protestant domination, is more a battle about institutions and their implications for individual identities than about resources. A solution to satisfy the Catholic side could have long-run distributional consequences. But the economic systems on either side of the border have a great deal in common, and are likely to be increasingly linked in the European Union. This does not prevent the most fiercely contested ideological policy-making process in the United Kingdom, in which the communities repeatedly show where they stand through the ballot box, and their leaders are acutely aware of their political constituencies.

The position taken here, then, is that many policy processes start from strongly asserted ideological commitments. In some cases, however, these commitments are so dominant that alternatives are not on offer in the programmes of effective opposition parties. In this case the apparent consensus which runs through the policy process may lead the ideological origins of the policies to be disregarded.

Where ideological conflict is open and positions are strongly contested, the political party roles in the policy process will be very evident, particularly at the early stages of a policy process. After that, if a policy-making process is to occur, either a measure of compromise is reached or (and this is the part that the more complacent accounts of the process tend to disregard) some opponents accept the inevitability of defeat, leaving the stage for the detailed decision making to others. The example discussed above of Northern Ireland is one where ideology remains dominant at the time of writing, as the 'peace process' runs erratically on and on. The point is that, if to evolve into an effective policy-making process (as opposed to being an impasse in which actors continually reassert their disagreements), it will have to reach a stage where the participants work together in a more relaxed way over details.

As policy processes evolve, there are at least three routes for opponents to take: to maintain formal opposition in parliamentary 'set pieces', to settle for small compromises which reduce the perceived negative impact of the policy, or to withdraw from the contest completely.

Hence strongly contested party politics is most likely when there are big issues at stake. The ideological elements in a policy are likely to be revealed at an early stage of a policy process – perhaps in manifestos or statements at party meetings. Broad groups – generally mobilised in political parties – will compete on a public 'stage' about the issues. Then, assuming the proponents of such a policy innovation think they can win through to enact something, they will press on to a more detailed policy formulation stage, in which broad opposition may still be evident, but in which (unless there has been a miscalculation about the general prospects for the policy) it may be increasingly muted or impotent. Detailed bargaining moves centre stage.

Agenda setting

At various places in this book, warnings have been given about the use of models of the policy process which see it as a sequence of stages in time. However, it is appropriate to insert at this point in the discussion a brief comment on 'agenda setting'. It has been suggested that ideological processes are particularly associated with this initial formulation of policy ideas. Agenda setting is in many respects an ideological process, translating an issue into a policy proposal. Parsons (1995, p. 87) gives an example of a sequence: issue – people sleeping in the streets → problem – homelessness → policy – more housing. Then he argues:

> We may all agree what an issue is but disagree as to what exactly the problem is, and therefore what policy should be pursued. If we see people sleeping on the streets as a problem of vagrancy, then the policy response may be framed in terms of law enforcement and policing. (p. 87)

There is an extensive literature on social problems (see, for example, Becker, 1966; Berger and Luckman, 1975) which explores the way in which (a) personal 'troubles' are interpreted as social issues (Mills, 1959); (b) those issues are defined as problems requiring solutions; and (c) appropriate solutions are identified. Models of society and of the nature of social pathology will influence that process. These models will influence views about the extent to which state intervention is appropriate and about the form any such intervention will take. Another name for such models is ideologies.

Hence, inasmuch as political organisations are formed around ideological positions, or have their activities framed by ideologies, they are likely to play crucial roles as agenda-setters. Another way of seeing party political activists is as 'policy entrepreneurs': 'people who are willing to invest resources of various kinds in hopes of a future return in the form of policies they favour' (Kingdon, 1984, p. 151).

However, party activists are by no means the only 'policy entrepreneurs'. Pressure groups and even comparatively isolated intellectuals may also be engaged in this activity. Furthermore, much political party activity – particularly in those contexts where ideology plays a comparatively low key role in party politics – may be seen not so much as involving policy entrepreneurship as using other people's ideas in efforts to frame electorally appealing programmes. In this sense they may be seen as '"policy brokers" – whose dominant concerns are with keeping the level of political conflict within acceptable limits and reaching some "reasonable" solution to the problem' (Sabatier and Jenkins-Smith, 1993, p. 27).

Bargaining processes

While party political processes, often embodying ideological stances, are particularly evident at the early stages of a policy process, it does not follow that bargaining is absent. Rather the statements above concern relative dominance *when* there is a policy issue at stake on which broad party mobilisation is likely. Many policies do not originate in this way. In each of the sections into which this discussion has been divided, we will find issues about policy origination arising.

In this part of the discussion, it is important to remember that organised groups in society are not just reactive. They are very likely to press for political actions which enhance their interests. This is the simple 'demands' model of politics, celebrated in pluralist and public choice theory, and enshrined in models like Easton's (see pp. 19–21). They may, of course, make their demands in an open way to political parties, and in doing so they may find these embraced in a political package put to the electorate: for example, in a manifesto. The danger for them in doing this is that the policies will acquire a party political tinge, from the way in which they are presented to the public and linked to other objectives. Other routes into the policy process may be preferable to them.

The discussions in Chapter 4 about the way pluralist theories have been adapted into 'corporatism' and into the notions of 'policy networks' and 'policy communities' draw attention to the ways in which interest groups and the state are linked into frameworks which facilitate consensual and often covert forms of bargaining over policy issues. For the doctors or the farmers to pursue interests through overt alliances with political parties may be a dangerous strategy. It is much better for these groups to be linked into policy-making institutions in which they can negotiate with ministers and officials over their policy concerns.

Of course, the extent to which bargaining processes can be covert depends upon the extent to which there is public controversy. We may contrast, to take some examples from recent UK political history, the fierce open politics of the 'poll tax', income maintenance reform (in the 1986 Social Security Act) or rail privatisation with legislation to change the way mentally ill people are treated or to consolidate the law dealing with the protection of children. The last two examples are ones where the parties were not really divided. The numbers of legislators with detailed knowledge of the issues were limited, and they mostly had such knowledge because of specific briefing by interest groups. Much of the detail of the legislation was settled behind the scenes – between civil servants and representatives from the groups within the 'policy community'.

The examples in the last paragraph represent extreme cases. In between there are examples – education and health policy reform – where the politicians took broad stands on either side, clothing what they had to say in pro- or anti-market ideologies. Nevertheless, at the more detailed stages of the policy-making processes it is possible to find: (a) changes made by the government after representations from or negotiations with interest groups; and (b) amendments moved by legislature members from both government and opposition, which were inspired by interest groups.

A final group of policies in the United Kingdom are ones which excite high levels of conflict, but where that conflict is not orchestrated along straightforward political party lines. These are often matters of moral or religious conflict – abortion, divorce, capital punishment, liquor licensing, etc. The politics of these issues may be described as 'ideological' in the broad sense; it is manifested, however, in an intense interest group politics, offering what perhaps in the United Kingdom comes nearest to the pluralist model of politics. The political parties will tend to seek ways to handle them which minimise the damage that might be caused by the fact that they cause divisions in their own ranks.

The examples in this discussion have been drawn from the United Kingdom. It is very important to bear in mind the importance of political institutions and political culture in influencing the relative importance of party politics, bargaining and the administration in the policy process. The contemporary UK political system drives many issues into a framework dominated by political parties. A country with a less simplified party system (the Netherlands, for example) or a less integrated legislative system (the United States, for example) will experience the unifying influence of ideology and the fragmentary influence of bargaining rather differently.

Bargaining will go on throughout the policy-making process (and beyond: see the next chapter), but it is particularly likely either where pressure groups are themselves the initiators of policy or at the stages in the policy process when broader aspirations are translated into action. It is likely to be both overt and covert – which is appropriate may be a matter for tactical decision by the interest groups. In particular, there will be trade-offs to consider between the possibility of embarrassing the government and attracting wider support on the one hand, and the importance of maintaining a 'policy community' in which there is a relatively privileged access to power (see Smith (1993) ch. 4 on the way these issues cause change in policy communities).

Administrative processes

The last two sections set the parameters for this one. Under what circumstances are administrators inside the system (but not simply put there to advance the cause of a particular party or group) the initiators of policy? And at what stage do they get involved in policy processes they have not themselves initiated? There are some complex, and controversial, issues wrapped up in those two questions.

The assumption that top administrators are problem-solvers, likely to want to make improvements in policy some of which entail much more than adjustments at the implementation stage, is built into much of the prescriptive literature on the policy process. As suggested above, the 'rational model' is largely founded on this assumption. In this case it is the expertise of the permanent officials which is seen as providing the justification for their role in policy making. But then the way in which value issues and factual issues are intertwined makes it difficult to draw lines and determine limits to their participation.

Take, for example, 'community care' policy in the United Kingdom. A decision – presumably taken by a politician, and certainly with a strong ideological tinge to it – made in the early 1980s led to a situation in which large numbers of low-income people were able to get help from the social security system towards care in private residential homes, without any evaluation of the extent to which such care was essential. Hitherto most care was in public sector homes and was very strictly rationed by local authorities. Presumably it was initially regarded as a good idea to support a private sector development. But this decision created a heavy burden on the social security budget. It also led to anomalies whereby people could get care much more easily in some areas than others. Considerations of financial control and equity led to a view that some integrated system of decisions about the need for care was required, involving a single authority. The search for a solution was essentially conducted by permanent officials (Audit Commission, 1986; Firth, 1987). After that the minister accepted the case for change, appointed a trusted adviser to investigate – which meant, of course, consulting the interested parties (Griffiths, 1988) – and subsequently promoted legislation (see Fimister and Hill, 1993). Here is an example of administrator-initiated change, with strong expert participation, in a relatively politically charged area – since questions of both privatisation and public expenditure control were involved. The issue was really one of getting a needed reform set up in a way which would satisfy the ideology of the dominant politicians.

Dunleavy and O'Leary refer to the 'professionalisation' of government to suggest that, in areas where expertise is important, issues are pulled out of the general political arena into the more private politics of 'policy communities':

> In the professionalised state the grassroots implementation of policy, and major shifts in the overall climate of debate in each issue area, are both influenced chiefly by individual occupational groups. Professional communities act as a key forum for developing and testing knowledge, setting standards and policing the behaviour of individual policy-makers and policy implementers. Knowledge élites are crucial sources of innovations in public policy-making . . . in areas where professions directly control service delivery the whole policy formulation process may be 'implementation skewed'. (1987, pp. 302 3)

This leads us on, however, to two questions much debated in studies of civil services: the extent to which a permanent civil service in practice engages in manipulating political policy input processes in order to retain its dominance; and alternatively, the extent to which that civil service takes its own ideological 'colour' from its political masters (particularly when the same party is in power for a long while).

These questions were explored a little in the preceding chapter (pp. 80–5). In fact the two alternative propositions above both attribute powerful roles to administrators, albeit with administrators allegedly on top in the first case and politicians in the second. An alternative is to see the two groups together as 'functionaries', both elected and non-elected (Lindblom and Woodhouse, 1993, p. 4). Lee, writing about UK local government, has similarly seen integration of the two groups in this way:

> It is misleading to think of the County Council primarily as a body of elected representatives who make decisions of policy and then order officials to execute them. Although such a view constitutes the theory, the reality is vastly different. It is better to regard the system of county government as a body of professional people placed together in a large office at County Hall, who can call upon the representatives from all places throughout the area which they administer. Some of these representatives by sheer ability and drive make themselves indispensable to the successful working of the machine; others merely represent points of view which come into conflict with it. (1963, p. 214)

It is appropriate to point out that Lee is describing a County Council, in a relatively uncontroversial period for UK local government, which had been dominated by Conservative or conservative-minded independent councillors. But this is not an exceptional situation for a local or even a national government.

Dyson's analysis of 'strong' and 'weak' states, discussed in the previous chapter, suggested that in the strong state civil servants are carriers of a tradition of service to the state which is seen as providing a context for the more temporary concerns of politicians (see pp. 92–4). Where do parties fit into a policy process in which administrators tend to play a strong role? Or, alternatively, how are political and administrative roles fitted together? Much depends here upon other aspects of the constitution. If electoral systems tend to produce unified programmatic parties, then there is a potential tension between the two elements in the policy-making process. Here the generalisations about the early and later parts of the policy process are likely to be relevant. But much is going to depend upon the extent to which either one party is largely dominant (as in Sweden until recently) or there is a relatively low level of conflict between the parties (as in Germany). France is perhaps the most interesting case inasmuch as the constitution of the Fifth Republic gives administrators considerable autonomy. Commentators on France suggest that the period in which Mitterrand came to presidential power with innovatory socialist policies, but was then forced first to water them down and then to accept 'cohabitation' with a prime minister of a different political persuasion, was a crucial testing time for French democracy (Ritchie in Harrop, 1992).

An alternative perspective on the strong states is supplied by those where multiparty systems dominate or have dominated (the Netherlands, Belgium, the French Fourth Republic). In these the party political input is largely seen very early in the policy process – in the issues that are contested in elections and in the compromises that occur between the elements in a coalition – after which the kind of administrator/politician accommodation described above in the quotation from Lee seems to apply. In general this is the way Dyson sees the strong states as coping with the democratic demands of political parties, even to the extent that they (as in Germany) accept 'a deep party "penetration" that influences appointments and promotions within the public bureaucracy' (1980, p. 260).

Another very much more modern twist to all the issues about the way the politician/administrator boundary is organised comes with two approaches to government which, while they have echoes in the past and particularly in pre-democratic regimes, are currently assuming increasing importance: public/private partnerships and the delegation of public tasks to quasi-independent or independent organisations.

In many respects this is a subject for the discussion of implementation. Certainly this is how governments tend to present such developments, emphasising Woodrow Wilson's politics/administration distinction or stressing 'we' still make the 'policy', 'they' are responsible for 'operations'. Invoking the already-criticised Wilson distinction indicates that this should be viewed with caution.

Leaving aside the new ways in which this now brings politicians into concerns about 'implementation', it will be seen that an 'agent' is likely to develop very real concerns about the way in which the policy it operates is constructed. If it is confronted with something unexpectedly expensive (as in the example of the social security funding of community care above) or something unworkable (as the UK's Child Support Agency found its initial legislative brief), it is likely to lobby (probably covertly) for policy change. The agent with a contract to carry out a specific task with a specific sum of money is a politically interested party (a new actor in the bargaining part of the game), particularly likely to behave in the way predicted by public choice theory. This theme is explored further in Chapters 7 to 9.

This discussion of administrative roles in the policy process has had to deal with what is perhaps the most ambiguous part of the initial policy process. It is certainly the most difficult to research, because so much of the action is private (in the United Kingdom we have to wait 30 years for the publication of official papers and even then some items are protected for longer, some are purged and many were never committed to paper records in the first place). The fact that there have been so many attempts to draw the politics/administration distinction or to delimit the political roles and interests of permanent officials indicates the complexity of this issue. The achievement of the ideal that civil servants should be just 'managers' or just concerned with 'means' is fraught with difficulty. Furthermore, it has been evident that many politicians want civil servants to play central policy-making roles (see Campbell and Wilson, 1995). Indeed, they often even want them to play 'political roles' – anticipating political risks and handling controversial issues.

Advocacy coalitions

Some writers on the policy process – particularly those with prescriptive rather than descriptive concerns – would regard the exploration of the respective roles of politicians, pressure groups and administrators as rather beside the point. They pick up on the work of the analysts of group processes, who have portrayed the importance of policy communities (see Chapter 3, pp. 70–4), to stress the extent to which the policy process must be seen as involving:

> 'advocacy coalitions' . . . people from a variety of positions (elected and agency officials, interest group leaders, researchers, etc.) who share a particular belief system – that is, a set of basic values, causal assumptions, and problem perceptions – and who show a nontrivial degree of coordinated activity over time. (Sabatier and Jenkins-Smith, 1993, p. 25)

Parsons argues that the advocacy coalition ideas offer a 'powerful framework for organizing and mapping the wide range of ideas which have emerged in the study of public policy and policy analysis' (1995, p. 199). But he is critical of the way Sabatier and Jenkins-Smith go on to use it to frame hypotheses about the way the policy process works. It needs to be seen in the context of the political culture from which it emerged, that of the United States. From a prescriptive point of view, it offers a model to assist with the provision of advice to those who want to secure policy change in a fragmented institutional context. The next section explores further some of the variations between societies in this respect.

The impact of institutions and culture on policy making

The above discussion of policy making, with its distinctions between the roles of party politics, bargaining and administration, has emphasised that the three are mixed in varying combinations and often in all stages of the process. It has also suggested that there will be differences between the policy issues at stake, depending upon the interests involved. It has also been stressed that the relationships among the three elements identified will vary according to the political culture and the institutional structure. Some further comments on this are appropriate here.

The discussion of institutions in the previous chapter has suggested that the policy-making process will be influenced by constitutions, rules, political structures and standard operating procedures. Each of the three elements in policy making discussed in this chapter will be influenced by these.

The nature of the party political system will be important for the way ideological issues figure in the policy process. This itself is likely to be influenced by the nature of the electoral system, whether it is one that tends to channel the political argument into a limited number of parties (as 'first past the post' systems tend to do), so that compromise has to occur within the parties, or one with many parties which can offer more distinctive positions, but which then need to compromise with each other in order to enact policies.

The shape of the party system is clearly not merely a product of the electoral system, it is also likely to be related to other aspects of the constitution. The United Kingdom and the United States have similar electoral systems, but these have to relate to very different systems of government: the centralised and unitary system in the United Kingdom, and the federal system with its division of powers between the two houses of Congress and the president at the centre. It is the latter difference that seems to be particularly important for the much greater salience of bargaining in the United States.

As suggested in the discussion of the different ways of dealing with the issue of civil service loyalty and responsibility in the previous chapter, rules and conventions about the role of the administration are similarly important in determining how public officials operate in relation to policy making.

But can one just read off the answers to the questions posed here for comparative studies from an examination of formal structures? Clearly one cannot: structures are themselves products of earlier policy processes, influenced by battles over political values. They themselves undergo change – written constitutions are amended or reinterpreted, and the assumptions about unwritten ones like the United Kingdom's are modified. Changing views of the civil service role in the United Kingdom were explored a little on page 83. Federal/state relationships in the United States and central/local relationships in the United Kingdom have changed considerably in the recent past.

There is a body of often rather speculative work on political culture (see Peters (1995) ch. 2 for a discussion of the applicability of this to public administration; see also Pye and Verba, 1965; Gibbins, 1989). Among the questions this has addressed are the following:

- Why is a positive role for the state more readily accepted in some societies than others?
- What explains variations in public trust of governments?

● Why are parties which are relatively integrated by a common ideology (in particular, social democratic parties) more important in some societies than others?

Issues like these tend to be used to explain why ideological politics is more in evidence, what structures bargaining processes or why administrations are given the space to work on the solution of policy problems. The consideration of them raises issues about differences between societies in terms of the extent to which there is acceptance of a strong role for the state, a topic which was explored at the end of Chapter 4.

An alternative approach to distinguishing policy-making systems is to consider the extent to which differences in 'policy style' can be detected. This idea has been developed by Richardson (1982), in relation not merely to national differences, but also to differences in the policy issues at stake. It is an approach linked to ideas about 'policy communities' (see pp. 72–4) – hence the suggestion is that different policy styles may be manifested in different policy communities even within the same country, let alone between countries. Smith (1993) picks this idea up in his discussion of the distinction between 'policy networks' and 'policy communities', suggesting that features of the United States make the former more likely than the latter. This is another way of saying that bargaining processes are more likely to be evident in such a large country with a complex constitutional structure.

Richardson explores his concept of policy style in terms of two dimensions:

● An anticipatory style as opposed to a reactive one.
● A consensus-seeking style as opposed to one which tends to impose decisions on society.

This model is then used to identify four quadrants:

1. Anticipatory and consensus seeking.
2. Anticipatory and imposing decisions.
3. Reactive and consensus seeking.
4. Reactive and imposing decisions.

In terms of the notions of party politics, bargaining and administrative politics, type 1 may be linked with high levels of administrator influence and type 2 with the salience of ideology. In type 3 bargaining is clearly in evidence. Type 4 is authoritarian, but without any very evident ideological direction.

As at the end of Chapter 4, we have finished with some suggestions about ways in which the themes explored have to be recognised as manifesting themselves rather differently in different societies, states and situations. The work discussed in this last section is essentially tentative, beginning a process of setting the agenda for fruitful comparative work.

CHAPTER 6

IMPLEMENTATION

Synopsis

This chapter will look at the contribution made to the study of the policy process by the 'discovery' of the importance of implementation. It will outline some of the ideas that have emerged from the 'top-down' work on this theme. It will then go on to examine the criticisms of this work, particularly as embodied in the alternative 'bottom-up' approach. It will explore the issues raised by the debate between the two approaches by examining a number of examples. These suggest that it is important to take into account the forms that policies assume, the issues they deal with and the institutional contexts in which they are implemented. It will be shown how the top-down/bottom-up debate raises important issues about accountability and about the best methodology for implementation studies.

Introduction

In the United States in the early 1970s and in Europe later in that decade, there emerged a wave of studies examining the implementation of public policy. Their rationale was that there had been, in the study of public policy, a 'missing link' (Hargrove, 1975) between the concern with policy making and the evaluation of policy outcomes. We should perhaps beware when academics claim to have discovered a new topic or a 'missing link': they are very good at dressing up old concerns in a new language and thereby claiming originality. The absence of theory and literature on implementation before Pressman and Wildavsky's seminal work (1973) on that topic has been exaggerated: for example, many organisational studies are *de facto* concerned with this phenomenon. Furthermore, a concern with the relationship between policy making and administration is as old as democratic politics (Wilson, 1887). Nevertheless as empirical research in political science developed in the first half of the twentieth century, there was perhaps a relative neglect of the study of processes by which policies are translated into action. They were regarded as mundane and taken for granted. As Gunn argues: 'Academics have often seemed obsessed with policy formation while leaving the "practical details" of policy implementation to administrators' (1978, p. 1).

Hence, the explosion of implementation studies represents an important advance in policy analysis. Yet, like so many paradigm shifts in the social sciences, this new intellectual development has come to be seen as having its own limitations. The case for the treatment of implementation as a separate topic from policy making was made in Chapter 1 and at the beginning of the previous chapter. At the same time, warnings were given about the too ready adoption of the 'stagist' view of the policy process.

The very strength of the study of implementation, in stressing the importance of that process as distinguishable from the policy-making process, and deserving of attention in its own right, has tended to lead to an overemphasis on the distinctiveness of the two processes. There has been a tendency to treat policies as clear-cut, uncontroversial entities, whose implementation can be quite separately studied. This has raised both methodological problems and problems about the extent to which the very practical concerns of implementation studies may involve, explicitly or implicitly, identification with some actors' views of what should happen.

The top-down model for the study of implementation

In a number of public policy studies textbooks, a distinction is made between policy making, policy implementation and the evaluation of policy outcomes. A model is often drawn which bears some relationship to Easton's (1965a) portrait of the political process, which was discussed in Chapter 1, of inputs going into a decision system and producing outputs. Those who use models of this kind stress, quite rightly, the need to try to disaggregate the decision system so that it is not so much of a black box. Usually this involves making a distinction between policy making and implementation.

For many who make this distinction, implementation is defined in terms of a relationship to policy. Hence, Van Meter and Van Horn define the implementation process as 'Those actions by public or private individuals (or groups) that are directed at the achievement of objectives set forth in prior policy decisions' (1975, p. 445). In a similar vein, Pressman and Wildavsky say: 'A verb like "implement" must have an object like "policy"' (1973, p. xiv). The pioneering implementation studies therefore argue that the process of putting policy into action is deserving of study, and that it is wrong to take it for granted that this process will be smooth and straightforward. Indeed, in many ways these studies are concerned with the discovery that many things go wrong between policy formulation and output. Hence Pressman and Wildavsky subtitled their book 'How great expectations in Washington are dashed in Oakland; or why it's amazing that federal programs work at all, this being a saga of the economic development administration as told by two sympathetic observers who seek to build morals on a foundation of ruined hopes'.

One senses here some of the frustration felt by many Americans about the failures, or limited successes, of the 'War on Poverty' and 'Great Society' programmes of the late 1960s. Pressman and Wildavsky were not the first observers of this apparent gap between federal aspirations and local reality; there was a similar body of literature on the limitations of Roosevelt's reformist interventions in American society (see, in particular, Selznick, 1949). Clearly an important preoccupation in this work is the concern with the problem of intervention from the top of a federal system; it comes through similarly in other analyses of American social policy with less of an emphasis on implementation *per se* (see Marris and Rein, 1967; Moynihan, 1969).

However, the concern with American federalism does not destroy the value of this approach for the study of implementation in other societies. Indeed, if analysed in this manner, it raises important questions about the ways in which policy transmission occurs, or fails to occur, through multigovernment systems. Certainly a great deal of the analysis in Pressman and Wildavsky's book is concerned with the extent to which successful implementation depends upon linkages between different organisations and departments at the local level. They argue that, if action depends upon a number of links in an implementation chain, then the degree of co-operation between agencies required to make those links has to be very close to 100 per cent if a situation is not to occur in which a number of small deficits cumulatively create a large shortfall. They thus introduce the idea of 'implementation deficit' and suggest that implementation may be analysed mathematically in this way.

This notion of cumulative deficit, if co-operation is less than perfect, has similarities to the approach to the study of administration developed in the United Kingdom by Christopher Hood (1976). He suggests:

> One way of analysing implementation problems is to begin by thinking about what 'perfect administration' would be like, comparable to the way in which economists employ the model of perfect competition. Perfect administration could be defined as a condition in which 'external' elements of resource availability and political acceptability combine with 'administration' to produce perfect policy implementation. (p. 6)

Hood goes on to develop an argument about the 'limits of administration' (his book title) which focuses not so much on the political processes that occur within the administrative system as on the inherent limits to control in complex systems. This is similarly the concern of a two-volume contribution to the subject by another British writer, Andrew Dunsire (1978a, 1978b). Hood and Dunsire, although they use examples from real situations, are concerned to link organisation theory with the study of implementation to provide an abstract model of the problems to be faced by persons attempting top-down control over the administrative system. The results are very complex, and seem likely to be hard to operationalise in actual empirical studies.

A rather less elaborate and more explicitly practice-related version of the top-down approach is provided in a short article by Gunn (1978), subsequently elaborated in Hogwood and Gunn (1984), in which ten preconditions necessary to achieve perfect implementation are set out:

1. Circumstances external to the implementing agency do not impose crippling constraints.
2. Adequate time and sufficient resources are made available to the programme.
3. Not only are there no constraints in terms of overall resources but

also, at each stage in the implementation process, the required combination of resources is actually available.

4. The policy to be implemented is based upon a valid theory of cause and effect.
5. The relationship between cause and effect is direct and there are few, if any, intervening links.
6. There is a single implementing agency which need not depend upon other agencies for success or, if other agencies must be involved, the dependency relationships are minimal in number and importance.
7. There is complete understanding of, and agreement upon, the objectives to be achieved; and these conditions persist throughout the implementation process.
8. In moving towards agreed objectives it is possible to specify, in complete detail and perfect sequence, the tasks to be performed by each participant.
9. There is perfect communication among, and co-ordination of, the various elements involved in the programme.
10. Those in authority can demand and obtain perfect obedience.

Gunn's list epitomises the top-down approach to implementation. It takes as its central purpose the provision of advice to those at the top on how to minimise implementation deficit.

Similar work has been produced in the United States (notably by Sabatier and Mazmanian, 1979). Policy is taken to be the property of policy-makers at the 'top'. The issues to be tackled are as follows:

● The nature of policy – see that it is unambiguous.
● The implementation structure – keep links in the chain to a minimum.
● The prevention of outside interference.
● Control over implementing actors.

Developments of these notions have been many and varied. There has been a concern to examine how the nature of policy may have an impact, with attempts to develop Lowi's (1972) typology of policies (see pp. 11–12) to explore how this may influence the implementation process. Hargrove (1983) argues: 'It is assumed that it is possible to classify types of policies so that the categories can be used as a basis for predicting the implementation process within each category.' He goes on to amplify this: 'The plausibility of using a typology as a point of departure follows from the idea that different kinds of policy issues will evoke different sets of participants and levels of intensity according to the stakes presented by the issue.' Implicitly this suggests that underlying the question of whether some kinds of policy may be harder to implement than others are issues about the probability of outside interference.

Significantly, Hargrove suggests that redistributive policies are harder to implement than distributive ones, while the success of regulatory policies may often rest upon the extent to which they have redistributive consequences. This is an interesting line of argument, but one that may be particularly rooted in the complexity of American politics. The issue of policy types is one to which we will return later (pp. 140–8), with the suggestion that differences in the implementation process may be rather more related to the extent to which it is easy to routinise processes.

Mountjoy and O'Toole (1979) have linked the theme of policy specificity with the notion that inter-organisational linkages create hazards for successful implementation. They identify some policies which avoid these hazards because of the clarity of their mandates and the security of their resources. Nixon (1980), looking at the handing down of policies from central to local level in the United Kingdom, has stressed the role of communication, perhaps a related notion to Mountjoy and O'Toole's mandate. Nixon emphasises the importance of clarity and consistency in the communication of policy. Both the notion of clear communication and the idea of mandate highlight the significance of an absence of ambiguity and compromise at the policy-making stage. This may be easier to achieve when conflict of interests is minimal than when disagreement exists among the various groups affected by a decision.

The work discussed above provides a variety of examples of the way the agenda for implementation studies has been established, principally by writers who accept some variant of the top-down approach. The examination of the implementation process must be concerned with the nature of policy, the inter- and intra- organisational context within which it is implemented, and the external world on which it is expected to impact. What has proved more controversial, however, is the way in which writers of the top-down school of thought handle both the concept of policy and the policy–implementation relationship.

Problems with the top-down model

The argument in this section will be complicated, since there are a number of different kinds of criticism of the top-down approach which apply differently to different representatives of that school of thought. Broadly the arguments separate out in the way suggested above, into those about the nature of policy, those about the interrelationship between policy making and the implementation process, and those about the normative stance adopted by students of implementation (particularly when this is implicit rather than explicit).

Pressman and Wildavsky were quoted earlier as approaching their definition of implementation by asserting that 'implement' is a verb that must have an object, 'policy'. In arguing in this way, they surely run the risk of catching themselves in a linguistic trap of their own making. As Wildavsky subsequently recognised, it is dangerous to regard it as self-evident that implementers are working with a recognisable entity that may be called a policy. In Chapter 1 it was shown that policy is indeed an extremely slippery concept. It may really only emerge through an elaborate process that is likely to include those stages which are conventionally described as implementation.

The definitions quoted in Chapter 1 (pp. 6–7) referred to the different characteristics of policy. However, the two rather different approaches to identifying policy indicated there – a general stance and a rather more concrete formulation – both entail problems for implementation studies, problems which are, in a sense, mirror images of each other. Policies defined as a stance (Friend *et al.*, 1974) may be relatively clear-cut, political commitments to specific action. The difficulty is that they are made much more complex as they are translated into action. Policies defined in more concrete terms are, as the definitions of Easton (1953) and Jenkins (1978) suggest, often so complex that we are unlikely to be able to identify simple goals within them. Friend's definition is really closer to the concept of policy used in everyday speech. It refers to the goals embodied in the 'Queen's speeches' or the President's 'messages to Congress', not to the complex phenomena which emerge at the end of the legislative process. Yet it is surely the latter with which students of implementation work.

The argument so far has been that implementation studies face problems in identifying what is being implemented because policies are complex phenomena. This needs now to be taken a stage further. Perhaps they are quite deliberately made complex, obscure, ambiguous or even meaningless. As was suggested in Chapter 1 with particular reference to the work of Edelman, in the most extreme case the policies which are the concern of politicians may be no more than symbolic, formulated without any intention to secure implementation. To what extent do politicians want to be seen as in favour of certain ideals or goals while actually doing nothing about them? Any system in which policy making and implementation are clearly separated, either by a division between legislature and executive (as in the United States) or by a division between levels of government or ministries and implementing agencies (present in most systems, but most clear in federal ones), provides opportunities for the promulgation of symbolic policies. In the United Kingdom, for example, many regulatory policies require parliamentary enactment but local authority implementation. Parliament may relatively easily pass laws allowing the control of certain activities or the provision of certain services, while not providing the resources to make action possible. Relatively small teams of local environmental health officials, for example, have to cope with a mountain of legislation designed to protect the public from the many potential health hazards – in restaurants, shops, etc.

Even when policies are not simply symbolic, it is important to recognise that the phenomena upon which action must be based are products of negotiation and compromise. Hence, as Barrett and Hill (1981) argue, many policies have the following characteristics:

- They represent compromises between conflicting values.
- They involve compromises with key interests within the implementation structure.
- They involve compromises with key interests upon whom implementation will have an impact.
- They are framed without attention being given to the way in which underlying forces (particularly economic ones) will undermine them (p. 89).

It must then be recognised, first, that this compromise is not a once and for all process but one that may continue throughout the history of the translation of that policy into action, and second, that the initial 'policy-makers' may be happy to let this occur as it enables them to evade decision problems. If the implementers are distanced from the original policy-framing process, and indeed are perhaps even in separate, 'subordinate' organisations, they may be perceived as responsible for problems and inconsistencies and for unpopular resolutions of these. Thus, in the United Kingdom, local authorities have been given responsibilities for supporting the rents of low-income people where the central government has failed to resolve a conflict between its desire to deregulate the housing market and its concern not to let increases in the cost of benefits to low-income rent payers escalate too rapidly. It has left it to the local authorities to use their discretion, at their own expense, to decide which high rents should be fully reimbursed. Similarly, even central executive agencies accountable to ministries seem to have been set policy goals which are incompatible with the resources they have been given (this has been an aspect of the implementation problems facing the Child Support Agency, an example discussed further later).

A further complication for the analysis of policies is that many government actions do not involve, as a reading of most of the American empirical studies of implementation would seem to suggest, the promulgation of explicit programmes requiring new activities. They involve adjustments to the way existing activities are to be carried out. The most common and obvious interventions of this kind are increases or decreases in the resources for specific activities. In this way, programmes are stimulated or allowed to wither away. What makes implementation studies even more complex, however, is that the relationship between resource adjustment and substantive programmes may be an indirect one. This is particularly a feature of UK central–local relations where, generally, central government does not explicitly fund programmes, but makes resources available to multipurpose authorities.

Indirect funding means that the study of the relationship between policy and implementation is by no means straightforward. Bramley and Stewart have shown how varied was the actual effect of public expenditure cuts in the United Kingdom in the late 1970s (in Barrett and Fudge, 1981). A study by Webb and Wistow (1982) looks at personal social services policy and demonstrates apparent implementation deficit because local authorities chose to disregard central guidelines and preserve social services expenditure, letting the impact of a reduction in central grants fall on other services. They refer to the central government minister subsequently boasting of his success in protecting social services from cuts. Yet Webb and Wistow's way of presenting these events, with its deference to the top-down approach, makes this appear more inconsistent than it really is, since they treat the initial cutting decisions as rational top-down policy making. The reality is of a government committed to cutting public expenditure, a bargaining process in which different spending ministers were forced to deliver specific shares in the cuts, and a cash supply control process in which lower-level actors (the local authorities) were able to do their own separate priority exercises. The ministry at the top did not have a *policy for social services spending*, in any very substantive sense.

Adjustments to the context in which decisions are made come not only in the form of resource change, but also in the form of structure change. These structure changes may or may not carry implications for substantive outputs. Hence services may be transferred from one agency to another, new rules may be made on how services are to be administered, or new arrangements may be made for policy delivery. These changes to the 'programme shell' (Knoepfel and Weidner, 1982; Whitmore, 1984) are common top-down interventions in public policy, but the analysis of their effects must rest upon an elaborate study of the way in which the balance of power is changed within the implementation system. In purposive language they are concerned with means not ends, therefore explicit goals cannot be identified, yet they may be of fundamental importance for outcomes and may embody implicit goals. The development in the United Kingdom and elsewhere which is transforming the way policies are delivered – replacing large bureaucratic departments by hived-off agencies, units that arc placed in a quasi-market situation or even private organisations operating as contractors for public services – must be seen not merely as restructuring the policy delivery system, but also as often transforming the policies themselves. The rules of the game may change the outcome of the game. This is a topic to which we will return in later chapters.

When the 'stance' definition of policy was contrasted with the 'interrelated decisions' definition (see p. 133), it was suggested that there is a process of concretising which goes on. It was also implied that there may be a difficulty about determining where policy making stops and implementation begins. This point should be further emphasised:

> to say that some policies are easier to implement than others one has to be able to identify the point at which they are packaged up ready for implementation. We may be able to say some commitments in party manifestos are easier to implement than others. We may equally be able to say that some Acts of Parliament are easier to implement than others. But in both cases such generalisation may be heavily dependent upon the extent to which aspirations have been concretised. (Hill, in Barrett and Fudge, 1981, p. 208)

The concretisation of policy continues way beyond the legislative process. There is something of a seamless web here, though it may be that it is possible to identify some decisions which are more fundamental for determining the major (policy?) issues than others. There is, however, no reason why we should always expect to find such decisions, nor is it the case that these decisions, when they exist, are invariably taken during what we conventionally define as the policy-making process. There are, on the contrary, a number of reasons why they may be left to the implementation process, of which the following is by no means an exhaustive list:

- Because conflicts cannot be resolved during the policy-making stage.
- Because it is regarded as necessary to let key decisions be made when all the facts are available to implementers.
- Because it is believed that implementers (professionals, for example) are better equipped to make the key decisions than anyone else.
- Because little is known in advance about the actual impact of the new measures.
- Because it is recognised that day-to-day decisions will have to involve negotiation and compromise with powerful groups.
- Because it is considered politically inexpedient to try to resolve the conflicts.

Considerations of this kind must lead us to regard the policy-making process as something which often continues during the so-called implementation phase. It may involve continuing flexibility, it may involve the concretisation of policy in action, or it may involve a process of movement back and forth between policy and action. Barrett and Fudge have stressed the need, therefore, 'to consider implementation as a policy/action continuum in which an interactive and negotiative process is taking place over time between those seeking to put policy into effect and those upon whom action depends' (1981, p. 25).

Lane (1987) highlights some of the key issues here in a paper in which, among a variety of approaches to implementation, he identifies 'implementation as evolution' (p. 532; see also Majone and Wildavsky, 1978), 'implementation as learning' (p. 534; see also Browne and Wildavsky, 1984), 'implementation as coalition' (p. 539, with important references to the essentially collaborative implementation implicit in corporatist relationships: see Chapter 4), and 'implementation as responsibility and trust (p. 541; this is a theme which we will explore further in Chapters 8 and 9). All of these imply a system in which close collaboration characterises relations within the policy system allowing policy to emerge in action.

The bottom-up alternative

These arguments lead on to the view that a model of the policy–implementation relationship in which the policy-making process can be seen as setting 'goals', the extent of whose realisation in action can be measured, provides an insufficient foundation for studies of implementation. It is this that has led various students of implementation to argue for a bottom-up rather than a top-down stance for the study of implementation. Elmore has coined the term 'backward mapping', which he defines as:

> 'backward reasoning' from the individual and organisational choices that are the hub of the problem to which policy is addressed, to the rules, procedures and structures that have the closest proximity to those choices, to the policy instruments available to affect those things, and hence to feasible policy objectives. (1981, p. 1; see also Elmore, 1980)

Focusing on individual actions as a starting point enables actions to be seen as responses to problems or issues in the form of choices between alternatives. One of Elmore's justifications for this approach derives not so much from the concern explored here about the difficulty in separating policy making and implementation, as from a recognition that in many policy areas in the United States (youth employment policy is Elmore's particular interest) implementation actors are forced to make choices between programmes which conflict or interact with each other.

The proponents of this approach argue that it is, by comparison with the top-down model, relatively free of predetermining assumptions. It is less likely to imply assumptions about cause and effect, about hierarchical or any other structural relations between actors and agencies, or about what should be going on between them.

The approach is expounded even more forcefully by Hjern and his associates (Hjern and Porter, 1981; and Hjern and Hull, 1982), who argue for a methodology in which researchers construct empirically the networks within which field-level decision-making actors carry out their activities without predetermining assumptions about the structures within which these occur. The author, in his work with Susan Barrett, has added his own support to the methodological argument for this perspective, arguing as follows:

> to understand the policy–action relationship we must get away from a single perspective of the process that reflects a normative administrative or managerial view of how the process should be, and try to find a conceptualisation that reflects better the empirical evidence of the complexity and dynamics of the interactions between individuals and groups seeking to put policy into effect, those upon whom action depends and those whose interests are affected when change is proposed. To do this, we have argued for an alternative perspective to be adopted – one that focuses on the actors and agencies themselves and their interactions, and for an action-centred or 'bottom-up' mode of analysis as a method of identifying more clearly who seems to be influencing what, how and why. (Barrett and Hill, 1981, p. 19)

What, in many respects, is being emphasised in this more action-centred mode of analysis is that the very things which top-down theorists like Gunn urge must be controlled are the elements which are difficult to bring under control. The reality, therefore, is not of imperfect control, but of action as a continuous process of interaction with a *changing and changeable policy*, a *complex interaction structure*, an *outside world which must interfere* with implementation because government action impinges upon it, and implementing actors who are *inherently difficult to control*. Analysis is best focused upon the levels at which this is occurring, since it is not so much creating implementation deficiency as recreating policy.

This emphasis, in the bottom-up critique, upon the complexities in the concept of policy and in the way it is made also suggests that implementation may itself be an ambiguous concept. Lane has argued that there is some confusion in the implementation literature between 'implementation or successful implementation as an outcome, and the implementation process or how implementation comes about' (1987, p. 545). The classical top-down studies are principally concerned with explaining why a successful outcome does or does not occur, and to do this they need clear goal statements to work with. These may be supplied by the policy-makers or imputed by the researchers. Without such yardsticks we may still study processes, but our activity is rather different. Sabatier, in an attempt to fuse the best ideas from both top-down and bottom-up processes, rightly suggests that the presence or absence of a 'dominant piece of legislation structuring the situation' (1986, p. 37) may help to determine which approach is appropriate. However, this may involve starting with a question-begging assumption that this structuring has in fact occurred. Obviously one can treat a piece of legislation as dominant. However, if you do so, the problems for explanation, in cases of implementation failure, tend to be either what others have done to subvert it, or what is wrong with it. Both of these may be oversimplified questions about both policy and its implementation context, and particularly about the relationship between the two.

Contrasting the two perspectives – further considerations

The implementation 'debate' described above has involved participants from a number of different countries, from different disciplinary backgrounds and often with very different policy issues in mind. Table 6.1 highlights contrasts between the two perspectives that tend to lead to them having very different preoccupations, and thus in some respects contribute to situations in which they do not really engage with each other. The next three sections will explore these three points.

Table 6.1 Comparing the 'top-down' and 'bottom-up' perspectives

	Top-down	Bottom-up
Policy rule framework seen as	Rigid	Flexible
Policy seen as	An input	An output
Accountability seen as depending upon	Deference to a legislative process	Adaptability to customer/ client/regulatee needs

The nature of policy rule framework

This issue is best explored through the use of examples. It has already been argued that the policy/implementation distinction largely rests upon a capacity – in many policy systems – to distinguish stages in the translation of policy into action. These stages involve increasing concretisation of policy – from a general commitment to action, through the formal enactment of a law, to the establishment of a series of guidelines to implementers, 'street-level' interpretations and thus eventually an 'output'. These stages may be recognised institutionally, in terms of formal rules and practices about the roles of various organisations in this process. The products of the stages may have specific legal forms, to which reference will be made in disputes about the meaning and impact of the policy. Constitutions, of varying degrees of formality and rigidity, will be likely to embody assumptions about these products and the legitimacy of the participants who shape them.

In other words, using UK examples to clarify this rather abstract paragraph, the study of the history of any particular policy is likely to involve an examination of the following:

- Political manifestos.
- The proposals in the 'Queen's speech' at the beginning of a parliamentary session.
- 'Green' and 'white' papers which set out policy objectives in general terms.
- Parliamentary debates.
- The Bill and subsequent Act which give the policy its primary legal shape.
- Regulations enacted after the passing of the Bill.
- Circulars, codes and other instructions to officials.
- Detailed notes, reports and accounts of working practice.

As suggested earlier, implementation is conventionally seen as involving the last two or three items in this list.

The central problem is that, while some policies pass out of the legislative stages with very clear rule structures, enabling implementation deficits to be easily identified, others are much less fully formed. A related issue – once we get into any comparative discussion of the policy process – is that national systems differ in their formal stages and in the extent to which these are regarded as crucial for the policy process. But before going on to this complication let us compare some UK examples.

Perhaps the best known British 'policy failure' in the 1980s was the attempt to transform the local taxation system, replacing a system of property taxation by a poll tax (Butler *et al.*, 1994). This policy was abandoned after widespread protest. Local authorities faced considerable implementation difficulties – in registering all liable to pay the tax, in enforcing payment and in administering rebates from full tax liability. Yet there was little ambiguity about the implementation task, and no local authority attempted to evade its implementation responsibilities or to reinterpret the tax to suit local circumstances. The intentions of central government were too explicit and the consequences for local government elected members and staff of non-compliance – both legal (suspension and prosecution) and practical (a serious cash deficiency) – were quite clear. Here then is a case where implementation problems can be analysed in a clear-cut 'top-down' way – policy objectives were quite specific and practical implementation problems can be explored in terms of the difficulties these objectives imposed.

It can generally be argued that, in the modern United Kingdom, taxation initiatives will reach the implementation stage with comparatively clear rule structures. These rules may be hard to implement and may be the subject of formal disputes in the courts, hence implementation deficit may be analysed, but political and social forces in UK society have taken taxation a long way from the vague 'tax farming' that characterised such policies in early medieval England, when implementers were charged to bring in money – to profit if they were good at it and be punished if they were not – by rulers who cared little about how it was done.

Similar points may be made about cash benefit systems. British income maintenance policy has evolved a long way from the de-centralised Poor Law in which a great deal of discretion was vested in local Boards of Guardians, to a modern situation in which all the main benefit systems (including the means-tested ones) have strong rule-based structures which facilitate computerised computation and the operation of formal appeal mechanisms. A widely discussed 'policy failure' from the 1990s – the Child Support Act of 1991 – has many features in common with the poll tax, with this time a central agency charged with a difficult and unpopular task. Students of implementation, in this case, can find their evidence in official auditing studies of error rates and delay, and in complaints to the ombudsman about administrative inefficiency.

These examples from taxation and social security may be contrasted with policies where there is a complex and dynamic relationship between rule structures and their interpretation. This is illustrated by two UK examples, both involving what have been regarded as controversial policy changes, driven by political commitments.

Glennerster *et al.* (1994) studied the early history of a health policy initiative designed to enable primary health care doctors to secure hospital services for their own patients by entering into contracts without reference to health authorities. These 'general practitioner fundholders' were allocated budgets based upon the size of their lists and past referral practices. The initial setting of these budgets was very much a matter of trial and error. Similarly, the establishment of rules to regulate this activity – to prevent possible abuses of autonomy and to cope with unexpected problems – was an evolutionary process, involving collaboration between the health authorities, the national Department of Health and the fundholders themselves.

Glennerster and his colleagues describe this as 'Lewis and Clark planning' (adapting an idea from Schultze (1968)). They say:

> The American explorers, Lewis and Clark, were merely told to find a route to the Pacific. They did so by finding the watershed, following the rivers to the sea using their wits as they went.
>
> The implementation of fundholding can be seen as a Lewis and Clark adventure – but in this instance there was telephonic contact between the field explorers and the equivalent of Washington and regular flights back to discuss progress with other explorers. (Glennerster *et al.*, 1994, p. 30)

The second example comes from a study of education policy. Here the issue is the development, under the 1988 Education Act, of a 'national curriculum' setting parameters for school teaching. In this case the legislation does little more than prescribe broad subjects to be included (maths, English, science, etc.), and organisations and procedures have been set up to determine more detailed content and to enforce compliance. Then even within the implementation process there is – not surprisingly, given the complexity of the issues – considerable latitude to enable individual schools and teachers to select topics to emphasise, approaches to teaching and so on. Bowe *et al.* (1992) use a concept from sociology and linguistics, 'texts' (Atkinson, 1985), to explain what is here being described as an implementation process. They argue:

> Texts carry with them both possibilities and constraints, contradictions and spaces. The reality of policy in practice depends upon the compromises and accommodations to these in particular settings . . .

our conception of policy has to be set against the idea that policy is
something that is simply done to people. (p. 15)

They go on to highlight the peculiar combination of 'Thatcherite policy-
making which rides roughshod over the sensibilities of teachers' (p.
15), lack of public confidence in teachers and low morale on the one
hand with the fact that it has depended upon a very complex interaction
between education officials, advisory bodies and the teachers themselves to make the national curriculum 'work'.

Thus Bowe and his colleagues argue:

> Policies . . . are textual interventions but they also carry with them
> material constraints and possibilities. The responses to these texts have
> 'real' consequences. These consequences are experienced in . . . the
> arena of practice to which policy refers . . . policy is not simply received
> and implemented within this arena rather it is subject to interpretation
> and then recreated. (pp. 21–2)

These two examples were selected because in both cases the authors
were using new ways to try to capture the complexity of the policy–
implementation relationship. Many others could have been chosen
from areas where policy implementation involves complex service
activities.

Similar issues arise in many areas of regulatory policy – some of the
earlier illustrations to support the bottom-up view came from that field.
In this area of policy, alongside the problems of complexity there may
be other features which complicate implementation: in particular, the
fact that the regulatee often understands the process better than the
regulators, that there are difficult trade-off judgements to be made
about the costs of compliance and that the ability of the regulatee to
evade control puts willing compliance at a premium. This has led Hanf
(1993) to see much regulatory activity as involving 'co-production'
between regulator and regulatee.

At its extreme – and this probably characterised much UK pollution
control until very recently – policy is essentially no more than the terms
that the regulator is able to reach with the regulatee. In industrial air
pollution control, the statutory concept of the use of the 'best practicable
means' to limit emissions had little meaning except in the context of
such an agreement (Hill, 1983). It certainly could not in any realistic
sense be described as defined in the policy-making process. Since then,
under pressure from the European Community for a more precise
approach, this 'policy' has moved on a little, but the policy emphasis is

still rather more upon ambient air quality targets than upon specific control over what goes up individual chimneys.

The last example and the preceding one – from education policy – essentially involve a need for creative policy interpretation at the 'street level'. This is a theme explored further in Chapters 8 and 9 with reference to discretion and the roles of 'street-level bureaucrats'.

There are very important areas of policy where the policy implementation distinction is even more blurred than in these examples from service provision and regulation. Oddly these do not seem to have been given much attention in the implementation literature, perhaps because they concern issues at the very centre of national politics – economic and foreign policy.

With the development in the twentieth century of a series of assumptions that government can control the working of the economy, there have developed policy processes in which political executives are central actors and policy adjustments are frequent and often carried out quickly and with a minimum of due process. Very often, therefore, these occur with little prior participation from legislatures. At best legislative roles are to endorse or evaluate developments afterwards. Particularly significant examples of interventions of this kind are adjustments to exchange rates and interest rates, together with government borrowing and other direct interventions into money markets.

In the case of the United Kingdom such interventions are particularly the responsibility of the chancellor of the exchequer, probably in consultation with the prime minister. Other cabinet ministers are involved on an *ad hoc* and generally unpredictable basis. The governor of the state-owned Bank of England is a regular participant, and Treasury officials obviously have important roles to play. Key figures from the European Union are likely to be involved, together with perhaps finance ministers from other nations (the United States and Japan, for example). In some circumstances representatives of international organisations are involved, such as the International Monetary Fund. The 1975 balance of payments crisis (Dell, 1991) and the efforts to control UK exchange rates by linking the pound to other European currencies in the 1980s and 1990s (Stephens, 1996) have stimulated accounts of these policy processes.

If the policy making/implementation distinction is to be based upon the model of stages in a formal process outlined above, then these policy processes are essentially implementation. They do not generally involve legislation; indeed, it may be unclear just where the formal authority to take action comes from. On the other hand, they do tend to involve key elected politicians – though as suggested by the UK example, they may be operated in consultation with unelected officials and even involve foreign participants. We have here an issue where implementation is very much under the control of the core executive, as Thompson's (1995) discussion of this (outlined on p. 85) suggests.

Much the same may be said about some of the key decision-making processes in foreign policy. Decisions may be made quickly and perhaps secretly by political leaders, leaving the legislature to follow along behind, perhaps even inhibited by a view that it is damaging to the national interest to be critical. If one examines events like the decisions to make and use atomic weapons, the Suez crisis (1956), the Falklands War (1982) and the Gulf War (1991), the political inquests followed much later. At the time of writing, incidents that involved a combination of UK foreign policy and economic policy concerning the sale of weapons have been the subject of intense inquiry into the lies and deceptions used to keep decision making from public or political scrutiny (Scott Report, 1996). In the United States, foreign policy raises particularly delicate constitutional issues because of the way presidents have used their prerogatives as head of the armed services to deploy force without consultation in situations in which the right to declare war belongs to Congress. In all these cases, the policy making/implementation distinction seems singularly meaningless.

Hence this discussion has drawn distinctions between situations in which rules for implementation are very much in evidence, situations in which implementation is very much a processes of developing and elaborating initial policy frameworks, and situations in which we need either to say that the implementation process *is* the policy-making process or to regard this distinction as meaningless.

In setting out these situations, different policy examples were used – tax and benefits, services, regulation, economic policy and foreign policy. It would be tempting to go on from the basic point, that in general terms the issue will affect the process, to advance a taxonomy of kinds of policy (reference has already been made on pp. 131–2 to Hargrove's attempt to work with Lowi's typology). This would, however, be a rash step to take. There is no necessary connection between policy area and the nature of the implementation process. The examples of tax farming and the early days of poor relief were indeed cited to suggest that, even in areas often highly regulated, alternative models involving extensive implementer discretion may be used. Conversely, attempts are regularly made to develop strict rule structures for services and for regulation. Not surprisingly, in economic and foreign policy, legislators regularly engage in attempts to curb executive discretion. Chapter 9 will explore further some of the pressures for and against the development of clear rules.

What is perhaps more important in relation to this continuum between very closed and very open implementation systems is to draw attention to the fact that variation will depend upon the characteristics of governmental systems and upon political culture. Nearly all the examples in the discussion above come from the United Kingdom. They therefore come from a system which is a peculiar mixture of extreme centralisation and considerable ambiguity about the 'hidden wiring' (Hennessy, 1995) of an unwritten constitution. There is thus considerable variation in control over implementation processes from issue to issue, where matters like centrality to the commitments of the government of the day and the capacity of outsiders to compel or prevent rule making may have a considerable influence.

Contrastingly, it is perhaps not surprising that issues about the capacity of policy-makers to influence implementation have been given particular attention in the United States, because of the ways in which federalism, the division of executive, legislative and judicial powers and the written constitution complicate executive action. As suggested above, ever since the New Deal in the 1930s, the exploration of ways to increase Washington's influence in Oakland, or wherever, has been a key preoccupation of those Americans who regard active federal government as important for their society. In the 1960s, the struggle against racial segregation in the Deep South and the efforts to develop new initiatives in welfare policy and in urban policy offered particularly salient examples.

Alternatively, the combination of quite complex and often de-centralised administrative arrangements in small consensual societies – like Sweden, Norway and the Netherlands – contributes perhaps to a relaxed view of delegated implementation in which the centre expects to play a 'steering' role in a context of trust. See, for example, Gustafsson (1991) on central–local relations in Sweden. It is perhaps appropriate to comment that the observations of Lane on this issue (see pp. 137–8) come from a Swede.

Underlying all this are a variety of concerns about accountability, the subject of the last section of this chapter and of Chapter 9. Clearly, issues about whether the legislature – as policy-maker – secures compliance and how it does it are central to concerns about democratic accountability. The way someone might want to talk about the policy making/implementation relationship in China, for example, might be very different.

Policy as input or output?

Before coming back to that sort of prescriptive issue, however, there is a need to give some attention to the second row in Table 6.1 – the distinction between policy as *input* and policy as *output*. It will be clear that, in the various cases discussed above where policy becomes manifest only in the implementation stage, it must be interpreted primarily as output. Where, however, policy is identified as input, it is logically the case that there must be some activity – new legislation, or an amendment of some kind to existing legislation – which receives attention. This is essentially a methodological point about the top-down/ bottom-up distinction. All the work with a clear top-down focus concerns how a new intervention is implemented. The bottom-up approach may also be used to the same end, as in Elmore's backward mapping methodology. But, in addition, in some of the bottom-up studies (see, for example, Kettunen, 1994) the focus is simply upon an ongoing activity. Clearly, very many studies of public policy practitioners – concerned with how teachers teach, regulators regulate and so on – operate in this way without needing to raise questions about whether new interventions from the top have any effect. Later in this book, we will find Michael Lipsky's work on 'street-level bureaucrats' exploring these issues in an essentially bottom-up way without needing to give attention to any specific policy innovation.

This may seem a rather obvious and unnecessary point to make, but it does appear that some of the top-down/bottom-up debate misses the point that it is clearly very different to be asking what effect a specific innovation has, as opposed to being concerned with how an implementation system works. One raises questions about the input/output relationship, while the other confines itself to the influences upon output.

Stances on accountability, and the prescriptive potential of implementation studies

A characteristic of the top-down approach to the study of implementation has been a concern to give advice to top actors about how they

Whether you favour one or the other approach, some combination of the two or one that tries to avoid either, depends very much on what you are trying to do.

If your primary aim is to understand an implementation process, a great deal is going to depend upon what activity you are interested in. If you are looking at one in which there is a quite explicit 'top'-initiated, goal-directed activity, it may be justifiable to use a 'top-down' methodology and work with a notion such as 'implementation deficit'. This may be particularly the case where a quantifiable output is available and explicit inputs can be measured. The UK experience with the Thatcher governments has offered a number of examples where government goals have been very clear. There have been cases of very determined top-down pursuit of clearly specified objectives (the sale of local authority-owned homes to their occupiers: see Forrest and Murie, 1991), cases where clear evidence of implementation problems ahead has pulled government back (the strange case of an identity card scheme to prevent football hooliganism) and dramatic cases of implementation difficulty leading to yet further policy innovation (the two cases of the 'poll tax' and the Child Support Act mentioned above).

Yet many events in the policy process do not involve such clarity. Examples can be found, even in the Thatcher years in the United Kingdom, of complex and confusing cases where central goals were not nearly so clear, or where central goal statements should be received with great scepticism – in fields like community care, employment policy, urban renewal and the prevention of crime. Yet if this is true of the unified, centralised, one-party-dominated United Kingdom, how much more true it is of societies where politics is dominated by compromises between federal units or coalition governments. Furthermore, as suggested above, concern may be with an ongoing process where explicit change is not initiated from above, or where there are grounds for scepticism about whether change efforts will carry through to the 'bottom'.

There are good grounds – from a methodological point of view – in situations like those set out in the previous paragraph, for not starting a search for influences on implementation at the top. This does not, however, need to be translated into a dogmatic bottom-up stance. Rather the trace for influences upon action may be initiated in a variety of ways and from a variety of positions. Organisational studies (see further discussion in the next chapter) have warned against taking hierarchy for granted. Equally it is a mistake to disregard aspects of hierarchical power. One of the author's students once challenged him – why either top or bottom, what about the importance of influences from the middle? Since much of his working life has been spent somewhere in the middle, he could only agree.

Any effort to develop implementation theory must face the difficulty – once it moves away from the attempt to develop checklists of pitfalls for the implementation process in the way described and criticised above – of becoming involved with the wide range of questions which have been raised in relation to policy making and the study of organisations. If we substitute the word 'doing' for implementation, we see how we are confronted by an attempt to develop a 'theory of doing' – or of action. Perhaps, therefore, this is not a very helpful way to proceed. Rather, as Susan Barrett and the author have suggested, it is hard to go beyond the identification of the key elements which must be analysed in the study of implementation, and the recognition of the overwhelming importance of the negotiation and bargaining which occur throughout the policy process:

> many so-called implementation problems arise precisely because there is a tension between the normative assumptions of government – what ought to be done and how it should happen – and the struggle and conflict between interests – the need to bargain and compromise – that represent the reality of the process by which power/influence is gained and held in order to pursue ideological goals. (Barrett and Hill, 1981, p. 145)

This general exploration of implementation – with its emphasis upon the significance of organisational complexity and upon the sources of variation in discretion in the implementation process – is now followed by three chapters which explore these issues more fully.

CHAPTER 7

THE POLICY PROCESS AS AN ORGANISATIONAL PROCESS

Synopsis

This chapter will start with a discussion of mainstream work on 'the theory of bureaucracy', rooted in the work of Max Weber, which has been very important for the study of the modern state. It will then move on from the essentially single organisation preoccupations of that theory (often, indeed, seeing the whole complex state in unitary terms) to attempts to develop a related body of inter-organisation theory. The latter is complex, but assumes considerable contemporary importance because of two concerns – with government as the regulator of other organisations, and with models of public service delivery in which other organisations may be involved and market or quasi-market processes created. The last is an important feature of the 'new public management' movement, so the chapter ends with a brief account of this.

Introduction

The policy process, and particularly those aspects of it that are described as implementation, generally occurs in a complex organisational context. The preceding chapter focused upon some aspects of this, stressing organisational complexity as an influence upon implementation. This organisational complexity must be seen as often involving a dual form – complexity within each single organisation, and in many cases further complexity because two or more organisations are required to interact with each other. Hence, in reviewing ideas from organisation theory in this chapter, there is a need to explore first aspects of *intra*-organisational processes and then *inter*-organisational dynamics.

The issues about the policy process as an organisational process are emphasised in discussions of the role of bureaucracy. In Chapter 4 it was shown that some of the key theories of the state – particularly élitist theories and public choice theories – concern themselves with issues about bureaucratic power, seeing it (particularly in public choice theory) as involving the domination of the policy process by those inside the organisational system. The word 'bureaucracy' is used both as a neutral descriptive term for a complex organisation – particularly a governmental one – and as a pejorative term to denote an impenetrable, ponderous and unimaginative organisation.

In many discussions of the role of organisations in the modern world, these complex 'bureaucracies' are seen as necessary evils. As Perrow puts it: 'Without this form of social technology, the industrialized countries of the West could not have reached the heights of extravagance, wealth and pollution that they currently enjoy' (1972, p. 5). The concern here is with 'bureaucratic' government – this wider reference helps to remind us that, inasmuch as there are 'problems of bureaucracy', these are not merely problems about government, and, indeed, part of the argument for governmental complexity lies in the complexity of the 'private' organisations to which government has to relate.

The argument about bureaucracy, highlighted by the frequency with which the term is used pejoratively, has two separate key concerns which we may describe simply as concerns about (a) accountability and (b) efficiency and effectiveness. One aspect of critiques of bureaucracy is to stress – as was suggested in parts of Chapter 4 – problems about making government organisations accountable to the people. The other aspect is to emphasise the extent to which they are unsatisfactory 'instruments' for the carrying out of policy, increasing costs and distorting outputs. In many critiques – and in particular in public choice theory – these two alleged defects are linked together. This is largely a consequence of the adoption of a narrow notion of accountability which emphasises cost effectiveness. But accountability embodies wider considerations than that. It is clearly possible to have organisations that are accountable but inefficient, or unaccountable but efficient. Furthermore, specific control efforts may differ in the extent to which they are directed towards dealing with either of the two issues, and may have to come to terms with the fact that efforts to increase accountability may decrease efficiency or vice versa.

For public policy, protagonists at both of the political extremes offer solutions to the alleged problem of 'bureaucracy'. For the extreme right, the solution is the allocation of goods and services by way of the market, with the role of government kept to a minimum. The market offers a mechanism which is accountable because the public are consumers able to make choices about what they purchase, and efficient because providers are in continuous competition with each other. The extreme left, alternatively, has seen a world in which capitalist power is overthrown as offering the possibility of free collaboration between equal citizens in meeting their needs. Both extremes embody a utopian element – in the case of the right, a belief in the feasibility of a really competitive market rather than an economy in which there is a tendency for monopoly to develop and for choices to be limited and manipulated; in the case of the left, a world in which big government is as unnecessary as big capitalism.

The utopianism of the right is more important for the modern political agenda than that of the left, partly because of the dominance of capitalist ideology and partly because the history of communism has offered so dramatic a betrayal of its idealistic roots. Yet nearer the centre of the political debate, the idealistic assertions of both camps offer key poles for debate about public policy, concerning the extent to which there are problems about organising the public sector and regulating the market sector. This takes us back to Perrow's neat aphorism. Inasmuch as there is a necessity for complex organisations to meet the needs of modern society, then governments are engaged in a combination of direct provision and regulation. Moreover, they have to cope with trade-offs between the two. In most of the twentieth century, the tendency has been for governments – at least in western Europe – to see direct provision as preferable to regulation in many areas of social and economic life. This has forced attention to issues about the control of their own large bureaucratic organisations. In the final quarter of the century, there has been something of a reaction against this approach. But this heightens the need for attention to regulation, essentially an issue about the relationships between government organisations and private or quasi-autonomous ones. The worries about 'bureaucracy' have not been dispelled, as many within the New Right suggested. Rather they take new forms, forcing us to reconceptualise bureaucracy in a more complex way. This reconceptualisation has been a key concern of work which sees late-twentieth-century innovations in the public sector as a 'new public management' movement (Pollitt, 1990; Hood, 1991).

These normative and prescriptive arguments are not the main concerns of this book. But they have coloured much theorising and research about organisational behaviour. And, as the previous paragraph suggests, they have had an impact upon innovation in public policy and particularly upon efforts to influence the implementation process.

Max Weber and the theory of bureaucracy

The work of a German theorist, Max Weber, active at the end of the nineteenth century and in the early years of the twentieth, was particularly important for the development of the theory of organisations. Furthermore, it was the organisation of government in the modern state that particularly concerned him. He observed the development of a powerful unified civil service in Germany, recognising its potential as an instrument of government and worrying about its implications for democratic accountability.

Weber embedded his theory of bureaucracy in a wider theory of social power. His discussion of bureaucracy is linked with an analysis of types of authority. He postulates three basic authority types: charismatic, traditional and rational-legal. He sees the last named as characteristic of the modern state.

Charismatic authority is based upon 'devotion to the specific and exceptional sanctity, heroism or exemplary character of an individual person' (1947, p. 328). It is a transitory phenomenon associated with periods of social turmoil; the essentially personal nature of the relationship between leader and follower makes the development of permanent institutions impossible, and accordingly it succumbs to processes of 'routinisation' which transform it into one of the other types of authority. Traditional authority, on the other hand, rests upon 'an established belief in the sanctity of immemorial traditions and the legitimacy of the status of those exercising authority under them' (p. 328). While charismatic authority's weakness lies in its instability, the weakness of traditional authority is its static nature. It is thus the case that the rational-legal type of authority is superior to either of the other two types.

Weber states that rational-legal authority rests upon 'a belief in the legality of patterns of normative rules, and the right of those elevated to authority under such rules to issue commands' (p. 328). The maintenance of such a system of authority rests upon the development of a bureaucratic system of administration in which permanent officials administer, and are bound by, rules.

Weber regards the development of bureaucratic administration as intimately associated with the evolution of modern industrialised society. Bureaucratisation is seen as a consequence of the development of a complex economic and political system, and also a phenomenon that has helped to make these developments possible.

Students of Weber have differed in the extent to which they regard him as a theorist who believed that bureaucracy can be subjected to democratic control. He was clearly ambivalent on that topic. While the use of bureaucracy as a pejorative term (see the discussion above) clearly pre-dates Weber, he must be seen as the theorist who effectively poses the dilemma – that here is an instrument that enables much to be done that could not have been done, but there is a need to be concerned about how it is used, how it is controlled and who controls it (Albrow, 1970; Beetham, 1987).

The strength of the bureaucratic form of administration, according to Weber, rests upon its formal rationality, a notion which a number of modern students of organisations have equated with efficiency. This translation of Weber's concept has led to some useful discussions of the relationship between formalism and efficiency, but has also given currency to a rather unsubtle characterisation of Weber's theory. Albrow (1970) shows how this confusion arose and provides the following clarification of Weber's position:

> The real relation between formal rationality and efficiency can best be understood by considering the means by which efficiency is commonly measured, through the calculation of cost in money terms, or in time, or in energy expended. Such calculations are formal procedures which do not in themselves guarantee efficiency, but are among the conditions for determining what level of efficiency has been reached. At the heart of Weber's idea of formal rationality was the idea of correct calculation, in either numerical terms, as with the accountant, or in logical terms, as with the lawyer. This was normally a necessary though not sufficient condition for the attainment of goals; it could even conflict with material rationality. (p. 65)

Weber's theory is seen as providing a number of simple propositions about the formal structure of organisations, a misconception that has contributed to his usefulness to students of organisations, but which does not do justice to the depth of his understanding of the critical issues in organisational sociology. As he outlines the characteristics of an organisational type that is important in complex societies because of its formal rationality, he naturally stresses the strength of that type rather than its weakness. Weber's aim is to define a widespread kind of organisation and explain why it is growing in importance, thereby offering sociological analysis rather than political polemic.

Weber lists a number of characteristics which, taken together, define bureaucracy. These characteristics are as follows:

- A continuous organisation with a specified function, or functions, its operation bound by rules. Continuity and consistency within the organisation are ensured by the use of writing to record acts, decisions and rules.
- The organisation of personnel is on the basis of hierarchy. The scope of authority within the hierarchy is clearly defined, and the rights and duties of the officials at each level are specified.
- The staff are separated from ownership of the means of administration or production. They are personally free, 'subject to authority only with respect to their impersonal official obligations'.
- Staff are appointed, not elected, on the basis of impersonal qualifications, and are promoted on the basis of merit.
- Staff are paid fixed salaries and have fixed terms of employment. The salary scale is normally graded according to rank in the hierarchy. Employment is permanent with a certain security of tenure, and pensions are usually paid on retirement (1947, pp. 329–41).

While Weber does not see these characteristics as prescriptions for organisation, many subsequent writers have seized upon their similarity to the model prescribed by others who were searching for the best way to organise. Pundits like Fayol (1916), a Frenchman writing around the time of the First World War, and Urwick (1943), an Englishman who was influential in both private and public organisations in the inter-war period, seek to set out rules and maxims for successful administration. But perhaps the most influential figure in the search for principles of organisation before the First World War was F. W. Taylor (1911). He was an American who tried to develop scientific principles for industrial management, based upon a series of generalisations which he claimed to be of universal application. His importance for this account is that he has been widely seen as the leading exponent of methods of organisation which rest upon treating human beings as units of labour to be used efficiently without regard to their needs, attitudes and emotions (Braverman, 1974). Hence a great deal of the subsequent concern about human relations in organisations emerged from the exposure of the limitations of 'Taylorism'. Despite this exposure, however, the influence of Taylorism lives on. Pollitt (1990) has described much modern managerialism in the public services as 'neo-Taylorism'. He argues:

> Taylorism was centrally concerned with the 'processes of determining and fixing effort levels' and can be seen as 'the bureaucratization of the structure of control but *not* the employment relationship' (Littler, 1978, pp. 199 and 185 respectively). It proceeded on the basis that . . . the work process could and should be measured by management, and then used as a basis for rewarding and controlling effort . . . This is not far, in principle, from the recent epidemic of electronically-mediated public-service systems of performance indicators, individual performance review and merit pay. (p. 16)

Taylor was working in the Ford motor company, a pioneer in mass production methods. Hence other theorists have spoken of 'Fordism' (Sabel, 1982) to describe an approach to organisation in which Taylorist methods are used to try to reduce workers to commodities, performing limited tasks in tightly regulated conditions for the lowest possible rewards. While public policy implementation is seen as less likely to embody circumstances in which such mass production is feasible, Taylorism or Fordism can be seen to offer one model for the public bureaucracy (see Pollitt, 1990). It is one model, moreover, which may be seen as solving the dilemma of accountability – at least as far as routine tasks like social benefit administration are concerned – by ensuring a rigid adherence to hierarchically (and thus perhaps ultimately democratically) determined rules. This is an issue to which we will return when we explore the relationship between rules and discretion in Chapter 8.

But that is only one way to take the Weberian model, seeking to make it simply a compliant instrument. Others suggested problems with this, and observed some of the tensions and contradictions in the 'ideal type'. In the 1920s and 1930s management theory gradually began to move away from a concern with the development of formal prescriptions for organisational structure towards a better understanding of organisational life. This development, while still firmly preoccupied by a concern with control over subordinates within the industrial enterprise, nevertheless eventually contributed to a transformation of the way organisations were understood.

The work carried out under Elton Mayo at the Hawthorne Works in Chicago during the late 1920s and early 1930s is often credited with effecting this revolution in industrial sociology (Roethlisberger and Dickson, 1939). This is an oversimplified view. The Hawthorne researchers were influenced by research on morale carried out during the First World War. They were also well aware of the progress being made in social psychology between the wars, and in particular they were influenced by the more sophisticated approach to human motivation that Freudian psychology helped to produce. The development of a more complex approach to social structure at this time, by sociologists and anthropologists, also had an impact on their work. In some ways, too, their thinking had been foreshadowed by the writings of Mary Parker Follett (1941) on management. For these reasons it makes more sense to say that the Hawthorne researches represent the most significant single advance in the understanding of human behaviour in a work context. They have had a colossal impact upon subsequent workers in this field, and it is only natural that the process of the simplification of the history of ideas has led to their being accorded a significance out of proportion to their true contribution.

There is not the space here to discuss in detail the findings of the Hawthorne researches, but their main importance lies in the way they shifted the emphasis in organisation theory away from a mechanical concern to discover the 'one best way' to organise work tasks, towards a recognition of the importance of human relationships for organisational performance. Their early research draws attention to the relevance of managerial interest in workers' activities for motivation and morale, while their later work throws light upon relationships within the work group.

The Hawthorne researches demonstrate the need to analyse organisations as living social structures. They indicate that, just as to discover that there are such and such a number of farmers, shopkeepers and labourers living in a village and that 'x' works for 'y' and so on is not to find out a great deal of significance about the social structure of that village, so to regard an organisation as merely a pattern of formal roles is likely to make it impossible to understand fully the determinants of behaviour, even formally prescribed behaviour, within that organisation.

Although these findings relate to the shop floor, to the lowest level in an organisation's hierarchy, subsequent research has demonstrated the validity of the findings for all levels. Interpersonal relationships within groups of office workers or within management have equally been found to determine work behaviour in a way that formal organisational rules in no way anticipate.

The development of the sociology of organisations

As the social sciences began to grow in importance in the United States in the 1940s and 1950s, two developments in organisation theory – one stimulated by the work of Max Weber, the other influenced by the more obviously relevant findings of Mayo and his associates – began to come together. Sociologists, using Weber's work (or their understanding of it) as their starting point, set out to show the importance of patterns of informal relationships alongside the formal ones. Social psychologists, on the other hand, sought to explore the conflict between human needs and the apparent requirements of formal organisations. Drawing on this work, administrative theorists sought to update the old formal prescriptive models with more flexible propositions based upon this new understanding of organisational life (Argyris, 1964; McGregor, 1960; Herzberg, 1966).

Once Weber's work became available to sociologists in the United States in the 1940s and 1950s, it was applied to organisational studies as a kind of model against which real situations might be measured. By treating it in this way, sociologists began to identify problems about the rational model of bureaucracy, often unjustly alleging that Weber had not been aware of them, but nevertheless usefully advancing organisational theory.

In some of this work it is suggested that there is likely to be a conflict within the bureaucratic organisation between the principle of hierarchy and the need to maximise the use of expertise. Gouldner makes this point in the following way: 'Weber, then, thought of bureaucracy as a Janus-faced organisation, looking two ways at once. On the one side, it was administration based on expertise: while on the other, it was administration based on discipline' (1954, p. 22).

Bureaucratic organisation is founded upon the need to make the maximum use of the division of labour. Such division is based upon the need to subdivide a task either because of its size or because it is impossible for a single individual to master all its aspects. In fact, in most cases both these reasons apply. The principle of hierarchy rests upon the notion of the delegation of responsibility to subordinates. If the superior could perform the whole of the task which is delegated, there would be no need to have subordinates. He or she will delegate part of the task either because of a lack of time to do it alone, or because he or she has neither the time nor the knowledge to perform certain parts of the task. Inasmuch as the latter is the case, it is obvious that in respect of at least part of the task the superior is less expert than the subordinate. But even in the former case this may also be true, since, particularly as far as tasks that require decision making are concerned, the subordinate will be in possession of detailed information which, in delegating responsibility, the superior has chosen not to receive.

It is for these reasons that, as far as the detailed functioning of any organisation with complex tasks to perform is concerned, it must be recognised that expertise resides primarily in the lower ranks of a hierarchy. And it is for these reasons that it is inevitable that there tends to be conflict between authority based upon expertise and authority based upon hierarchy in bureaucratic organisations.

This apparent inconsistency in Weber's theory has helped to provoke several valuable studies of conflict between experts and administrators within organisations. An allied topic that has also been explored is the conflict that exists for experts between professional orientation and organisational orientation in their attitudes to their work (Gouldner, 1957–8; Reissman, 1949).

A second important theme deriving from Weber's work concerns the relationship between rationality and rigidity. One of the earliest essays on this theme was Merton's (1957) discussion of bureaucratic structure and personality. This emphasis fits with the arguments about expertise within organisations. Its implications for the behaviour of bureaucratic employees will be explored further in Chapter 9.

This work led to an exploration of the relationship between organiational structure and organisational tasks. Thus, the question raised was whether the 'rational' structure may not be well adapted to some tasks but ill-adapted to others. Two British researchers, Burns and Stalker (1961), made one of the most important contributions on this theme. They drew a distinction between 'mechanistic' and 'organic' management systems. The former, involving structures broadly comparable to the Weberian model, are, their research suggests, most suitable for stable, unchanging tasks. The latter, by contrast, are best

> adapted to unstable conditions, when problems and requirements for action arise which cannot be broken down and distributed among specialist rules within a clearly defined hierarchy. Individuals have to perform their

special tasks in the light of their knowledge of the tasks of the firm as a whole. Jobs lose much of their formal definition in terms of methods, duties, and powers, which have to be redefined continually by interaction with others participating in a task. Interaction runs laterally as much as vertically. Communication between people of different ranks tends to resemble lateral consultation rather than vertical command. Omniscience can no longer be imputed to the head of the concern. (pp. 5–6)

Burns and Stalker base their dichotomy on experience of research into two contrasting industrial situations. Other sociologists began, however, to raise wider questions about the fit between organisational task and structure, by examining a wide range of work situations. Some other UK research played a seminal role in this development. First, Woodward (1965) developed a typology of industrial organisations based upon differences in technology. Then, later sociologists, notably a group working together at Aston University, began to argue for the recognition of the multidimensional nature of the determinants of organisation structure. Hence by 1975 researchers working in this tradition, which had become known as 'contingency theory', could suggest, for a study of UK local authorities, a complex interaction between contingent variables and structural variables as shown in Figure 7.1 (Greenwood, *et al.*, 1975, p. 5).

Conceptual framework summary

Contingent variables		Structural variables
Size		Differentiation:
Environment:		Committees
Population density		Departments
Socioeconomic structure		Functional specialists
Wealth		Integration:
Interdependence		Co-ordinating committees
Political structure:		Central departments
Party composition	Organisational filters	Chief executive officer
Electoral volatility	Ideas:	Management team
Ideologies:	Corporate planning	
Corporate planning	Administrative efficiency	
Administrative efficiency	Democracy	
Democracy		
Type of authority	Occupational cultures	
	Professionalism	
	Departmentalism	

Figure 7.1 Contingency theory

If you examine the range of 'contingent' variables set out in Figure 7.1, you find much more than the technologically determining variables present in Burns and Stalker or Woodward. You find variables which are external to the organisation in its 'environment', you find variables determined by the power structure in which it operates, and you find variables which will depend upon 'ideology' or what Child (1972) describes as 'strategic choice'. Some brief comments are essential about how the analysis of organisations has been elaborated in relation to these three issues.

Organisations have been recognised as being power systems in which structural features interact with and are affected by factors which make some participants within them more powerful than others. This has been called 'strategic contingencies theory'. It owes a great deal to a research report by Crozier (1964), which stresses the way in which particular participants in an organisation can dominate, and influence structure, by their indispensability. His main example concerns the role of maintenance workers whose contributions were essential whenever an otherwise highly routinised plant broke down. Developments of this theory have stressed the way it explains 'differential sub-unit power by dependence on contingencies ensuing from varying combinations of coping with uncertainty, substitutability, and centrality' (Hickson *et al.*, 1971, p. 229).

Yet even this approach tends to take internal contingencies as determinants of the power structure. There is a need to turn it the other way round too, accepting that contingencies and structures determine power, but also asking whether these should be taken for granted. It is important to ask to what extent they themselves reflect a pre-existing or external power structure, and to what extent organisations have been designed to reflect and reinforce this. Hence, various writers, notably Salaman (1979), Clegg (and with Dunkerley: 1977, 1979, 1980, 1989, 1990) and Benson (1977) have taken this emphasis upon the importance of organisational power much further, making, in what may be described as radical organisation theory, links with theories of power in society. Hence Salaman argues:

> What occurs within organisations, the ways in which work is designed, control applied, rewards and deprivations distributed, decisions made, must be seen in terms of a constant conflict of interests, now apparent, now disguised, now overt, often implicit, which lies behind, and informs, the nature of work organisations within capitalist societies. (1979, p. 216)

The internal and the external

Clearly it is important to make connections between issues about internal organisational power and the external context. While the modern radical theorists are right to emphasise the neglect of this theme in much organisation theory, it has never been absent from discussions of organisations. Within organisation theory the concern with environments or external relations of organisations has roots in earlier work.

Selznick, much of whose significant work was done in the 1940s and 1950s, remains one of the most sophisticated exponents of the dependence of organisations upon their environments. He emphasises the need to study organisations as institutions:

> The term 'organisation' thus suggests a certain bareness, a lean no-nonsense system of consciously coordinated activities. It refers to an expendable tool, a rational instrument engineered to do a job. An 'institution' on the other hand, is more nearly a natural product of social needs and pressures – a responsive adaptive organism. (1957, p. 5)

This is a nice distinction, but readers should beware that Selznick is using these two words 'organisation' and 'institution' in a special way, while many others treat them as more or less synonymous. By making this distinction, Selznick relates organisations both to their external environment and to the informal social systems that develop within them. But he goes an important step further, to relate external environment directly to the internal social system. Individuals within an administrative organisation bring with them certain social commitments and attachments. Then, in the course of their administrative duties, they have to take actions that affect the public. Their particular public may be single individuals or powerful organisations. The reactions of the public to any administrative actions must be taken into account, particularly if they have any bargaining power. In the course of time, a pattern of complex relationships may grow up between an individual and those people and organisations who constitute his or her public. At the same time, the individual will be involved in a similar network of relationships with colleagues, who will also be likely to be involved in a series of external relationships of the same kind.

Selznick has been criticised by Gouldner (1955) and by Perrow (1972) for too deterministic an approach to the study of organisations and for the neglect therefore of questions about power (see further discussion below). Nevertheless it would be foolish to underestimate the extent to which the environment, however much it too is manipulable, also places constraints upon organisational action. The following quotation from Selznick's classic *TVA and the Grass Roots* (1949) expresses this most clearly:

> All formal organizations are moulded by forces tangential to their rationally ordered structures and stated goals. Every formal organization – trade union, political party, army, corporation etc. – attempts to mobilize human and technical resources as means for the achievement of its ends. However, the individuals within the system tend to resist being treated as means. They interact as wholes, bringing to bear their own special problems and purposes; moreover the organization is embedded in an institutional matrix and is therefore subject to pressure upon it from its environment, to which some general adjustment must be made. As a result, the organization may be significantly viewed as an adaptive social structure, facing problems which arise simply because it exists as an organization in an institutional environment, independently of the special (economic, military, political) goals which called it into being. (p. 251)

Inter-organisational relationships

This concern with organisations and their environments raises questions about the extent to which inter-organisational relationships influence individual organisational action. The importance of this for the public sector is considerable, in view of the extent to which governmental activities involve sets of organisations rather than single entities. Some of the problems about inter-organisational co-operation were explored in the examination of implementation theory. Recognising the importance of collaboration between organisations in many areas of policy implementation, governments have been prone to argue the case for greater co-operation and to try to set up devices to facilitate joint planning. Theorists have sought to assist this task, in the process generating some very complex attempts to model the factors which affect inter-organisational collaboration. This discussion will identify some of the key themes in this literature.

The literature may be divided into analyses which emphasise – along the lines discussed earlier – that organisations have a range of internal concerns (about structuring tasks and securing compliance), those which follow from the work of people like Selznick in seeing organisations as

having a series of concerns about their relationships to their environments, and those which go further than this to see the very concept of
the 'organisation' as involving an arbitrary drawing of boundaries.

Theories which focus upon the internal concerns of organisations
naturally suggest that these will inhibit collaboration with others. The
focus is then upon situations in which 'exchanges' are likely to be in the
interest of organisations (Levine and White, 1961; for a wider discussion
see Hudson, 1987). It is possible to postulate a variety of situations in
which exchanges will be seen to be of mutual benefit to separate
organisations. Conversely, situations can be identified in which suggested
exchanges will be rejected as offering no mutual benefit or as benefiting
one party and not the other. Policy systems may be set up to try to
increase incentives to engage in exchange relationships. For example,
in the United Kingdom efforts have been made to enhance health and
social services collaboration by giving the former organisations extra
funds which can only be spent in joint projects with the latter (Challis *et
al.*, 1988).

Very many organisational activities intrinsically involve relationships
with others, including other organisations. Without exchanges, many
organisations will fail. In this sense a narrow concern with internal
relationships is likely to be self-defeating. Thus the manufacturing firm
needs exchange relationships providing inputs of raw materials etc. and
for the successful sale of outputs of produced goods. Economic 'market'
theory deals with these relationships, with price systems governing the
relevant exchanges. Organisational theorists have inevitably explored
the extent to which organisational exchanges in non-market situations
can be seen to involve activities in which, even if money transactions
are not concerned, there can be seen to be a kind of 'trading' (of power,
prestige, etc.).

The critique of public sector organisations particularly associated with
the 'public choice' theory involves attention to the extent to which
inefficiency and a lack of accountability arises because of a lack of
'market'-type constraints (see pp. 74–7). Organisations can be inward
looking and get away with it, or they may have monopoly power that
enables them to control their exchange activities in their own interests.

In the exploration of market exchanges, it has been recognised that
one of the problems faced by emergent capitalist enterprises was control
over the input and output relationships discussed above. In, for example,
the emergent oil industry in the United States in the late nineteenth
century, any company engaged in refining faced problems from the

instabilities associated with erratic crude oil extraction on the one side and from difficulties in organising distribution on the other. The result was efforts to integrate and extend control in both directions. The classic success story in this respect was Rockefeller's Standard Oil Company. Indeed, it was such a success that the US government was pressured into breaking it up, in the interests of the enhancement of competition (Yergin, 1991). This is an example of a market organisation trying to control its environment. Notwithstanding liberal economic theory's hostility to monopoly or oligopoly, this is 'rational' behaviour from the organisation's point of view. Furthermore, even from a wider perspective, the stability that activity imposes upon a production system may be in the public interest, reducing uncertainties and costs (see Chandler (1977) for an economic historian's perspective on these issues).

These costs have been described as 'transaction costs' (Coase, 1937; Williamson, 1975, 1985). When separate organisations trade with each other, the process of finding the best bargain is not cost free. Furthermore, when that trading needs to be on a regular basis, there is likely to be a need for a 'contract' setting out obligations on either side, lasting for a period of time and ultimately renegotiable. Making, monitoring and revising contracts entails costs. Both sides are likely to seek long-run stability. One way of doing this is through amalgamation. That may be by agreement or, as in the case of the build-up of the Standard Oil empire, one organisation may have the market power to be able to acquire others.

Williamson (1975) has gone on to analyse these issues in terms of a contrast between 'markets' and 'hierarchies'. His supposition is that, while in general market relationships are superior because of their flexibility and because of the role competition can play in keeping down costs, this may not apply if 'transaction costs' are high. When these are high, the incorporation of suppliers, distributers, etc. into hierarchies may become a desirable strategy.

Williamson's dichotomy relates to another dichotomy between Fordism and post-Fordism (Piore and Sabel, 1984; Aglietta, 1987; Elam, 1990; Jessop, 1992). The heyday of the Ford motor company involved routinised production on an assembly line. It also involved the incorporation of many elements in the production and distribution process into a single hierarchical organisation. Post-Fordism entails either or both of (a) fragmentation of activities within an organisation and (b) the hiving off of parts of the process into separate organisations. In the business world today, choices are not simple ones between 'market' and 'hierarchy', rather they are about a range of alternative ways of controlling exchange relationships – internal markets, franchising, subcontracting, etc.

Williamson's work has been generalised into forms of contingency theory (Donaldson, 1985), and has been challenged by writers who see issues of power and of control over environmental uncertainties as of greater explanatory value than Williamson's original approach (see, for example, Minzberg, 1983).

The literature on markets and hierarchies, like so much of the work explored in this book, is concerned both to assist the analysis of the behaviour of firms and to contribute to debates about what ought or ought not to be done about oligopoly. But why look at it in a discussion of public organisations? It suggests answers to questions about the design of organisations. The reasons for exploring it here are as follows:

● There are significant attempts by governments to take note of the public choice critique of bureaucracy and to try to transform some hierarchies into markets; contracts between public organisations or between public and private organisations are becoming an increasing feature of the public policy process (these are discussed in the next section).

● Even without contracts the issues about transaction costs are relevant to the exchange relations between public organisations, and there are issues about the consequences of choices between forms of organisation which incorporate many functions under one department and forms which leave them in separate bodies (see Flynn, 1993; Walsh, 1995).

However, Thelen and Steinmo, among others, argue that seeing 'institutions as efficient solutions to collective action problems, reducing transaction costs . . . in order to enhance efficiency' begs 'the important questions about how political power figures in the creation and maintenance of these institutions' (1992, p. 10).

A general problem with the use of the concept of 'exchange' is that it tends to direct attention to comparatively equal transactions. The Standard Oil story outlined above was about the growing capacity of one organisation to control its transactions with other organisations. Similarly, since, as critical theory argues, intra-organisational relationships involve power inequalities, so too do inter-organisational ones. Perrow (1972) attacks Selznick's disregard (see above) of the factors which enable some organisations to have a considerable measure of control over their domains and over the domains of others. There is therefore a need to explore the inequalities and 'power dependencies' in organisational interactions (Kochan, 1975; Aldrich, 1976).

Analysis of this subject needs to be sited within an overall analysis of social power, as explored earlier in this book. One writer who has done this, Benson, has criticised writers who concentrate on the problems of securing the co-ordination of public services and neglect the broader influences which affect co-ordination. Benson maintains that inter-organisational analysis is at one level concerned with examining the dependency of organisations on each other for resources such as money and authority, but at another level it must focus on the interests built into the structure of a particular policy sector. Benson defines a policy sector as 'a cluster or complex of organisations connected to each other by resource dependencies and distinguished from other clusters or complexes by breaks in the structure of resource dependencies' (1983, p. 3). Defined in this way, the concept of policy sectors has similarities to the policy communities discussed in Chapter 4. As well as examining the interests built into a policy sector, Benson suggests that it is necessary to examine the systems of rules which govern relationships between these interests. In essence, then, there is a need to explicate the interaction between the surface level and the 'deep structure which determines within limits the range of variation of the surface levels' (p. 5).

Thus, according to Benson, a complete analysis of inter-organisational relationships needs to explore three levels in the structure of policy sectors (p. 6). First, there is the administrative structure: that is, the surface level of linkages and networks between agencies held together by resource dependencies. Second, there is the interest structure: that is, the set of groups whose interests are built into the sector either positively or negatively. These groups comprise demand groups, support groups, administrative groups, provider groups and co-ordinating groups. The interest structure is important in that it provides the context for the administrative structure, which cannot be adequately understood except in terms of the underlying power relations manifested within the interest structure. In turn, the interest structure has to be located within the third level: that is, 'the rules of structure formation'. In advanced societies, these rules are principally those which relate to the maintenance of capital accumulation.

Benson summarises his argument in the following terms:

For each policy sector, then, it would be necessary to explore the impact of deep rules of structure formation. These would not determine the structure of the sector in every detail. It is reasonable to assume some measure of autonomy for the other levels – administrative organisation and structural interests. In broad terms, however, the events at those levels are to be explained at the level of rules of structure formation. The rules limit and enable action at other levels. Social science accounts which do not consider these deeper rules are to varying degrees incomplete. (1983, p. 31)

One of the issues this raises is: what precisely is the relationship between levels? While the main thrust of Benson's argument is that action at the surface level cannot be understood without reference to the interest structure and the rules of structure formation, he is careful not to suggest that the relationship between levels is simply deterministic. Indeed, in discussing how changes might occur within sectors, he notes the possibility that the administrative structure might become independent of the structural underpinnings and that bureaucracies might develop a life and logic of their own.

Benson's theory clearly takes us back to some of the ideas about structural determinism explored in Chapter 3, particularly those ideas which derive from Marxist theory. A somewhat similar position is reached, in a way which is less determinist and draws less upon the concept of 'interests', by the institutionalist theorists discussed in Chapter 4. Thus March and Olsen argue:

Institutional theories supplement exchange theories of political action in two primary ways: first, they emphasise the role of institutions in defining the terms of rational exchange . . . Second, without denying the reality of calculations and anticipations of consequences, institutional conceptions see such . . . as occurring within a broader framework of rules, roles and identities. (1996, p. 250)

DiMaggio and Powell (1983) explore – in a way which similarly rejects 'functionalist or Marxist explanations' (p. 156) – what they call 'isomorphic processes' which tend to make organisations similar to one another. They offer a series of hypotheses on this topic, including factors like internal organisational uncertainties and external resource dependencies to explain this convergence.

Another way into this issue, without using structuralist theory, is to recognise that individual members of organisations also have other affiliations. They belong to families, voluntary organisations, political parties, churches, etc. These may mean commitments to other organisations which interact with the organisation which employs them. This may seem a rather trivial point, but there are circumstances in which it is definitely not. The most significant of these for public policy is where they are members of professional groups extending across a number of organisations. The impact of this is then further enhanced inasmuch as there are intra-organisational divisions, with different professional groups in separate sections or hierarchical systems. To describe this phenomenon Ouchi (1980) has added 'clans' as a third element to be looked at within organisational relationships, alongside markets and hierarchies. Degeling, analysing hospitals as organisations, writes of them as often

> locales in which members of distinct authority structures are loosely linked in the provisions of services. The separateness of medicine, nursing, allied health and hotel services, recognised in the formal structure of most hospitals, attests to the past capacity of these occupational groups to stake out and preserve their control over particular aspects of treatment provision. (1993, p. 33)

Laffin (1986) identifies how these professional communities may have an influence upon relations between organisations, and DiMaggio and Powell (1983) argue that professional communities are important in generating convergence in organisational structures.

A related issue is the need to recognise that individual organisational participants have careers which may spread across one or more organisations. Studies of the UK civil service have thus suggested that Treasury dominance over the system stems, among other things, from that body's capacity to control career moves, and in particular its tendency to take promising young civil servants from other departments for a period and to bring the most successful back into its ranks later in their careers (Heclo and Wildavsky, 1981; Campbell and Wilson, 1995). This is perhaps a comparatively simple case of organisational dominance.

A less explored example, particularly pertinent to this discussion, concerns the dramatic personnel changes occurring in some of the organisations particularly affected by the establishment of quasi-market systems in the United Kingdom, which may involve fairly rapid moves between purchasers and providers or between local government and the health service. Where individuals come from and where they hope to go to must surely influence their willingness to engage with others. Those who have explored ways to enhance inter-organisational co-operation have explicitly suggested the fostering of roles which help individuals to look outwards from their own organisation (Friend *et al.*, 1974; Hudson, 1987; Huxham and Macdonald, 1992). A variety of devices may be adopted to this end: the setting up of special joint units, the designation of collaboration as a key ingredient of a work task, the temporary secondment of staff and so on. The success of these ventures depends upon some of the considerations already discussed – the feasibility of meaningful exchanges, the overall power context, the extent to which there are shared values. But inasmuch as they must be seen in terms of individual motivation as well as organisational motivation, there are key considerations to take into account about the extent to which they yield rewards – explicit or implicit, financial or psychic – for the persons involved.

This discussion has ranged briefly over a variety of sometimes difficult theory. This has been necessary to explore the complexity of the issues involved in inter-organisational relationships, which often frustrate naive efforts to devise structures to cope with their perceived negative effects.

The impact of 'new public management'

New approaches to the organisation of the public sector designed to get away from the traditional bureaucratic model are having a significant effect upon both intra- and inter-organisational relationships. These are therefore given special attention in this section.

The expression 'new public management' (NPM) is useful shorthand for a variety of innovations, widespread across the world, which are 'dominating the bureaucratic reform agenda' (Hood, 1991, p. 3), and have been designed to deal with alleged shortcomings of the old bureaucratic model. There is a danger that the use of this shorthand expression conveys a unified and compatible set of initiatives. In a later essay, Hood (1995), despite having established himself as the leading analyst of the phenomenon, attacks the view that NPM is a 'new global paradigm' and highlights some of the inconsistencies within the work of its leading exponents.

Hood identifies seven 'doctrines' to which 'Over the last decade, a "typical" public sector policy delivery unit in the UK, Australia, New Zealand and many other OECD countries would be likely to have had some exposure' (1991, p. 4). He does not mention the United States, but perhaps the most influential of all the NMP tracts, a book by Osborne and Gaebler (1992), comes from that country. The seven doctrines Hood identifies are:

1. 'Hands on professional management in the public sector'.
2. 'Explicit standards and measures of performance'.
3. 'Greater emphasis on output controls'.
4. '. . . disaggregation of units in the public sector'.
5. '. . . greater competition in the public sector' (to this may be added actual privatisation).
6. '. . . private sector styles of management'.
7. '. . . greater discipline and parsimony in resource use' (adapted from Hood, 1991, pp. 4–5).

Hood indicates that NPM has been attacked for its concern to place issues about efficiency before equity (Pollitt, 1990), but argues that NPM advocates would assert that efficiency 'can be conceived in ways which do not fundamentally conflict with equity (Hood, 1991, p. 20, citing Wilenski, 1986). This takes us into value issues which are not the concern of this discussion.

Another conflict within NPM seems to be between the two concerns about bureaucracy which have been highlighted in this chapter – efficiency and accountability. Some of the NPM movement's concerns come directly from the public choice attack upon traditional public bureaucracy which links the two concepts. However, some of the ideas – notably items 1 and 4 in Hood's list – have their roots in Peters and Waterman's (1982) concerns about human relations in the organisation, and the desire to create organisations where 'excellence' can be achieved by a committed workforce left to perform delegated tasks without undue surveillance. This argument draws upon the evidence from organisational sociology discussed on pp. 161–4. It seems to conflict with the public choice view that public sector managers cannot be trusted to operate autonomously.

This same tension occurs in relation to the public choice distrust of professionalism – characteristically defended in terms like those used by Peters and Waterman to argue for the flexible and creative post-Fordist enterprise. A particular feature of NPM in practice has been an attack upon the traditional autonomy claims of the established professions – medicine, teaching, etc. Interestingly, the new 'hands-on professional' managers are seen as a countervailing force to the traditional professionals (Hoggett, 1996).

If the ideas are taken together as a package, these conflicts may be resolved to the satisfaction of the New Right perspective by stressing that market discipline imposes its own accountability. Managerial autonomy does not enable managers to 'buck the market'. They are the missionaries for the new realities. Others, like the 'aristocratic' old professions, it is argued, must learn to come to terms with market discipline.

For others, not wedded to the New Right perspective, this mixture of measures seems to preserve the autonomy of those 'hands-on' managers at the top while ensuring the efficiency of response by lower-level workers to their demands through the increased insecurity entailed in the combination of strict standards and competition from alternative providers (Hoggett, 1996).

A characteristic of NPM in the United Kingdom (and probably in Australia and New Zealand too) is that it has been very much a 'top-down' movement. Reform of central administration has not involved decentralisation. The 'disaggregated units' that Hood refers to have been subject to tight controls. For example, the agency-based UK social security system operates in a more routinised way than ever in its history (Ling, 1994). There are grounds for arguing – with respect to the prison service or the role of the agency set up to secure payments form absent parents – that the operational freedom consists merely of a freedom to take the blame. At the lower levels, UK local government experienced over the decade from 1985 to 1995 steadily tightening financial control, strong steering to ensure that its interpretation of NPM was compatible with that of the government, and requirements to accept and stimulate competition that weakened its capacity to respond to local political forces (Walsh, 1995; Butcher, 1995; Hoggett, 1996; Deakin and Walsh, 1996).

A set of alternative ways of conceptualising NPM has been put forward which recognise the force of the Peters and Waterman critique of bureaucracy, accept the importance of performance measures as indices to be shared with the public, but reject the market orientation of much of the rest of the thinking. This approach tackles the issue of accountability not by the adoption of market devices, but by trying to put bottom-up notions of accountability in place of the traditional top-down ones (Stewart and Clarke, 1987; Hoggett, 1991).

This discussion of NPM has run briefly through a number of themes, all of which will be explored further in the next two chapters. This introduction to the topic has been designed to show how NPM is a response to dilemmas about public bureaucracy that go back at least as far as Max Weber's time, and draws upon the sociological analysis of organisations stimulated by Weber's work and by the arguments about Taylorism or Fordism as well as the public choice critique. It is important to note how these ideas have travelled quickly from country to country, promoted by fashionable gurus.

While the writer has probably failed to disguise his suspicion of the NPM movement, this account has not been designed as a thorough critique of it. Research evaluations of the key developments have been slow to emerge and have produced equivocal findings. There are grounds for a view that the achievements of NPM will be limited. This is based upon two arguments. One is that realistic competitive 'markets' are hard to create. The evidence for this comes from studies of the behaviour of the private sector – here the discussion of transaction costs (pp. 167–9) is relevant. There are very strong reasons why actors will try to secure long-run stable non-competitive relationships.

The other argument brings us back to the theme of accountability. While the quest for cost minimisation seems to have been a central motive for the adoption of NPM, other political concerns make it very hard to leave 'hands-on' managers, hived-off agencies and local contracting systems alone. After all, particularly in a centralised political system like the United Kingdom's, who do we turn to but our elected politicians when the local hospital, school or bus service is inadequate? Consumerism is a very blunt alternative weapon. There is a whole series of structural reasons why, in the vital short run at least, alternative choices are unavailable. Furthermore, inasmuch as service delivery matters can be delegated to private or autonomous organisations, any reduction of the role of government in relation to provision is likely to need to be counterbalanced by increases in regulatory activities.

CHAPTER 8

RULES AND DISCRETION IN PUBLIC POLICY

Synopsis

The relationship between rules, which specify the duties and obligations of officials, and discretion, allowing them freedom of choice of action, has been a particular preoccupation of literature on public law. It is therefore the starting point of this chapter. Concerns about state power and the role of the judicial system in offering mechanisms for the control of that power have led on to some fruitful theoretical work on rules and discretion. However, these legal preoccupations tend to involve an approach to these concepts which sees rules very much in a statutory context and discretionary actions as involving not so much individual choice of courses of action (which many will take for granted as inevitable) as particular cases of legitimate departure from action prescribed by a legal rule structure. A later section widens attention to the way these phenomena are handled in organisational sociology and related work, in the exploration of hierarchical control, its effects and its limits. The discussion leads on to some wider issues about organisational behaviour which are then explored further in the next chapter.

Introduction

Exploration of the relationship between policy making and implementation and the issues about organisational and inter-organisational relations, involve a variety of issues about the extent to which super-ordinate actors (including organisations) impose rules upon subordinate

177

ones. These may be explored in terms of legitimacy, and be taken back to a variety of arguments about democracy and accountability: that is, about the rights some actors have to impose constraints on others. This is not the approach taken here, though it must be acknowledged that it is an issue that lurks in the background all the while. However, the book does have as a central focus the description of policy processes, among which efforts and claims to control loom large. The feasibility of such efforts has been explored to some extent in looking at implementation and the relationships between organisations. This exploration can be taken forward further by looking at (a) the way substantive issues affect efforts to control and (b) the kinds of claim made to legitimise either the making and enforcement of rules to impose control or the absence (more likely the partial absence) of such rules. It is the latter phenomenon which is described as 'discretion'. The efforts of lawyers to deal with the rules/discretion relationship provides a good starting point for such a discussion.

Rules and discretion in public and administrative law

In the United Kingdom, the absence of a written constitution gives debate about public law a peculiar shape, deriving from the fact that the primary source of law is Parliament, the main arguments about the limits to parliamentary power rest upon a peculiar body of legal tradition known as 'common law' and the main remedies for the citizen have emerged out of an arcane procedure under which the Crown was petitioned to consider remedies against the excesses of its own officials. The central concern is whether the rules applied by public officials have the formal sanction of Parliament and whether departures from those rules (discretion) are formally authorised (or not formally proscribed) by statute. A secondary concern is the capacity of the court system – as supplemented in the modern world by simpler grievance procedures such as tribunals and ombudsmen – to respond to situations in which citizens (singly or in organised groups) regard official behaviour as falling outside these statutorily determined boundaries.

These lead to a third concern, with potentially major political implications, about the inadequacy of the existing constitutional and legal system as a bulwark against the arbitrary exercise of power by either elected politicians or appointed officials.

The peculiarities of the UK system (shared, of course, by some

Commonwealth countries) contrast with the systems of countries with written constitutions and a supreme adjudicative body entrusted with the protection and interpretation of these constitutions. In such countries – of which the United States is clearly a very influential example for all readers of English – an additional test of the legitimacy of any action related to the policy process will be its compatibility with the constitution.

The American constitution was, of course, a product of political action, and can be amended by political action. There are potentially wider ways of testing the legitimacy of action – in relation to broad principles setting out human rights and limitations upon governmental action. These are set out in various supra-national declarations which, while also in the first place created by political decision-making processes, may offer – if there are usable enforcement mechanisms (such as the European Court) – another avenue of redress to the aggrieved citizen.

Thus issues about the legitimacy of official rules, and the related discretions they may explicitly or implicitly convey, may be disputed with reference to their specific source, to their constitutional context or to wider principles. There is a fairly universal debate on this, particularly focusing upon the extent to which discretionary powers are either inevitable or legitimate. However, its more detailed form in any country is likely to be influenced by the more specific constitutional context. Inevitably, therefore, a significant part of the following discussion has been shaped by UK concerns.

Traditionally, UK administrative law textbooks give attention to administrative discretion as a 'taken-for-granted' phenomenon within the political system. They point out that the concern of the courts has been with: (a) whether or not discretionary powers which are exercised have been clearly delegated by statute; (b) whether the exercise of those powers is within the boundaries of natural justice (are they exercised reasonably and with regard to due process?); and (c) the principle that if a statute grants discretionary powers, then the officials using them should not devise rules which in practice fetter that discretion.

The role of the courts in relation to administrative discretion is an interesting phenomenon in its own right. The textbooks provide a portrait of the law as trying to keep administrative discretion under control. The law is presented as the defender of the citizen against the arbitrary exercise of power. Wade (1967), for example, perceives administrative law as an attempt to ensure that the 'whole new empires of executive power' conform to the principles of liberty and fair dealing. This perspective leads Wade to argue that the key issue is ensuring that the law can control 'the exercise of the innumerable discretionary powers which Parliament has conferred on the various authorities' (p. 4). His emphasis is on ensuring that such authorities do not act *ultra vires* by exceeding their statutory power or following the wrong procedures. Authorities cannot escape such control by being offered statutes that give them unlimited power, since 'in practice all statutory powers have statutory limits, and where the expressed limits are indefinite, the courts are all the more inclined to find that limits are implied. The notion of unlimited power has no place in the system' (p. 50).

Two things complicate this boldly stated model of the 'rule of law'. One, outside the terms of reference of this book, is the difficulties citizens have in using the law to protect themselves from the executive. The other, very much within our terms of reference, is that these so-called statutory powers are very complicated. One view, abandoned by any realistic critic of the UK legislative system at least fifty years ago, was that all rules should be embodied in formal Acts of Parliament. The reality is that there is a great deal of subordinate rule making – not only in 'regulations' which are hypothetically open to parliamentary scrutiny, but also in a variety of departmental guidance circulars, codes and working instructions to officials.

The very institutional complexity of the policy system – as explored in the previous chapter – means that there is a wide range of bodies which have responsibilities to interpret and perhaps amplify their statutory mandates. Hence, it is not possible to draw a simple distinction between statutory rules, deriving from the legislature, and the discretion of officials. The intermediary departments, agencies, local governments and so on which can be seen, from the old-fashioned perspective, as discretionary actors themselves engage in subordinate rule-making processes. A considerable body of case law governs these processes.

Modern writing on discretion involves an approach to the examination of the role of law in public policy implementation in which discretion is recognised as a fundamentally important phenomenon, and not as an undesirable manifestation of the collectivist state which ought to be eliminated, as earlier legalistic analyses such as those by Dicey (1905) and Hewart (1929) had suggested. At the same time, the older concern about the threat posed by discretion to the rule of law is still alive. Not surprisingly, there are significant cultural differences between societies in the extent to which the issues about discretion are regarded as susceptible to judicial control, with a strong emphasis on this theme coming from the United States.

While, as this chapter proceeds, attention will shift to discretion as decision making by individual officials which is not entirely pre-programmed, it is important to stress at this stage how complex the relationship is likely to be between an originating statute and an official action. The problem this poses for the aggrieved citizen is, of course, that it may be difficult to determine the real basis of a decision.

Defining discretion and explaining its presence: the legal theory approach

In any administrative system regulated by law, discretion will be embedded in a rule structure – at the very least in a form which will make it clear that only in a very specific set of circumstances can officials do what they like (probably the laws which come nearest to this form are those which give certain officials very strong powers to act in the interests of public safety or to prevent the entry into the country of foreigners deemed to be a threat to the regime). This embedded character of discretion leads to a rather confusing argument. Perhaps the most influential definition of discretion is Davis': 'A public officer has discretion wherever the effective limits on his power leave him free to make a choice among possible courses of action and inaction' (1969, p. 4). Others have used quite restrictive definitions, reserving the concept for only some of the phenomena embraced by Davis' definition. For example, Bull (1980) and Donnison (1977), in their separate discussions of social security discretion, draw a distinction between judgement, where the simple interpretation of rules is required, and discretion, where the rules give specific functionaries in particular situations the responsibility to make such decisions as they think fit. This seems to be drawing an unnecessary distinction. If all discretion is embedded to some extent in a rule structure (being what Dworkin (1977) has called 'the hole in the donut'), then Bull and Donnison are merely drawing a distinction between more and less structured discretion, or what Dworkin has called weak and strong forms (p. 31).

The approach here is to use the concept of discretion in the wide sense embodied in Davis' definition. This is partly influenced by a belief that social scientists should try to avoid imposing their own restrictive definitions of concepts used in everyday speech. But it is also justified by the fact that this discussion is concerned to see to what extent discretion is a useful concept with which to explore delegated decision-making processes.

The use of a wide definition like Davis' implies a concern with almost all decision-making situations, since, as Jacques (1967) points out, almost all delegated tasks involve some degree of discretion. A study of discretion must involve, by implication, a study of rules, and may alternatively be defined in that way as being concerned with the extent to which actions are determined by rules. This also means that students of discretion must be concerned with rule breaking, since in real-life situations the interpretation of the extent to which rule following allows discretion merges imperceptibly into the witting or unwitting disregard of rules.

Davis' definition comes from a book in which he argues for the rule structure within which discretion is exercised to be drawn as tightly as possible. He argues: 'Our governmental and legal systems are saturated with excessive discretionary power which needs to be confined, structured and checked' (1969, p. 27). Later in the same book he argues:

> we have to open our eyes to the reality that justice to individual parties is administered more outside courts than in them, and we have to penetrate the unpleasant areas of discretionary determinations by police and prosecutors and other administrators, where huge concentrations of injustice invite drastic reforms. (p. 215)

Davis argues that citizens' rights to procedural justice can best be achieved through earlier and more elaborate administrative rule making and in better structuring and checking of discretionary power (p. 219). Davis is thus concerned with the need for the public organisation to control the discretionary power of the individual public officer, and he feels that this should be primarily attempted through rules which are open to public inspection.

In the United Kingdom, Jeffrey Jowell carried forward the kind of concern about discretion shown by Davis in the United States. Jowell's definition of discretion is like Davis'. He defines it as 'the room for decisional manoeuvre possessed by a decision maker' (1973, p. 179), and argues that the key need is to ensure that decision-makers cannot make arbitrary decisions. However, Jowell lays a far greater stress than Davis upon difficulties in reducing administrative discretion. In particular, he shows how many of the considerations with which decisions must be concerned are inherently difficult to specify in rules. Legislators are concerned to prevent *dangerous* driving, to ensure that food is *pure*, and that factories are *safe*. The provision of clear-cut rules to define what is safe or dangerous, pure or polluted, is often difficult. It may be that legislators need the help of the experts who are to enforce the law to provide some specific rules. In this sense, discretion may be limited at a later date when experience of enforcement enables explicit rules to be devised. It may be that conflict over the legislation has led to the blurring of the issues, and that legislators have evaded their responsibility to make more explicit rules. But it may be the case that the translation of standards into explicit rules is so difficult as to be practically impossible.

Jeffrey Jowell provides a valuable discussion of the problems of fettering discretion where concern is with the enforcement of standards. He argues that standards may be rendered more precise by criteria, facts that are to be taken into account. However, he argues that 'the feature of standards that distinguishes them from rules is their flexibility and susceptibility to change over time' (p. 204). Very often, too, standards involve questions of individual taste or values. Jowell quotes with reference to this point an appeal court case in which the judge was unable 'to enforce a covenant restricting the erection of "any building of unseemly description"' (p. 204). Jowell similarly suggests that situations in which unlike things have to be compared, or which are unique and non-recurring, cannot be regulated by reference to a clearly specified standard. He argues:

> It is not difficult to appreciate that it would be asking too much of the English football selectors to decide after a public hearing and with due representation, to state reasons why the national interest would be served by having X rather than Y or Z to play centre forward in the coming match. (p. 206)

This issue about standards has been taken up in other legal writing on discretion. Hence Dworkin's (1977) distinction between strong discretion, where the decision-maker creates the standards, and weak discretion, where standards set by a prior authority have to be interpreted. Galligan (1986) is similarly concerned to analyse discretion in this way, identifying that decision-makers have to apply standards to the interpretation of facts. These distinctions may seem very academic; they are, however, important in administrative law for distinctions between decisions which are within an official's powers and ones which are not, and therefore for determining whether intervention by an appeal body is appropriate.

Issues about conflicting facts arise where evidence is ambiguous, or where individuals present different versions of the same events. One of the surprising aspects of some of the less sophisticated attacks on discretionary administration by lawyers is that, in practising their own profession, while they talk of facts and law and of proof and disproof, they very often require judges and juries to decide between conflicting evidence. The proper distinction to make is not between the precision of judicial decision making and the imprecision of much administration, but between the extent to which procedural safeguards for the individual, or due process, exist in each situation. Here again Jowell's work is helpful, since he distinguishes between two approaches to the control of discretion: 'legalisation', the 'process of subjecting official decisions to predetermined rules' and thus, of course, the elimination of discretion; and 'judicialisation', involving 'submitting official decision to adjudicative procedures'.

Jowell does not accept a simple dichotomy between rules and discretion as suggested by Davis, but rather argues that discretion 'is a matter of degree, and ranges along a continuum between high and low' (p. 179). At first glance, rules may appear to abolish such discretion, 'but since rules are purposively devised . . . and because language is largely uncertain in its application to situations that cannot be foreseen, the applier of a rule will frequently be possessed of some degree of discretion to interpret its scope' (p. 201). This last comment suggests that any study of discretionary decision making requires a consideration of social processes internal to the organisation and a study of the attitudes and beliefs of those who have to interpret the rules.

Jowell's arguments quoted above suggest a need to relate any evaluation of discretion to the substantive issue involved. He suggests some reasons why discretion may be inevitable. His football selection example highlights not merely the issue of standards, but also the relevance of expertise and the significance of 'polycentric' issues where many factors interact (Baldwin, 1995, p. 29). This suggests a need to identify types of decision situation in which discretion is more necessary.

Mashaw (1983, ch. 2) draws a distinction between three different models of justice in relation to administrative decision making:

- The *bureaucratic rationality* model, which demands that decisions should accurately reflect the original policy-makers' objectives.

- The *professional treatment* model, which calls for the application of specialist skills in complex situations, and where intuitive judgements are likely to be needed.
- The *moral judgement* model, where fairness and independence are important.

Clearly the first and the third sound rather similar. Mashaw acknowledges this, but goes on to argue that the moral judgement model should be seen as 'value defining' (p. 29). It is likely to involve rather more discretion inasmuch as what is at stake is value issues and judgements like those Jowell emphasises in relation to 'standards'. Perhaps it may be added, though Mashaw does not make this point, that situations of this kind – like the disputes between neighbours about pollution, which he cites as an example – may require to some extent a 'bottom-up' decision process and a measure of flexibility to allow for participation by the members of the public affected.

The second model is, on the other hand, self-evidently the one which offers a justification for official discretion.

Mashaw's analysis aims to offer a rationale for determining the 'acceptability' of any particular decision system. But Baldwin's objection to this is to ask 'acceptable to whom?' (1995, pp. 40–1). He goes on to argue: 'it can be questioned whether the judges of a bureaucratic process are to be the consumers of services, the general public, the management of the agency, the front-line officials, the government, the media, or some other grouping' (p. 41).

Baldwin goes on from this critique to offer his own 'five rationales for legitimacy claims' (pp. 41–6). These are as follows:

1. The 'legislative mandate claim', resting upon evidence of parliamentary authorisation.
2. The 'accountability or control claim', using a variety of wider accountability justifications, including general legislative oversight or more immediate forms of participation as alternatives to simple evidence of a legislative mandate.
3. The 'due process claim', which rests upon the transparency of the decision process and/or the availability of avenues for appeal.
4. The 'expertise claim', referring to 'polycentric issues' and Mashaw's 'professional treatment model'.
5. The 'efficiency claim', arguing that 'stated objectives are being achieved in an effective manner, and . . . that economically efficient actions are being taken' (p. 46).

Baldwin's 'legitimacy claims' clearly relate to the whole range of issues about rules and discretion. They may be used to justify primary rule (law) making processes (particularly claim 1), secondary rule making (particularly 2 and 3) and the delegation of discretionary powers (particularly 4 and 5). They may well be used in combination.

Finally, Baldwin argues for his typology on the grounds that it can be used both in relation to 'normative *judgements* as to legitimacy and *descriptions* of legitimacy' (p. 48). It is the latter that is the primary concern here. In his discussion of this, Baldwin quotes Beetham: 'the social scientist, in concluding that a given power relationship is legitimate, is making a judgement, not delivering a report about people's beliefs in legitimacy' (Beetham, 1991, p.13). Arguments used for rules or for discretion rest upon one or more of these justifications.

Some contributors to the debates about discretion within a series of sponsored workshops on discretion in social policy held in the United Kingdom in 1979–80 expressed scepticism about the value of a priori definitions of discretion. For example, Gilbert Smith (1981) argues:

> the merits of specifically 'discretionary decisions' as a weapon in the research worker's conceptual armoury are dubious. It seems likely to backfire and give rise to a great deal of definitional debate which confuses as much as it clarifies. The *a priori* definitions of discretion tend to be either arbitrary or prejudiced. (p. 67)

This discussion has shown how important the debate about rules and discretion is for the examination of some issues in public law. It has suggested, however, that the relationship between rules and discretion is complex, and that what is particularly important is claims or justifications for the presence or absence of either phenomenon. Thus, while not agreeing with Gilbert Smith, it is suggested that the concept of discretion needs using with some care in any analysis of the policy process. This case for care can be further explored by considering the way in which organisational sociology has dealt with these issues. This is done in the next section.

Rules and discretion in organisational sociology

All work, however closely controlled and supervised, involves some degree of discretion. Wherever work is delegated, the person who delegates loses some amount of control. To approach the concept in this way is, of course, to examine it from the perspective of superordinate authority. Viewed the other way round, the equivalent phenomenon is rules which apparently guarantee benefits or services, but which nevertheless have to be interpreted by intermediaries. It is in the twin contexts of task complexity and the delegation of responsibility that the phenomenon of discretion becomes of salient importance. In complex organisational situations, gaps readily emerge between intentions and outcomes. Logically, people running one-person businesses have discretion, but the concern here is with it as a relational phenomenon. The problems about discretion are perceived, not surprisingly, as arising when one person's discretionary freedom may subvert the intentions of another.

Running through much organisation theory – and in particular through the work of those writers who are seeking to help those whom they see as being in control of organisations to determine the right way to approach the delegation of tasks – is therefore a concern about the balance between rules and discretion, even when different words are used. Hence Simon, in his classic work *Administrative Behaviour* (1957), emphasises the importance of the various premises upon which decisions are based. Rule making and control within organisations are concerned with the specification of premises for subordinates. Simon argues:

> The behaviour of a rational person can be controlled, therefore, if the value and factual premises upon which he bases his decisions are specified for him. This control can be complete or partial – all premises can be specified, or some can be left to his discretion. Influence, then, is exercised through control over the premises of decision. (p. 223)

One reservation must be made about this statement: namely that, as suggested above, the notion of total control in an organisational context is unrealistic. Otherwise it is a valuable statement of the place of discretion in a hierarchical relationship. Simon goes on to suggest that what occurs within an organisational system is that a series of areas of discretion are created in which individuals have freedom to interpret their tasks within general frameworks provided by their superiors. He quotes a military example relevant to the 'modern battlefield':

> how does the authority of the commander extend to the soldiers in the ranks? How does he limit and guide their behaviour? He does this by specifying the general mission and objective of each unit on the next level below, and by determining such elements of time and place as will assure a proper coordination among units. The colonel assigns to each

battalion in his regiment its task; the major, to each company in his battalion; the captain, to each platoon in his company. Beyond this, the officer does not ordinarily go. The internal arrangements of Army Field Services Regulations specify that 'an order should not trespass upon the province of a subordinate. It should contain everything beyond the independent authority of the subordinate, but nothing more'. (p. 224)

Thus Simon recognises the importance of discretion even in the most hierarchical and authoritarian organisation.

Dunsire (1987a) has seized upon the interesting reference to the 'province' of the subordinate in this context. He portrays organisational activities as involving 'programmes within programmes'. In a hierarchy, subordinate programmes are dependent upon superior ones, but they may involve very different kinds of activity. He elaborates an example of a railway closure to show that, while activities such as the rerouting of trains, the selling of railway property and, at the very end of the chain, the removal of ballast from abandoned tracks are necessarily dependent upon superior decisions about the closure, the way they are carried out is not predetermined by the decisions taken at the top of the hierarchy. He argues that decisions at the higher level are of high generality, those at the bottom of high specificity. This does not mean, however, 'that a worker at a high specificity level necessarily has a smaller amount of discretion (in any of its senses) than a worker at a high generality level' (p. 221). This approach helps us to make sense of the use of the concept of discretion in relation to professional hierarchies, such as education or medicine. The organisational or planning activities at the top of such hierarchies set contexts for, but do not necessarily predetermine, decision making at field levels, where very different tasks are performed and very different problems have to be solved.

All the writers who have been concerned about the complexity of organisations have acknowledged that there are related problems of control, co-ordination and communication between these different provinces and linking these programmes within programmes (see Dunsire, 1987b). Attention has been drawn to the interdependence involved, and therefore to the fact that, in a hierarchical situation, superiors may be dependent upon subordinates. This is taken further by Gouldner, who shows that the top-down presentation of hierarchical relationships, with superiors promulgating rules to restrict the discretion of the subordinates, may sometimes be turned on its head. He draws attention to the development of rules which limit the discretionary freedom of superiors in the interests of their subordinates. The classic discussion of this occurs in Gouldner's *Patterns of Industrial Bureaucracy* (1954), in which he shows the part that workers may play in securing rules to protect their interests. Overall his emphasis is upon the appeal to rules, by either party, in a situation in which a previously obtaining relationship breaks down:

> Efforts are made to install new bureaucratic rules, or enforce old ones, when people in a given social position (i.e. management or workers) perceive those in a reciprocal position (i.e. workers or management) as failing to perform their role obligations. (p. 232)

Gouldner is concerned about the many functions of rules in situations of social conflict. He draws our attention, therefore, to the extent to which rules and discretion must be studied in the context of relationships in which the parties on either side seek to influence the freedom of movement of the other.

It is important to move away from the older emphasis in organisation theory which saw the rules/discretion relationship from the perspective of superiors concerned to limit discretion, as far as acceptable, in the interests of rational management. Instead attention should be directed towards the extent to which both rules and discretion are manipulated and bargained over within hierarchies. Fox (1974), coming to the examination of this issue from a concern with industrial relations, has interestingly related rule imposition to low-trust relationships. He picks up the top-down concern with detailed prescription and shows how this creates or reinforces low-trust relations:

> The role occupant perceives superordinates as behaving as if they believe he cannot be trusted, of his own volition, to deliver a work performance which fully accords with the goals they wish to see pursued or the values they wish to see observed. (p. 26)

A vicious circle may be expected to ensue. The subordinate, who perceives that he or she is not trusted, feels little commitment to the effective performance of work. This particularly affects the way the remaining discretionary parts of the work are carried out. The superior's response is to try to tighten control, and further reduce the discretionary elements. The irreducible minimum of discretion left leaves the subordinate with some weapons against the superior; the prescribed task is performed in a rigid, unimaginative and slow way.

Hence, some rather similar phenomena may emerge by different routes. One may be defined as discretion, the other as rule breaking.

The former emerges from a recognition of the power and status of implementers (this word is used deliberately instead of subordinates). This is the high-trust situation described by Fox, and applies to much professional discretion within public administration. The latter is seized by low-level staff regarded as subordinates rather than implementers, who, in practice, superiors fail to control. One is legitimised, the other regarded – by the dominant elements in the hierarchy – as illegitimate. To the member of the public on the receiving end, they may be indistinguishable.

Etzioni (1961) has suggested that organisational participants will be likely to have one of three kinds of involvement: 'alienative', 'calculative' or 'moral'. He also argues that the exercise of power may be categorised as 'coercive', 'utilitarian' or 'normative'. These two sets of concepts are then put together to suggest 'congruent' and incongruent matches. Where there is moral commitment normative power can be exercised: for example, within a religious order. Where there is calculative commitment, utilitarian power is likely to be exercised, through monetary rewards. Alienative involvement is characteristic of the orientation of the prison inmate, who therefore needs to be the coerced. Individuals may expect a very different kind of leadership according to whether their orientation to the organisation is 'alienative' 'calculative' or 'moral'.

Where this analysis leads is to suggest that there will be control problems if the matches between involvement and power are 'incongruent'. The relevant point for this discussion is that the imposition of rules involves a relatively coercive approach, or at least a utilitarian approach to the exercise of power. It involves comparative distrust. As such, it may tend to erode a moral orientation to the organisation.

Much of the organisation theory explored here indicates that discretion and rule breaking cannot be simply contrasted. Actors may be faced with situations in which rules conflict, in which rules are ambiguous, or in which so many rules are imposed that effective action becomes impossible (see, for example, Long's discussion of US tax laws (1981, pp. 206–7)). In these situations, choices are made between rules, or about the spirit in which they are to be respected. Hence occasions arise in which subordinates can paralyse the organisation by working to rule, obsessively following rules which under normal operating conditions everyone tacitly recognises as only to be applied in unusual situations. The next chapter will explore the issues about 'over-conforming' bureaucrats who create problems because they apply the letter and not the spirit of the law. The author has elsewhere discussed the way in which social security officials may operate when they suspect fraud. They are able to operate rules and procedures in a heavy-handed way to ensure that claims are fully investigated and that claimants are made fully aware of the consequences of detection (Hill, 1969). If, however, they operate like this in more normal situations, they will severely slow down the processing of claims and deter genuine applicants.

Alternatively, Blau (1955) shows how front-line bureaucrats disregard rules to enable them to relate more effectively to their peers and to the members of the public with whom they deal. In this sense, rule bending or breaking operates as a substitute for discretion to generate a responsive organisation. However, there are issues to be raised here about the legitimacy of such adaptation, and the extent to which it may be used to favour some clients but not others. In the next chapter, the discussion of Lipsky's work on 'street-level bureaucracy' returns to this theme.

The previous chapter explored the extent to which the 'new public management' movement has seen the rigid bureaucratic organisation as an inefficient device for public policy. The 'search for excellence', or 'reinvented government', has involved an attempt to put a 'post-Fordist' form of administrative organisation into place to combat this bureaucratic 'disease'. Yet it was shown in that discussion that there is something of a conflict between this remedy for inefficient government and the 'public choice' theory which sees bureaucratic autonomy as a key cause of the uncontrollable growth of government. In the context of this discussion, it is also necessary to note the conflict between the case for the flexible organisation in which staff have high discretion and the use of rules to secure accountability.

The solution to this dilemma has been seen to involve two ideas. One of these is that control should deal with broad general parameters, leaving much detail to be settled at the 'street level'. This is the idea of the loose/tight organisation 'steering' not 'rowing' (Osborne and Gaebler, 1992). Steering is seen as involving the setting of the financial framework and the specification of a range of incentives (Kickert, 1995, pp. 149–50). It must be questioned how much this is really new, and how much it is merely another approach to analysing the hierarchical structure of discretion emphasised in the points quoted from Simon and from Dunsire above (pp. 187–8) (see also the criticism of Kickert in Hoggett (1996)).

The other approach to control involves emphasis upon retrospective controls requiring the collection of output data. On the basis of such data, rewards or sanctions are applied. The crucial sanction may be the termination of a contract, if a quasi-market system is operating. Some commentators on UK public policy in the 1990s have seen developments of this kind as a retreat from accountable public administration (Baldwin, 1995). Others have seen them as a rather bogus loosening of control – taking out some actors who might have played a role in accountability such as local government (see Glennerster *et al.*, 1991) while financial constraints and fear of sanctions reinforce strong central control (Deakin and Walsh, 1996). Some forms of managerial control have been enhanced at the expense of professional autonomy, particularly where those managers hold values compatible with the pro-market right (Hoggett, 1996).

At the same time, it is necessary to draw another lesson about the use of rational devices in the control of administrative behaviour – for example, management by objectives and quantitative staff assessment – from Blau's old study (1955). He demonstrates how performance indicators used in the evaluation of work may distort bureaucratic behaviour. Individuals not only set out to cook their own performance statistics, but choose to emphasise those activities which will maximise the score achieved by themselves and their agency. Quantitative rather than qualitative performance becomes emphasised. It is through the use of output rather than outcome measures, whose collection and analysis is facilitated by computer technologies, that much retrospective control over discretion is sought. This is one of the ingredients in the curious mix of apparent neo-Fordism with a reversion to Fordism in the public sector (Pollitt, 1990; Hoggett, 1996).

This brief excursion into the treatment of discretion in organisation theory suggests, therefore, that there are a number of reasons why discretion is likely to be an important phenomenon in bureaucracies. At times confusion emerges between notions of organisation flexibility in which discretion, particularly professional discretion, is accepted as an inherent feature, and notions of conflict between formal requirements and informal behaviour (or more explicitly between rule making or enforcement and rule breaking). This confusion may be a reflection of the fact that in reality these phenomena are confused. Organisations are not simply fixed entities within which informal behaviour may develop. They are in a permanent state of change with both new rules and new forms of rule breaking occurring as conflicting interests interact.

The granting of discretion may be a conscious ingredient of the formal design, at one extreme, or a reluctant concession to organisational realities at the other. Conversely, new limitations upon discretion may stem from attempts by superiors to assert their hierarchical rights, or from aspirations of subordinates to introduce greater certainty for their activities. In this last sense, therefore, there is no simple equation between rule making and hierarchical control or between the preservation of discretion and subordinate freedom.

This final point needs emphasising further. Baumgartner (1992) criticises the legal concern that discretionary behaviour is unpredictable, and argues that 'social laws' make it predictable. Her essay analyses the impact of a variety of sociological features of official encounters upon their outcomes. In some respects she caricatures the legal approach – the preoccupation of people like Davis with the regulation of discretion is based as much upon a concern about the social biases which enter into it as upon its unpredictability. However, this sociological perspective is important in reminding us that 'rules' may be as readily 'made' in the course of official behaviour as promulgated by policy makers and managers. These 'rules', moreover, may have characteristics which give them a power which is difficult to resist. Feldman, in an essay in the same volume as Baumgartner's, offers a clever analogy:

> The difference between the formal limits and the social context limits to discretion can be likened to the difference between a wall and a rushing stream of water. The wall is firm, clearly delineated, and it hurts when you run into it. The rushing stream . . . moves; its speed varies; it is more powerful in the middle than on the edges. It does not always hurt to go into the stream; indeed it may at times be pleasurable. The wall, however, can be assaulted and broken down while the stream rushes on creating a path for itself against the mightiest resistance. (1992, p. 183)

Aspects of this will be considered further in the examination of some ideas about influences upon bureaucratic and professional behaviour in the next chapter.

Conclusions

In examining rules and discretion, several issues need to be given attention. First, the complex interaction of the two concepts must be emphasised. Issues about rigid rule frameworks are implicitly issues about the absence of discretion. Concerns about excessive discretion are concerns about the limitation of the rule systems within which it is embedded. Hardly ever, in the discussion of public policy, is there either absolute rule dominance or unstructured discretion.

Second, therefore, as stressed throughout this book, policy (in which rules and discretion are mixed together) must be seen in a wider social and political context, which is likely to affect the way discretion manifests itself and the attempts that are made to control it. We should note Prosser's dissatisfaction 'with the "black box" model of discretion . . . in which the determined legislative purpose is "shone into" an administrative agency, but then "refracted" by the various influences affecting the exercise of discretion' (1981, p. 149). Discretion may arise from ambiguity, sometimes deliberate, in public policy.

Third, while acknowledging political reasons why discretionary power may be conferred, the discussion has not disregarded the extent to which this phenomenon arises as a consequence of inherent *limits* to control. Hence attention has been given to questions about standards, to polycentric issues, and to some of the supervision problems which must face those who seek to control discretion. As Prottas (1978) argues, echoing the general point made in many references to discretion within organisations:

> A general rule in the analysis of power is that an actor with low 'compliance observability' is relatively autonomous. If it is difficult or costly to determine how an actor behaves and the actor knows this, then he is under less compulsion to comply. (p. 298)

Fourth, as this last observation reminds us, there is a need to analyse discretion as a facet of organisational life, in a complex relationship to rule breaking. It is important to relate discretion to issues about organisational complexity, reward systems, motivation and morale. It also must not be forgotten that, as was shown in the previous chapter, organisations themselves need to be seen in their social contexts. These themes are picked up again in the next chapter.

Fifth, we should not disregard the extent to which the concern about discretion is a normative one. Under what circumstances may discretion be said to be a problem, and for whom? To what extent does the balance established between discretion and rules distribute differential advantages and disadvantages to the parties involved, and particularly to the members of the public affected by the policy?

Finally, in noting that discretion has been regarded as a problem, we should recognise that a variety of strategies of organisation control have developed to try to deal with it. The traditional approach has been to try to control it through tighter rules and procedures (as discussed in Chapter 7). More recently, identification of the ubiquitous nature of the phenomenon has led rather to attempts to structure it. This is one of the key preoccupations of the 'new public management' movement.

The applicability of many of these ideas to various areas of policy is explored further in the next chapter, after a range of further issues about the behaviour of bureaucrats and professionals have been introduced.

CHAPTER 9

BUREAUCRATS AND PROFESSIONALS IN THE POLICY PROCESS

Synopsis

The chapter starts by examining three issues which emerge from the literature on individual behaviour in organisations: (a) the extent to which 'bureaucratic personalities' give organisational activities and perhaps particularly public sector ones a negative and perhaps conservative aspect; (b) a development of that theme, the nature of the pressures upon what have been called 'street-level bureaucrats' and the significance of these for interactions with the public; and (c) the theme of professionalism, seen as offering, on the one hand, an answer to the problem of the rigid rule-bound bureaucrat and, on the other hand, a model for policy delivery in which accountability to politicians, management and the public is particularly weak.

The last part of the chapter then works through these themes, relating them to the discussion of discretion in the previous chapter and to the impact of contemporary developments, with reference to different kinds of policy issue.

Introduction

There has been an extensive debate, particularly in the United Kingdom, about the part top officials play alongside politicians in the policy process. This has been linked to arguments about the nature of the power structure, with questions being raised about the class position of civil servants. Some references were made to these issues in Chapters 4 and 5. This chapter looks at rather different issues – the roles of lower-level officials in the implementation process. The bureaucrats in the title refer generically to public officials, including many who prefer to be seen as professionals rather than bureaucrats.

Chapter 6 set out the view that a great deal of policy is in fact made, or modified, in the implementation process. Chapters 7 and 8 amplified this argument with reference to the characteristics of organisations and the ways that policies are framed in terms of a combination of rules and discretion. Both chapters made some references to issues about the roles of middle- and lower-level employees. The traditional bureaucratic model was shown in Chapter 7 to have come under criticism – particularly from the 'new public management' movement. On the other hand, public decision making was shown in Chapter 8 to require consistent behaviour, with discretion contained within a framework of rules. This chapter extends such analysis by focusing more closely upon behaviour.

Bureaucratic behaviour and the bureaucratic personality

The administrative organisation typically has a complex structure of a kind which many writers have described as bureaucratic. But, for a number of commentators, bureaucracy implies something more than a complex organisation. For them, bureaucracies are characterised as rigid and slow, with effective action hampered by red tape. Although the main arguments on this topic are concerned with the inherent limitations of elaborate formal procedures, several writers have sought to show that bureaucratic rigidity is in some respects a consequence either of the impact of working in a rule-bound context upon the personalities of individuals, or of a tendency for bureaucracies to recruit people with inflexible personalities.

In the study of public bureaucracy, the organisation personality theory links up with a theme which has had a place in popular mythology for many centuries, a theme which several European novelists have developed most effectively, the portrayal of the clerk in public service as an individual whose life becomes dominated by the complex rules which have to be followed in dealings with the public.

Reference was made in Chapter 7 to a pioneering essay on organisational sociology by Merton (1957), which takes up this theme and attempts to explain the conditions under which bureaucratic personalities are likely to be found. Merton argues as follows:

- An effective bureaucracy demands reliability of response and strict devotion to regulations.
- Such devotion to the rules leads to their transformation into absolutes; they are no longer conceived as relative to a set of purposes.
- This interferes with ready adaptation under special conditions not clearly envisaged by those who drew up the general rules.
- Thus, the very elements which conduce towards efficiency in general produce inefficiency in specific instances (p. 200).

The position of those in authority is markedly simplified if subordinates are submissive individuals conditioned to following their superiors uncritically, and much of the literature on authority suggests that many subordinates will be of this kind. Moreover, the implication of much managerial training is that the successful operation of a system of authority will depend upon creating bureaucratic personalities. On the other hand, some of the more sophisticated writers in this field have recognised that there are severe dangers in creating over-submissive subordinates, and that there are advantages to be gained from having bureaucrats who are unwilling to be excessively bound by formal rules. Moreover, subordinates will resist overformalisation, and so it may be said that they will try to avoid becoming bureaucratic personalities (see the work of writers like Mayo, McGregor and Argyris discussed in Chapter 7).

In his essay, Merton argues that in Weber's analysis of bureaucracy 'the positive attainments and functions of bureaucratic organisation are emphasised and the internal stresses and strains of such structures are almost wholly neglected' (1957, p. 197). He contrasts this with the popular emphasis upon the imperfections of bureaucracy. Merton argues that bureaucrats are likely to show particular attachment to rules that protect the internal system of social relationships, enhance their status by enabling them to take on the status of the organisation, and protect them from conflict with clients by emphasising impersonality. Because of their function in providing security, rules of this kind are particularly likely to be transformed into absolutes. In this sense, policy goals are distorted as means are treated as ends.

Merton's essay is applied to bureaucratic organisations in general, but there are reasons why it may be particularly applicable to public administration. First, public officials are placed in a particularly difficult position *vis-à-vis* their clients. They may be putting into practice political decisions with which they disagree; they are facing a public who cannot normally go elsewhere if their demands are unsatisfied, as they often can with private enterprise; and the justice of their acts is open to public scrutiny, by politicians and sometimes by courts of law. They are thus under particular pressure to ensure that their acts are in conformity with rules. Rules are bound to play a major part in their working lives.

Second, the careers of public officials are normally organised very much along the lines of Weber's bureaucratic model. Indeed, in this respect at least, state bureaucracies often come very close to Weber's ideal type. The demand for fairness in selection and promotion leads to the development of highly regularised career structures. It tends to be very difficult to justify dramatic or unconventional promotions, and therefore public service careers are likely to be oriented towards what F. Morstein Marx (1957) has called 'the economics of small chances'. Marx explains this expression in the following way:

> In the first place, the ideology of service itself minimises the unabashed display of consuming ambition. In some respects, indeed, service is its own reward. Moreover, the mass conditions to which personnel policy and procedure must be addressed in large-scale organisations cry out for recognition of the normal rather than the exceptional. Meteoric rise of the outstandingly able individual is therefore discouraged quite in the same way as favouritism and disregard of rules are discouraged. Advancement, if it is not to attract suspicious or unfriendly eyes, must generally stay in line with the 'normal'. Exceptions call for too much explaining. All this tends to make reward for accomplishment something that comes in small packages at fairly long intervals. (p. 97)

Such a career structure obviously puts an onus upon conformity, and will tend to create a situation in which, if a public official becomes conspicuous for disregarding rules, it will be more likely to hamper than enhance his or her career.

Marx's book is interesting in developing the picture of the public official as a bureaucratic personality as a result of the factors discussed above. He therefore characterises the public service as 'the settled life' in which security is valued above high rewards (p. 102). He says 'the merit bureaucracy is not the place for those who want to make money, to rise fast, to venture far, or to stand on their own'. Marx concedes that senior public officials are usually required to be of a reasonably high calibre, but suggests that those who compete for entry will be mostly the 'solid – as contrasted with the brilliant but restive, for instance' (p. 102).

Marx goes on to suggest that the career structure he describes in this way reinforces the pressure for uniformity within a government bureaucracy which arises from the political need for equity and consistency. Thus he claims: 'When the common rule and the common mind combine, the natural consequence is a narrowness of perspective – a weakness more aggravating than mediocrity in administrative performance' (p. 103).

Marx suggests, then, that the bureaucratic personality will be both a product of the fact that only certain types of people choose to join the public service – or, indeed, the fact that selection procedures may pick out certain types of people – and a product of the bureaucratic environment. The two influences upon personality operate to reinforce each other. In the same way, Merton (1957) recognises this interaction as a key problem for research. He asks:

> To what extent are particular personality types selected and modified by the various bureaucracies (private enterprise, public service, the quasi-legal political machine, religious orders)? Inasmuch as ascendancy and submission are held to be traits of personality, despite their variability in different stimulus situations, do bureaucracies select personalities of particularly submissive or ascendant tendencies? And since various studies have shown that these traits can be modified, does participation in bureaucratic office tend to increase ascendant tendencies? Do various systems of recruitment (e.g. patronage, open competition involving specialised knowledge or general mental capacity, practical experience) select different personality types? (p. 205)

There are, therefore, a number of related issues to consider here:

- The extent to which certain types of people choose to embark on bureaucratic careers.
- The impact of selection processes in selecting certain types from among those who seek to enter bureaucratic careers.
- The extent to which personalities who do not fit the organisational environment drop out in the course of their careers.
- The extent to which success or failure in climbing a career ladder is associated with personality characteristics.

Merton and Marx are, of course, attempting to analyse systematically the widely accepted stereotype of the bureaucratic official. But because it deals with a stereotype, the bureaucratic personality theory runs into difficulties. On the most superficial level, the public official's role is difficult to distinguish from the role played by a very high proportion of the employed persons in a modern complex society – in which case there is nothing very special about the role of the public official. On the other hand, if an attempt is made to analyse roles more deeply, it will be found that distinctions can be made both between the many different roles in a public bureaucracy, and also between alternative adjustments to formally similar roles. The bureaucratic personality theory is both too specific, in trying to single out certain kinds of organisational role in a context in which most people are organisational employees, and too general, in implying the existence of uniformity of roles in organisations where such uniformity does not exist.

A secondary criticism of the theory can also be made: there is a tendency to assume the existence of bureaucratic personality, when in practice such behaviour may be a means of protecting the individual from total involvement in the work situation. On this theme a more recent vein of writing is relevant. It focuses on the pressures upon bureaucrats, and helps to explore, more effectively than the bureaucratic personality theory, how policies become reshaped as public officials seek to bring some order into their own lives. This is the work on street-level bureaucracy by Michael Lipsky (1980) and his associates. For these writers the issue is not the apparent total rule conformity suggested by Merton, but rather the way in which officials make choices to enforce some rules, particularly those which protect them, while disregarding others.

Street-level bureaucracy

The theory of street-level bureaucracy is set out in Lipsky's book with that title. It is further developed in work by two of his former research students, Weatherley (1979) and Prottas (1979). Lipsky says of his book: 'I argue that the decisions of street-level bureaucrats, the routines they establish, and the devices they invent to cope with uncertainties and work pressures, effectively become the public policies they carry out' (1980, p. xii).

He argues that this process of street-level policy making does not involve, as might be hoped, the advancement of the ideals many bring to personal service work but rather the development of practices which enable officials to cope with the pressures they face. He says:

people often enter public employment with at least some commitment to service. Yet the very nature of this work prevents them from coming close to the ideal conception of their jobs. Large classes or huge caseloads and inadequate resources combine with the uncertainties of method and the unpredictability of clients to defeat their aspirations as service workers. (p. xii)

Lipsky argues that street-level bureaucrats develop methods of processing people in a relatively routine and stereotyped way. They adjust their work habits to reflect lower expectations of themselves and their clients. They

often spend their work lives in a corrupted world of service. They believe themselves to be doing the best they can under adverse circumstances and they develop techniques to salvage service and decision-making values within the limits imposed upon them by the structure of work. They develop conceptions of their work and of their clients that narrow the gap between their personal and work limitations and the service ideal. (p. xii)

Thus Lipsky handles one of the paradoxes of street-level work. Such workers see themselves as cogs in a system, as oppressed by the bureaucracy within which they work. Yet they often seem to the researcher, and perhaps to their clients, to have a great deal of discretionary freedom and autonomy. This is particularly true of the many publicly employed semi-professionals – people like teachers and social workers who secure a degree of that autonomy allowed to professional workers. These are the people whose roles Lipsky and his colleagues are particularly interested in.

Lipsky analyses the paradox, suggested above, in the following way. He outlines the many ways in which street-level bureaucrats are able to manipulate their clients. He stresses the non-voluntary status of clients, suggesting that they only have limited resources inasmuch as the street-level bureaucrat needs their compliance for effective action (p. 57). This is a view supported by two other American writers, Hasenfeld and Steinmetz (1981), who argue that it is appropriate to see bureaucrat–client relationships as exchanges, but that in social services agencies serving low-status clients the latter have little to offer except deference. They point out, as does Lipsky, that 'clients have a very high need for services while the availability of alternatives is exceedingly limited' (Hasenfeld and Steinmetz, 1981, pp. 84–5). Accordingly, 'the power advantage social-services agencies have enables them to exercise considerable control over the lives of the recipients of their services' (p. 85). Clients have to wait for help, experience 'status degradation', have problems in securing access to information, and are taught ways to behave (pp. 89–92). They possess a generally weaker range of tactics with which to respond.

Lipsky also stresses that the street-level bureaucrat cannot readily be brought under the control of a superior. He argues:

> The essence of street-level bureaucracies is that they require people to make decisions about other people. Strcct-level bureaucrats have discretion because the nature of service provision calls for human judgement that cannot be programmed and for which machines cannot substitute. (p. 161)

In this sense, Lipsky portrays the street-level bureaucrat as making policy, carrying out a political role determining 'the allocation of particular goods and services in the society' (p. 84). Weatherley summarises this view, as follows:

> a view of policy as determining front-line behaviour is insufficient for explaining what workers actually do and why, and how their activities affect clients. Of course, teachers do teach, caseworkers dispense public assistance, public defenders defend indigent clients, and doctors treat patients, and their work activities are certainly responsive to public policy. But their activities are also responsive to a number of other influences over which the policy maker and administrator may only have limited or no control. The pyramid-shaped organisation chart depicting at the bottom the front-line worker as passively receiving and carrying out policies and procedures dispensed from above is a gross oversimplification. A more realistic model would place the front-line worker in the center of an irregularly shaped sphere with vectors of differing size directed inward. (1980, p. 9)

Elsewhere in Lipsky's book the street-level bureaucrat's role is portrayed very differently. He speaks of it as an 'alienated role' (1980, p. 76), stressing such classic features of alienation as that work is only on 'segments of the product', that there is no control over outcomes, or over 'raw materials' (clients' circumstances), and that there is no control over the pace of work. Lipsky also emphasises the 'problem of resources': street-level bureaucrats face uncertainty about just what personal resources are necessary for their jobs, they find that work situations and outcomes are unpredictable, and they face great pressures of inadequate time in relation to limitless needs.

Is there in Lipsky's work, therefore, an element of inconsistency, or can the contradictions in his analysis be explained? Perhaps he is providing a new variant on the Marxist dictum, 'Man makes his own history, even though he does not do so under conditions of his own choosing.' This is certainly partly the case. Street-level bureaucrats make choices about the use of scarce resources under pressure; contemporary fiscal pressure upon human services makes it much easier for officials to emphasise control than to try to put into practice service ideals.

But Lipsky does not really try to link his analysis to a macro-sociological perspective which would enable him to claim that the illusory freedom of street-level bureaucrats only operates as an instrument of class oppression and manipulation, and not in any other direction. His analysis, perhaps even more pessimistically, tends to show that the street-level bureaucrat's freedom to make policy is largely used to provide a more manageable task and environment. He talks of 'defenses against discretion', emphasising, as Smith (1981) and Zimmerman (1971) have, the extent to which street-level bureaucrats develop rigid practices which may be described by the observer as involving rule conformity, even though the rules are imposed upon themselves. Lipsky stresses patterns of practice as 'survival mechanisms', a perspective which is echoed in a UK study of social workers which, using older American theoretical work on organisational roles by Everett Hughes (1958), has a great deal in common with Lipsky's work. This is Satyamurti's (1981) study of English urban social work teams, in the years immediately after their reorganisation in 1971. There she speaks of the use of 'strategies of survival' by social workers under pressure, which nearly always lead people with the 'best of intentions' to do 'less for clients than they might have' and often to behave in 'ways that were positively damaging' (p. 82). The conclusion of this literature is that difficult work environments lead to the abandonment of ideals and to the adoption of techniques which enable clients to be 'managed'.

Lipsky argues that there is a problem about matching limited resources to apparently much greater needs, recognised by all sensitive members of social services agencies. Accordingly, therefore, considerable efforts are made to prioritise need and to develop rational ways to allocate resources. The problem is that 'theoretically there is no limit to the demand for free public goods' (1980, p. 81). Therefore it is important to accept that welfare agencies will always feel under pressure. Lipsky says that the resource problem for street-level bureaucrats is often irresolvable 'either because the number of people treated . . . is only a fraction of the number that could be treated, or because their theoretical obligations call for higher quality treatment than it is possible to provide to individual clients' (p. 37). Adjustments to caseloads further the quality of work, but leave the worry about quantity, and vice versa. It is always possible to make out cases for new resources. Marginal changes in those resources will not necessarily result in visible changes in stress for individual workers.

This equally seems to provide support for the cynical cutting of caseloads. Certainly Lipsky suggests that this is how it is sometimes seen. An agency which has great difficulty in measuring success or providing data on quantity of 'output' is inevitably vulnerable to cutting. Lipsky cogently shows how this response heightens the feeling of stress for individual workers, and thus intensifies the recourse to the manipulation of clients. Retrenchment and redundancy are particularly threatening to the remaining vestiges of altruism in the human services. In this sense, it may be suggested that incremental growth does little to relieve stress, but incremental decline intensifies it considerably.

A substantial section of Lipsky's analysis is concerned with the way in which street-level bureaucrats categorise their clients and respond in stereotyped ways to their needs. There is a large body of American research on which he is able to draw. In particular, many studies of the police have shown how distinctions are made between different kinds of citizen, which enable officers to develop responses in uncertain situations. It has been argued that it is misleading to attribute police racism simply either to the predisposition of recruits or to pressures from peers. In addition, stereotyping offers short cuts to decision making on how to approach people, how to determine whether to act on suspicion and so on (see Brown, 1981). Lipsky argues that such is the need for street-level bureaucrats to differentiate clients 'that it seems as useful to assume bias (however modest) and ask why it sometimes does not occur, than to assume equality of treatment and ask why it is regularly abridged' (1980, p. 111). Giller and Morris (1981) offer evidence of similar stereotyping in UK social work in their essay, 'What type of case is this?'

An issue that is related to simplifying assumptions in categorising different kinds of client is the adoption of stereotyped responses to clients in general. Lipsky speaks of these as 'psychological coping mechanisms', and elaborates the importance of simplified views of the client, his or her situation and responsibility for his or her plight to facilitate this (1980, ch. 10).

Richard Weatherley (1979) has specifically applied the street-level bureaucracy perspective to the study of the implementation of special education reform in the state of Massachusetts. A new law, enacted in 1974, required schools to operate much more sophisticated procedures for assessing needs for special education and to develop individualised programmes for children. The problem for staff was that they were required to do this without significantly more resources. 'Administrators were caught between the requirements to comply with the law, which they took quite seriously . . . and the certainty that their school committees would rebel against expenditures that led to increased taxes' (Weatherley and Lipsky, 1977, p. 193). Accordingly a response to the reform was developed which accommodated to the new requirements without substantially disrupting established ways of working. Implementation involved the adjustment of the law to local needs and requirements (see also Hudson (1989) for a discussion of the applicability of Lipsky's theory to similar policy contexts in the United Kingdom).

In his last chapter, Lipsky connects his concerns about street-level bureaucracy with some of the discussion of professionalism in bureaucracy. Are professionals different, and can the enhancement of professionalism provide a corrective to forms of bureaucratic behaviour outlined in Lipsky's analysis? The presence of professionals in bureaucracy can make some difference to the ways in which policy is implemented, but this does not imply that the answer to the normative question posed by Lipsky is a clear 'yes'. Professional power is a sub-category of bureaucratic power in this context, with some distinctive characteristics of its own which raise equally important value questions.

Professionalism in the bureaucracy: solution or another problem?

The critique of the Fordist organisation (see pp. 157–61), particularly that influenced by the work of Peters and Waterman (1982), seems to offer a solution to the problems about bureaucracy outlined by Merton, Morstein Marx and Lipsky. It suggests that organisational employees should be expected to have and use expertise, and be trusted by their managers to use discretion to tackle their work tasks in an adaptive way. In short they should be 'professionals'.

The paradox about this solution is that it conflicts both with that other theme in new public management – public choice – which sees public employees as untrustworthy and professionals as the most likely of all to distort the organisation in their own interests, and with a wider body of literature (from the left as well as the right) which has warned against professional power. Before looking at some more specific aspects of this issue, there is a need to consider the standard critique of professionalism.

Sociologists have made many attempts to define professions. An influential essay by Greenwood (1957) suggests that 'all professions seem to possess: (1) systematic theory, (2) authority, (3) community sanction, (4) ethical codes, and (5) a culture' (p. 45). However, this list of attributes of a profession mixes occupational characteristics with societal treatment of that occupation. Systematic theory, ethical codes and culture fall into the former category, and authority and community sanction into the latter. An analysis of professions needs at the very least to separate the occupational characteristics which give some groups high prestige, and corresponding power if they possess scarce and needed skills, from the way in which the state and society treat them. In practice there is a very complex interaction between these two groups of factors. It is more fruitful, therefore, to see a profession as an occupation whose members have had some success in defining 'the conditions and methods of their work' and in establishing 'a cognitive base and legitimation for their occupational autonomy' (DiMaggio and Powell, 1983, p. 152).

This can be explained better by exploring the issues about one, particularly powerful, profession: medicine. Of course, it is true that doctors possess expertise, and that the public, in its quest for good health, values that expertise. But much medical knowledge is accessible to all. What is also important about the position of the medical profession today is that the state has given the profession a monopoly over many forms of care, allowed it to control its own education and socialisation process, and created, in the United Kingdom and elsewhere, a health service in which it plays a dominant part (Harrison *et al.*, 1990; Moran and Wood, 1993).

There is a vein of writing on professions within organisations which sees professional power and autonomy as threatened by bureaucratic employment (see Wilensky, 1964). This is misleading, since professionals may secure dominant roles within organisations. However, to explore that argument fully would be to depart from the main object here, which is to emphasise ways in which professionalism is a source of power *within* organisations. The core of this argument is contained in the example of the doctors quoted above. They have succeeded in persuading politicians and administrators that the public will receive the best service if their discretionary freedom is maximised, and if they are given powerful positions in the organisations which run the health services. As suggested in Chapter 5 (pp. 119–20), these claims may extend beyond issues of service delivery to make the policy process 'implementation skewed' (Dunleavy and O'Leary, 1987, p. 323).

The arguments about expertise, linked with the emotive nature of our concerns about health and the social status which the profession acquired before medical services were provided on any large scale by the state, have reinforced this professional claim to dominance. Other, later established professions, with a weaker base either in expertise or social status, have claimed similar privileges – teachers and social workers, for example.

Ironically, the argument about the role that professions may play in bureaucracy has been fuelled by the contrast popularly drawn between the concepts of bureaucracy and professionalism. As Friedson (1970) has argued:

> In contrast to the negative word 'bureaucracy' we have the word 'profession'. This word is almost always positive in its connotation, and is frequently used to represent a superior alternative to bureaucracy. Unlike 'bureaucracy' which is disclaimed by every organisation concerned with its public relations, 'professions' is claimed by virtually every occupation seeking to improve its public image. When the two terms are brought together, the discussion is almost always at the expense of bureaucracy and to the advantage of profession. (pp. 129–30)

Hence professionals stress their altruism, arguing that they are motivated by an ethic of service which would be undermined if their activities were rigidly controlled. In some respects this is a question-begging argument. If public servants are given a high degree of autonomy, their actions need to be motivated by ideals of service. The maintenance of ethical standards is important if a group of people have extensive influence on the welfare of individuals. However, the ethical codes of the major professions are often concerned more with protecting members of the group from unfair competition from their colleagues, or 'unlicensed outsiders', than with service to the public. Moreover, even the public concept of 'good health' is to a considerable extent defined for us by the medical profession; in particular, the measures necessary to sustain it, or restore it when it is absent, are largely set out in terms of the activities of the medical profession, when in practice many other aspects of our lifestyles and forms of social organisation are also important (Kennedy, 1981; Illich, 1977).

There is, of course, more to medical prestige than expertise, hence Greenwood's fourth and fifth attributes: 'ethical codes' and 'a culture'. We trust and respect doctors, and ask them to take responsibilities far beyond those justifiable in terms of expertise. They are allowed to take decisions on when the life-support systems may be withdrawn, to ration kidney machines and abortions, to advise on where the limits of criminal responsibility may lie and so on. Such powers have emerged gradually as a complex relationship has developed between the state, society and the profession – the last of which has become legitimate partly as a result of the evolution of its ethics and culture, and partly because those with power in our society have been willing to devolve authority (see Johnson, 1972). The two phenomena, moreover, have been closely interrelated – internal professional control has made feasible the delegation of responsibility, but equally the latter has made the former more necessary to protect professional autonomy.

Occupations like medicine are not accorded the status of professions simply by virtue of their own characteristics. Professional status cannot simply be won, as some of the aspirant occupations seem to assume, by becoming more expert and devising an ethical code. It depends upon the delegation of power, and on the legitimisation process in society. In the case of the doctors, this legitimisation process may well owe a great deal to our fears about ill-health and their special expertise; nevertheless some theorists have argued that it must also be explained in class terms. Johnson (1972) and Parry and Parry (1976) have analysed the way in which medical power was established during the nineteenth century, through a developing relationship with other powerful groups in society. It is clearly relevant, therefore, to raise questions about the comparable autonomy enjoyed by other established professions whose expertise is much more accessible (lawyers, for example). Dunleavy (1981) has provided an interesting analysis of the influence on public policy and implementation of one such group, the architects, tracing the close connections between conventional professional wisdom and economic interests within the building industry.

The argument for professions based upon the idea that they possess inaccessible expertise is not sufficient on its own. Attention must be paid to the situations in which this expertise is used. The key issues here are two.

The first of these is indeterminacy: the extent to which it is impossible to predetermine the situations in which expertise will be used. It is the complexity of situations that doctors have to face and the extent to which solutions to medical problems are not always of a kind that can be programmed automatically. If they were, we would merely have to enter our symptoms into a computer and it could offer solutions. Of course, in very many situations this is possible; the difficulty is that judgements may be needed where the solution is not obvious or where there are reasons to distrust the obvious. Paradoxically, of course, indeterminacy is most evident when expertise does not offer ready solutions.

The second issue is invisibility: the extent to which detailed surveillance of work is impossible. Under an anaesthetic we have to trust the surgeon to react quickly to the unexpected. We cannot debate the implications of what has been found. It is equally inappropriate to have a manager looking over the surgeon's shoulder asking for an account of what is happening, or a medical committee waiting to be convened to debate the next step.

These two issues of indeterminacy and invisibility are not peculiar to the classic cases of professional decision making, like medicine. They apply, too, to the police officer alone on the beat and coming upon the unexpected around a corner. While the police are not seen as 'expert' in the medical sense, there is a similar issue here about seeing that they are as well trained as possible, to enable them to interpret the unexpected. But the case of the police reminds us of the need to go back to the issue of community sanction. There needs to be a sort of social contract – despite all that the sociologists have reminded us about the potential for collusion between powerful groups – in which the decision-maker is trusted to exercise discretion in situations which are indeterminate and invisible.

This concept of 'trust' is crucial – it was explored in the last chapter in relation to Fox's (1974) analysis of discretion in organisations. The argument against Fordism within organisations rests fundamentally upon the idea that desired creative responses to exceptional situations occur when individuals have been trusted to exercise discretion. Where it is hoped that public officials will play an active role in developing new approaches to their tasks and more sophisticated service to the public, there may be a strong case for granting them a high degree of autonomy. In individual services there is a need to make a choice between the case for a reliable service which can be changed only by initiative from the top, and a less predictable service which may nevertheless be flexible in practice. The organisation which makes extensive use of professionals is one in which there is high expertise in the lower ranks, a complex task to perform, difficulties in developing effective patterns of supervision and a need for flexibility and openness to change. A strong group of arguments for autonomy come together. In this sense, professionals are street-level bureaucrats who have been able to develop special claims to autonomy. But, as suggested above, they claim to differ from other public officials in that their relationships with their clients are governed by ethical codes and by altruistic values which others lack.

Professionalism versus bureaucracy – or is there a third alternative?

This discussion has reached a point at which two conflicting concerns about public employees have been highlighted – one a concern about bureaucracy with more flexible forms of organisation seen as the solution; the other a concern about control, with professionalism seen as suspect. There are close parallels here with the issues about the presence or absence of 'top-down' control over implementation explored in Chapter 6. In any search for resolution of this conflict, there is a need to look again at the multitude of different tasks that officials concerned with the implementation of public policy are required to perform.

A good starting point for consideration of task diversity is the examination of the different justifications for discretion examined in the previous chapter. Mashaw, in particular, offers a useful approach in his three 'models' of justice. Table 9.1 adapts a table from his book to establish a structure for our discussion.

Table 9.1 Task diversity and models of discretionary justice

Model	Primary goal	Organisation	Example
Bureaucratic rationality	Programme implementation	Hierarchical	Income maintenance
Professional treatment	Client satisfaction	Interpersonal	Medicine
Moral judgement	Conflict resolution	Independent	Pollution control

Source: Adapted from Mashaw (1983), p. 31.

In Chapter 8 it was suggested that both the 'professional treatment' and the 'moral judgement' model offered justifications for high discretion. It was also suggested that Mashaw's label 'moral judgement' was a little unsatisfactory, and that what it was all about was the determination of standards in situations in which there are disputes between individuals, by contrast with 'professional treatment' where there is a response to individual need in a situation of relative indeterminacy.

It is the claim to privilege a 'private' professional/client relationship, however, as nothing to do with anyone else, which lies at the heart of contemporary controversy about personal service professionalism. The next section, therefore, examines this issue, and is followed by a section on Mashaw's 'moral judgement' category. The 'bureaucratic rationality' issue is left to last, to explore the question: is this always qualitatively different to the other two?

Professional treatment: a special case of public policy implementation

The case for regarding professional treatment – particularly medical treatment – as a special case of public policy implementation has been set out above in terms of the issues of expertise, indeterminacy, invisibility and trust. The case against is that these issues are used to obscure professional power, used to deliver a protected work environment, occupational control and high rewards. This is a long-running argument. To what extent is its configuration changing, in favour of those who seek to exercise control over professionalism?

The start of an answer to this question was offered above. It was apparent that it is possible to show that a high percentage of professional work situations do not involve indeterminacy and do not have to be invisible. The rare and unexpected diagnostic situations, the medical or surgical emergencies where it is not possible to stop to debate or to consult a protocol, form but a small percentage of many doctors' work. Television hospital dramas give us a distorted view of a profession which is much more routine much of the time. Protocols are increasingly being developed to govern medical decision making, offering rules for many situations, and yardsticks against which actions can subsequently be judged. Computerised decision models are being developed for many conditions.

The second part of the answer concerns the fact that, as suggested at the end of the previous section, individual clinical decisions are not merely the concern of the practitioner and patient – at least as far as publicly financed medicine is concerned. In a situation of resource constraints (which must be regarded as a normal situation for a publicly financed health service), a response to the needs of any patient involves claims on scarce resources and must thus – taking an overall view – be to some extent at the expense of a response to others. This issue comes to the fore most poignantly where there is manifestly a lack of resources relative to an identified need – as is the case with various forms of treatment for kidney disease or in a hard-pressed emergency unit. But it is evidently present wherever there are waiting lists for treatments and operations. It may further be contended that there is a ubiquitous requirement for all clinical work to be planned and organised against a backcloth of resource issues.

Hence there seems to be a case against professional discretion, as traditionally defended in arguments about the sanctity of the doctor/ patient relationship and the needs of good medical practice. However, alongside the difficulties already raised about the residue of special indeterminant and invisible situations there are two further complex issues about the exercise of control over discretion. One of them is the problem of trust, already explored, but with particularly serious implications if low trust generates low morale among people required to perform a difficult and stressful task. This is where the logic of Etzioni's theory leads (see p. 190).

The other difficulty concerns the question: who is to do the controlling? There are five alternatives here (or obviously some combination of them): elected politicians, lay managers, professionally qualified managers, other professional colleagues and patients. There are problems about each of these groups.

The notion of control by elected politicians - in any large-scale system – goes back to much that has been discussed earlier in this book (particularly in Chapters 5, 6 and 8) about the difficulties of achieving and enforcing very specific policy prescriptions in relation to a complex activity. There may be a way forward in relation to politicians with a localised and specific remit, and we will return to this at the end of the discussion.

Clearly, the standard control model for the policy process involves appointed managers working within a remit supplied by politicians. The intense need for cost control over services like health has increased the propensity to see lay managers as having a key role to play. This view has been reinforced by the availability of new technologies (computerised medical records, systems to identify the costs of 'normal' medical procedures like that offered by the identification of 'diagnosis related groups' (DRGs), etc.). These may enhance, at the expense of professional service staff, the power of those who monitor their work, creating new kinds of 'professional dominance' from accountants, lawyers and managers (see Alford (1975) and Ham (1992) on 'corporate rationalisers', and developments of this theme in Harrison *et al.* (1990) and Flynn (1991)).

These new groups of lay managers may be seen as new professions, offering countervailing roles against the medical professionals. Not surprisingly, they are viewed with suspicion by the latter. It may be argued *inter alia* that some of the claims to expertise by these new professionals are every bit, if not more, open to objection than the expertise of the old professions (particularly inasmuch as they centred upon a claimed capacity to be able to measure and cost complex phenomena), and that control by this group brings us no nearer to true 'public accountability'. Finally, inasmuch as the stock in trade of this group is phenomena that are measurable, the producers of the information – the doctors etc. – are in a position to be able to manipulate their data.

Hence the third alternative, control by managers who are drawn from the ranks of the service professionals themselves. There has been a long-standing argument about this approach to the management of professionals: do these managers retain their old professional loyalties or become co-opted to the ranks of the lay managers? There seems good reason to believe, confirmed by research in which Pieter Degeling and the author are engaged, that the truth lies somewhere between these two positions. These 'managers' obviously offer scope for the development of a more sophisticated shared accountability, but do not, of course, open up the system to public accountability in the widest sense.

The fourth alternative is merely a variation on the third – the creation of a cadre of people who are involved in management but still practising their profession, or even more the generation through collegial shared participation in management issues of forms of collective self-management. This is a managerial model widely favoured by professionals. There are well-founded suspicions that – particularly when review processes are not shared outside the professional group (medical audit, for example: see Harrison and Pollitt (1994)) – this approach to management preserves traditional professional domination.

The fifth alternative – control by patients – seems to offer the best approach to true public accountability. The problem is that, while we are all patients some of the time, comparatively few people are patients all the time. And when we are patients we are likely to be more aware of individual need than of its collective context. Of course, medicine is a special case – other professionals (in education, in particular) may have more continuous relationships with a large and relatively stable group who may find it easier to see themselves in context (when invited to participate in control).

The market way around the patient accountability problem is to let conflicting demands for scarce services push up prices, thus regulating demand and perhaps drawing in new suppliers. It would be to depart too far from the brief of this book to explore the problems about this solution. The key point here is that this is a book about 'public policy', and strong political forces rule out this solution to public health rationing problems.

The 'quasi-market' ideas around in health policy, on the other hand, do involve one group of public officials in the role of purchasers, required to make contracts with service providers. There may then be competition between providers. These contracting processes may enhance efficiency through competition. They may also enhance accountability by making the terms and conditions under which services are provided more visible. As practised in the United Kingdom at present, they do not really start to engender accountability to customers in an individualistic sense, but they may help to sharpen awareness of the political rationing dilemmas.

This leads us to an approach to professional accountability which has been widely canvassed and which offers a kind of combination of political accountability and patient accountability, by stressing localised 'political' control mechanisms. Thus Lipsky argues for a new approach to professional accountability in which there is more emphasis upon client-based evaluation of their work (Lipsky, 1980, ch. 13). Similarly, Wilding (1982) writes of the need to realise 'a new relationship between professions, clients and society' (p. 149), precisely because others have so little control over them. Stewart and Clarke (1987) offer a related approach – though their concern is with local government and not with the health service – in terms of the idea of a 'public service' orientation committed to accountability to local citizens' groups. We will return to this theme in the final chapter. The main, perhaps rather dismissive, point to make here is that it represents rather more an aspiration than a properly tried form of accountability. It also leaves the issues about discretion as ones which are seen not as absolutely controlled, but as matters for consultation between affected parties. This leads logically to a discussion of Mashaw's 'moral judgement' model.

The moral judgement model and regulatory policy

Doubts have already been expressed about whether Mashaw's label 'the moral judgement model' satisfactorily encapsulates our second category of situations in which the characteristics of policy have an influence upon the extent of discretion in the roles of those who put it into practice. There are many situations where the key official role involves regulation – a form of law enforcement where the state has prescribed or is seeking to control certain activities. These activities have much in common with criminal law enforcement – and studies of that give us many insights into the exercise of discretion. Law enforcement is particularly difficult where there is an absence of unambiguous support for the enforcing agency. Studies of the police have drawn attention to the particular difficulties where there is an absence of people who regard themselves as victims (drug and alcohol offences, prostitution and traffic offences where no one is injured), or where there are groups in the community that will try to protect the criminal. Public health inspectors, pollution control officials and factory inspectors, as law enforcement agents, have to operate in a similar way to the police. The difficulties which beset the police are even more likely to apply in relation to the wide range of civil law regulatory tasks which concern officials like this – where the 'offenders' see themselves as engaged in carrying out their legitimate business, not as polluters or producers of impure food etc.

But Mashaw's moral judgement model particularly highlights two other conditions which often apply to these regulatory situations. First, what is being enforced by the regulator is a standard – about unreasonably high levels of pollution etc. – which is likely to be disputed. There are particular problems here about the translation of scientific evidence on levels of risk entailed to the public by specific phenomena (Nelkin, 1992; Barker and Peters, 1993). Second, there are likely to be conflicts of interest between those who are the source of the alleged problem and those who are affected by it. On top of all this the second alleged 'interest' is often a latent one, for one of the following reasons:

- The 'victims' whom the regulators have a duty to protect do not know they have a problem (when, for example, pollution cannot be detected by the sense of smell etc.).
- They regard the problem as the lesser of two evils (when they perceive it as a choice between a polluted environment and unemployment: see Crenson, 1971; Blowers, 1984).
- They are quite satisfied with a situation that others consider unsatisfactory (residents suffering from dementia in a poor quality care home, for example).

In some cases the conflict is between a quite specific individual interest and a very general public interest. In all these situations, enforcement is likely to be controversial and the enforcers may lack clear-cut forms of public support. The consequence is that – while it may be theoretically possible to formulate firm rules about what constitutes violation of a regulatory code and to prosecute when that occurs – the fact that what is at stake is arguable standards of performance and that regulation is fairly easily circumvented leads to the use of a flexible approach in which officials bargain with those they have to regulate. Their objective is likely to be voluntary acceptance of constraints on behaviour by the regulatees.

In many systems, regulatory activity therefore works not with absolute rules but with principles about best practice established by expert officials and operationalised using discretionary powers (see Hill, 1983). The relationship between rules and discretion in these situations may involve 'framework laws', with officials and regulatees negotiating to fill in the details so that gradually the law becomes more codified (see case studies in Hanf and Jensen (forthcoming), particularly on Sweden).

What is often involved in these cases, given that officials need to work very closely with the objects of their regulatory activities, is a process of bargaining between regulator and regulatee (Peacock, 1984; Hawkins, 1984). Such bargaining will not merely deal with costs and consequences, but will also be likely to take into account past behaviour (has the compliance record of the regulatee been satisfactory?) and the likely impact of any outcome on the behaviour of others. Hanf has described this process as one of 'co-production', in which the determinants of regulatory behaviour need to be seen as 'embedded in the social worlds within and outside the regulatory agency' (Hanf, 1993, p. 109). While the field of pollution control provides particularly good examples of this 'co-production', it is also evident in other cases where complex activities are being regulated – for example, the running of a private residential care home or nursing home.

A particularly important contribution of studies of law enforcement to our understanding of discretion in situations like these has been their emphasis upon the way in which bias operates. From an initial concern simply to demonstrate that social class, gender and race affect discretionary decision making, studies have gone on to explicate the ways in which these effects occur. They do not arise merely from prejudice, but also from situational characteristics of the enforcement official's task. Such phenomena as the relationship between the official and the community being 'policed', the way the official's day-to-day work is organised, the particular sources of stresses and conflicts in the task, and the way the official is encouraged to define law enforcement problems have been shown, particularly by the police discretion studies, to influence the pattern of formal enforcement action.

In this context it is important to bear in mind that much regulation is a private activity, not open to scrutiny by politicians and the public. The justification for this is the need to preserve commercial secrets. In such situations, biases are relatively easily hidden. It has been alleged that regulators working in circumstances like this are subject to 'capture' by the enterprises they are regulating – the regulators are often former employees of that industry, they have to work closely with those they regulate and they are likely to form a view of what control is feasible largely determined by those whose activities they are required to curb. Capture is particularly likely when the regulatees are big and powerful organisations. Regulators may take much weaker lines with them than with smaller enterprises.

Obviously the regulatory agencies dispute this sort of interpretation of their activities, stressing that their close understanding of the processes they are regulating makes it difficult for those they are regulating to deceive them or hide undesirable practices. They stress that an informed regulator can educate and encourage better practices, helping an enterprise to achieve better pollution control or a care home to offer more sympathetic services to residents more effectively in this way than through formal sanctions. The success of this approach may also depend upon the extent to which there is consensus about the desirability of the policy goals.

In the interpretation of this argument, the examination of the role played by sanctions may be important. Court cases where polluters are prosecuted for the violation of agreements help to establish the parameters of a control system, indicating what is clearly unacceptable and warning possible future violators. It is evidence to the public that the regulatory system does have some 'teeth'.

It is finally important to bear in mind that the issues about the balance between rules and discretion are likely also to apply to the courts which have the ultimate enforcement powers in these circumstances. Judges must be seen as just as much exercisers of discretion as the officials whose actions they may scrutinise. This is a perspective being given increasing recognition in the United Kingdom, a country which has hitherto treated its Law Lords with rather excessive reverence. In the United States, the political role of the Supreme Court has been more clearly identifiable for some time, together with the recognition that, at least in the short run, the evolution of the law depends upon the dispositions of sometimes fairly eccentric elderly people (see Bickel, 1970; Scheingold, 1974, among others).

A UK analysis of the politics of the judiciary concludes:

> Judges are concerned to preserve and to protect the existing order. This does not mean that no judges are capable of moving with the times, of adjusting to changed circumstances. But their function in our society is to do so belatedly. Law and order, the established distribution of power both public and private, the conventional and agreed view amongst those who exercise political and economic power, the fears and prejudices of the middle and upper classes, these are the forces which the judges are expected to uphold and do uphold. (Griffith, 1977, p. 214)

Thus, an approach to the study of discretion in administrative law which seeks to counteract the discretionary behaviour of officials with the rule of law may come up against a further set of discretionary actors, the judges.

Recapitulation: rules and discretion in the professional treatment and moral judgement cases

Before going on to the areas of policy where it is argued that official action can be more totally confined by rules, it is worth briefly recapitulating the central concerns of the previous two sections. The argument is that in both the professional treatment and the moral judgement cases there are reasons why systems are likely to have sought to find some sort of balance between rules and discretion in which both are significant. Key issues have been stressed which tip the balance in the discretion direction – indeterminacy, standards, trust, enforcement difficulties. All apply to both sections, though indeterminacy and trust were explored in the professional treatment section, standards and enforcement difficulties in the moral judgement one. Against the arguments for discretion are counterpoised arguments for rules. Discretionary decision making is likely to involve disregard of wider resource and rationing considerations and biases in favour of certain parties. Yet few will go so far as to lock doctors totally into what they have derided as 'cookbook medicine' or pollution control officers into enforcement actions which undermine employment opportunities in a neighbourhood. Hence the search for balance between rules and discretion.

The next section goes on to examine some kinds of public policy where the case for rule dominance seems very much stronger – yet there are still areas of discretion and analysts who are prepared to defend them.

The bureaucratic rationality model

The provision of cash benefits and its inverse, taxation, seem to fall into the category most naturally handled administratively, and judicially, by Mashaw's bureaucratic rationality model. Entitlements and obligations are naturally quantifiable, and there are strong expectations of pre-dictability in administration. Historically, these expectations have figured for a long while in the history of taxation, and some of the most fundamental political conflicts (the English Civil War, the American War of Independence, the French Revolution) have been concerned with rights with regard to taxation. In the case of social benefits, the assertion of rights has been a more modern phenomenon, involving a shift from a view of income maintenance as a discretionary gift from the rich to the poor, to a view of it as a citizens' right (Marshall, 1963). Partly because of this interesting evolution, partly because it is an area of public policy with which the author is particularly familiar, this discussion will focus upon the issues about the bureaucratic rationality model in income maintenance policy.

Mashaw's three models are set out in a book which reports research on the adjudication process with regard to American social security disability benefit claims. He describes this system as one in which 'over time the internal imperatives of bureaucratic rationality have triumphed by pushing professional judgment into a controllable hierarchical or evidentiary role and by making significant progress towards "bureaucratising" the hearing process to eliminate much of its "moral judgment" flavor' (Mashaw, 1983, pp. 45–6).

This comment highlights two crucial points. One of them is that decisions on the circumstances under which a claimed disability conveys a right to benefit constitute one of the key examples where a 'standards' issue enters into benefit decision making. A related example – not this time involving a medical judgement – occurs in relation to benefits for the unemployed, where systems invariably contain rules to prevent benefits being paid to those who deliberately leave work or are not trying to get work. Judgements are required about whether particular acts and aspects of behaviour fall into proscribed categories.

The other point is Mashaw's statement that the American system has pushed professional judgement into an 'evidentiary role'. This takes us back to the discretion/judgement distinction, which was described in the previous chapter (p. 181) as involving a rather unhelpful discrimination which masks the fact that discretion typically occurs within a rule framework. In other words, we have in Mashaw's example and in the unemployment benefits example, cases where a strong rule framework still requires elements of discretion.

In the development of the regulation of social security, the emergence of social insurance in many countries involved the construction of systems of benefits in which entitlement was, subject to detailed complications like those outlined above, broadly guaranteed by rules. Those who paid into such schemes have been deemed to have entitlements to take money out if they are old, sick or unemployed. These systems provided benefits for the emergent urban working class superior to those offered by the highly discretionary 'poor law' systems which had operated hitherto. They did not entirely replace the latter. In some countries (Australia, for example) social insurance never emerged, in others the social insurance system developed in a flawed way (the United Kingdom, for example). Even where strong social insurance systems were set up, new social problems (marriage breakdown, for example) have emerged. Moreover, today the insurance model is widely argued to be problematic because of the very extensive income transfers it is expected to effect. Accordingly, the rules systems related to social assistance schemes have come under scrutiny, and it has been argued that it is possible for these to be strengthened and for discretionary powers to be confined.

This issue has been particularly hotly fought in the United Kingdom, and the following discussion draws mainly upon the UK debate. But it has not been absent in the review of social assistance policy in other countries (see, for example, Hvinden (1994) on Norway, Hupe (1993) on the Netherlands, and Weatherly (1992) on Australia).

Until the mid-1960s, the UK social assistance system had a rule structure which contained very extensive discretionary powers (see Hill, 1969). The welfare rights 'movement' which developed in the 1960s focused on these. Campaigners argued that basic benefit scale rates were too low for most clients and that consequently additional payments – either lump-sum emergency needs payments or weekly exceptional circumstances additions – should be available as rights enforceable through an appeal system. They also drew attention to ways in which discretionary decision making involved discrimination against some claimants – the prejudices of officers operated against the 'undeserving poor' (migrants, single parents, etc.).

Titmuss (1971) attacked the arguments against discretion, condemning the alternative as likely to involve a rigid 'pathology of legalism' (p. 124), and argued 'that the real need was to achieve the correct balance between legal rules and administrative discretion' (p. 113). In particular, he was concerned that welfare rights tactics might pressurise the system towards an excessive itemisation of entitlement in terms of individual articles of clothing, furniture, etc. Donnison (1977), when in the key role of chairman of the agency which administered social assistance, argued that it was possible to establish a detailed rule structure for such a system. Reforms in the early 1980s attempted to do this.

Later, in 1986, the government rejected this approach, opting instead for a simplified rule structure for basic benefits, and a highly discretionary residual scheme (the 'social fund') to deal with exceptional situations. But the government gave the latter a rather different character to what had gone before by imposing cash limits on the fund, expecting most payments to be in the form of loans and expecting the administering authority to develop an internal system of working rules to try to ensure consistency.

Clearly this discussion does not want to get into the details of the rather complex history of UK social assistance. This brief story of the controversy about discretion has been set out to highlight several points.

There clearly has been in UK income maintenance policy a move from discretion to rules, driven by a political recognition of arguments about the 'rights' of beneficiaries, even in the absence of insurance-based entitlements. The debate about rights involved the recognition that the giving of rights in such a context *either* involves very detailed regulation *or* involves the setting up of a series of simple entitlement rules. The former approach both causes uncertainties about entitlements in the face of complexity, thus producing underclaiming, and offers 'handles' to skilled advocates who can use specific rules as precedents for new demands on the system. The latter approach either involves a very generous approach to need, or – politically a more likely eventuality – the enactment of constraints which leave many very poor people outside the net. The latter has been the case with the 1986 measures in the United Kingdom, with the 'social fund' as a limited attempt to mitigate the harshness of that decision.

A related example which highlights the two options here is to compare the UK approach to the support of housing costs with that adopted in most other countries. In principle, the UK approach takes full rent into account and accordingly poses some quite difficult discretionary problems (albeit framed in complex rules) about how to deal with unusually high rents and situations in which landlords and tenants conspire together to secure state benefits. Most other countries, however, impose explicit upper limits on the benefits provided (see Kemp, 1990).

Finally, let us go back to the issues about bureaucratic behaviour posed by the work of Merton, Morstein Marx and Lipsky. We see in these social security examples a movement which has tended to take discretionary powers away from low-level officials. Unlike doctors or pollution control inspectors, they have not been trusted to exercise extensive discretionary powers. Titmuss' (1971) paper contained arguments about ways to 'professionalise' them. Hupe (1993) has suggested that there have been efforts in the Netherlands to involve social benefit clients in a 'co-production' process in which they are consulted on discretionary options. The general thrust, however, has been to see social security officials as people who should not be trusted with extensive discretion.

But then, the challenge both posed by bureaucratic personality theory and implied by the notion of 'street-level bureaucracy' is that routine officials without discretion develop other ways to influence decisions. These ways include rule breaking or careless rule interpretation, officious rule enforcement which makes it difficult for the public to secure entitlements, failing to give information about entitlements and slow work practices which impose implicit rationing through delays. Particularly complex issues come up in relation to the prevention and detection of fraud, where systems, however rule bound, impose procedures which may be used with varying degrees of officiousness – from accepting statements at face value at one extreme to requiring detailed proof at the other. Officials who develop suspicions are almost inevitably left with choices about how to proceed. These phenomena about rule-bound systems – which could be illustrated copiously from the present-day United Kingdom, where the cost controls and staff savings required by the 'new public management' movement are producing short-cuts in procedures and increasing error rates – may be said (see the discussion on pp. 189–93) to involve 'discretion' by another name. At any rate they raise important concerns about how judgements are made and how they are explained to individuals in all aspects of official decision making As Sainsbury (1992) rightly argues, these have been rather masked by the way the UK debate on social security discretion became focused upon the margins of the system.

Conclusions

Since the implementation of public policy generally involves organisations, three chapters of this book have explored issues about them. This chapter started by focusing attention on the behaviour of organisational members. It found that writers have tended to highlight contradictory problems about public organisations. For some the problem is that they are full of rigid bureaucratic people – bound by rules, perhaps demoralised by rules and likely to manipulate rules. For others the problem is that public officials – particularly publicly appointed professionals – are not regulated enough: they are too free to 'make policy', exercising considerable discretion. The 'new public management' (NPM) movement claims to have ways to deal with both of these issues – the discussion of the inevitable trade-offs between rules and discretion suggested reasons to be sceptical about those claims. This is supported by Hood's analysis of the extent to which management changes under the influence of NPM produce 'side-effects and even reverse effects'. He borrows Sieber's (1981) notion of 'fatal remedies' – 'producing the opposite of the intended effect' – to analyse these (Hood, 1995, pp. 112–16). Among them the erosion of trust and the adverse effects of elaborate rule structures and reporting requirements loom large (see also the attack on the 'audit explosion' in Power (1994)).

The discussion in the later part of this chapter fused the concerns of Chapter 8 about the relationship between rules and discretion with issues about the affiliations of bureaucrats and professionals, exploring the ways in which different policies are likely to involve the mixing of rules and discretion in different ways. It suggested some factors which might influence this mix.

The discussion clearly did not resolve the debate between the two concerns. The main concern of this book is, of course, to highlight the issues not to prescribe solutions. The latter depend upon perspectives on accountability. These were explored a little in relation to medical management. The final chapter will pick up on some of these issues again because of their centrality for any efforts to use the examination of the policy process to help frame policy prescriptions.

CHAPTER 10

CONCLUSIONS

Synopsis

This final chapter is very brief. The main function of a textbook like this is to provide an overview of a wide range of ideas and theories. It is not appropriate to bring the whole exercise to a set of conclusions which argue for the selection of a single approach. Furthermore, only some of the theories have been presented as in distinct opposition to each other – and in many of these cases (as with the examples of pluralism and its critics or the top-down/bottom-up debate with regard to implementation), ways have been suggested of resolving the debates, or using them constructively in analysis. In many other cases, the theories can be used together – for example, fusing the network approach with the institutional approach, or recognising how legalistic approaches to the analysis of discretion need to be modified by sociological approaches. In the very first chapter, moreover, the approach to policy analysis used by Allison to explore the Cuban missile crisis was commended, showing that alternative approaches may be contrasted as offering alternative lenses through which to view reality.

This last point reminds us that, while at the extremes there are irreconcilable 'world-views' – pluralism and Marxism, for example – much of the time what are offered as theories are merely ways of trying to order reality in a very complex field. Institutionalism, policy networks, even probably élitism and corporatism, are not so much theories – of the kind from which testable hypotheses can be derived – as models or conceptual frameworks which help to organise our observations. This is more readily evident in relation to many of the ideas introduced later in the book: weak and strong states, agenda setting, street-level bureaucracy, Mashaw's model of discretion and so on.

The argument in the previous paragraph – with its specific comment on hypotheses – indicates that, as examined in this book, policy analysis must be seen as very much an interpretative art. If we are exploring the factors that play upon the policy process in the real world, we may try to make predictions. We may even try to advise policy actors about what will be likely to work and what will not. But this depends upon being able to offer a realistic interpretation of reality. We are hardly in a position to offer rigorous hypotheses, let alone discover situations in which they may be tested. This point was put explicitly with regard to institutional theory, with its concerns about the circumstances in which institutions constrain and the windows of opportunity for change. Much the same must be said of statements postulating the operation of structured and biased pluralism, models of policy communities, analyses of implementation structures, theories about inter-organisational relations and so on.

Some of the early analysts of public policy saw themselves as setting up a discipline of 'policy sciences'. Few modern writers on this subject would use such confident language. Where we do find perspectives that come close to this is in some of the work which offers analysis *for* policy, suggesting techniques to aid decision making (cost–benefit analysis) or ways to try to control the policy process (the rational model for decisions, the formulation of rules for top-down control over implementation). This book – as an exploration *of* policy processes – has not followed this path. Moreover, where some of this prescriptive work has been considered, the commentary has been severely sceptical.

This scepticism is fuelled by a recognition that policy processes are essentially political (with both a big and a small 'p'), as Gregory put it in a summing up of Lindblom's contribution to policy analysis: 'public policy making needs to be seen as an essentially political process, driven by a distinctive form of collective rationality' (1989, p. 151). What follows from this is not merely that there are always likely to be difficulties in following through a recommended procedure to control the policy process, but that there are likely to be conflicts over the values and interests built into any such procedures.

Two crucial value concerns lie behind any exploration of policy processes, and references to them have surfaced at various points in this book. One of them is efficiency, the other is democracy. While they are often seen as separate concerns and sometimes as conflicting concerns, it is also the case that disregard of democratic accountability can undermine efficiency as people resist alien impositions upon them. As Lindblom and Woodhouse express it, the quest must be to ensure that society enjoys *both* 'more reasoned and more democratic policy making' (1993, p. 7).

In any case, one of the most disturbing things about the way the word 'rationality' has been co-opted by those who want to talk about efficiency is that their discourse disregards the deep irrationality which arises when policy goals determined by élites are imposed upon unwilling citizens. To talk about rationality, as so much policy analysis literature does (often taking its cue from economics), without reference to ends or to the issues about who has the power to determine these ends is at least beside the point and at worst dangerous.

This book is influenced by a deep belief that people, as participants in policy processes (whether as those who try to influence decisions, those expected to implement decisions or those affected by decisions), need to understand what is going on. There was a joke that used to go around about Margaret Thatcher when she was prime minister that she was prone to assert that something must be done about the government. For her, at the centre of that government, it was bizarre to distance herself in such a way. But what was glaringly obvious about her also applies to all the rest of us. We are only too ready to distance ourselves from 'the government' or 'the state', seeing these as alien impositions upon us.

Much that has been said in this book seems to acknowledge that this is a plausible point of view. It will be evident that the author has a view of the policy process which emphasises biases in the system (recognising that even the Marxist perspective has important points to make on this), network complexity, institutional constraints and state power. It is also a view which stresses how difficult the implementation process is because of organisational complexity and the impossibility of operating models of simple rule-based control. In his gloomier moments the author is inclined to see the world as a capitalist 'garbage can' – biased against the interests of ordinary people, yet operating in incoherent and unpredictable ways.

Clearly the problem with such a pessimistic view is that it gives support to the 'anti-politics' politics of the New Right with its emphasis on 'state failure'. As one writer from that perspective puts it:

The biggest disease of the modern extended state is that it becomes neither a provider of public goods which cannot easily be provided by the market, nor a vehicle for redistribution to the less fortunate, but an engine for the provision of private benefits to interest groups. (Brittan, 1990, p. 12)

If, however, you believe that the market does not offer a satisfactory alternative model for solving distributive problems in society, or even if you accept the validity of market approaches to many issues but then think that this solution throws up considerable regulatory problems for society (a position taken by all but the most extreme right-wingers), then you must acknowledge a role for public policy in a complex society.

Perhaps some of the problem here is that we seem to be offered alternatives – state or market. In this formulation the state is increasingly seen nowadays as an external imposition upon us; by contrast the market is a place where we make choices (albeit often constrained ones). This view of the state is enhanced by another pair of apparent alternatives – state or society. Yet the ideal of the democratic state involves the control of state by society. In this formulation, that state is just as much 'us' as society – it is the instrument (or, more realistically, the set of instruments) by which we govern ourselves.

It is a certain despair about the viability of democratic self-government which engenders a phenomenon encountered by all who teach the courses for which this book is designed. Students who manifestly *do care* about public policies – about injustices in society, about pollution, about social problems (particularly those more personal ones that impinge on the lives of themselves and their friends – AIDs, alcoholism, homelessness and so on) – are inclined to 'switch off' when asked to think about political and administrative processes. This occurs notwithstanding the fact that these are processes – in which we all may be able to participate – to deal with policy issues about which we are concerned. As suggested above, the author sympathises with this feeling of impotence. It is arguable that teaching about policy processes in a way which emphasises biases and difficulties colludes with cynicism and indifference to politics. The only answer to this is that it is better to teach a realistic appreciation of the policy process than to try to indoctrinate people with a naive optimism about pluralism and the rationality of decision-makers.

The perspective of a book like this involves trying to take a difficult stance which says that the aspirations of the idealistic pluralists (Lindblom, for example) should be taken seriously and that the idea that goals should be embodied in policies and followed through in a predictable way is a good one, but that we must not underrate the difficulties or be fooled by those who dismiss our many concerns about reality as unconstructive radicalism.

Pieter Degeling often expresses the dilemma of policy analysis in terms of the notions of the 'sacred' and the 'profane'. We need to keep in sight the values embodied in the sacred discourse – of efficiency and rationality – while being able to recognise that much of the real discourse of policy processes is down to earth and cynical (in a word, profane). In studying and reflecting on the policy process, we must neither squeamishly refuse to recognise the profane nor become sucked so completely into the 'dirty' talk of practical people that we lose sight of the aspiration of modern government to solve problems in an effective and accountable way.

At this stage in the argument, we could proceed on to some solutions to the conflict between ideals and reality. But this book has aimed to describe rather than prescribe. There is a growing body of work which is seeking to resolve the problems explored here by reformulating our concepts of democracy in ways which facilitate power sharing and participation at various levels. Some of it has been mentioned fleetingly in the book: in particular in the discussion of the accountability aspirations of some of the people who have written about bottom-up implementation and about the fragmentation of policy delivery instruments. The policy process does not have to be dominated by the simple unitary state: indeed, since that state is being challenged from without (by supra-national institutions) as well as from within, change is very much on the agenda. Some of the literature about alternative models for democracy focuses upon ways to enhance pluralism and make it more balanced; others give attention to better ways to devolve power to sub-national governments. But there are also important issues being addressed about ways to increase the direct public accountability of the organisations which deliver public policies. It is also the case that the pro-market arguments for choice are beginning to be picked up in terms which supplement their naive belief in the power of consumers by suggestions that there are other ways in which citizens may be able to choose and then participate in the running of the institutions they have chosen. Key sources for some of these arguments are books by Bobbio (1987), Rendell and Ward (1989), Hirst (1994) and Cohen and Rogers (1995).

The more humble role of this book has been to raise questions about the way the policy process works, acknowledging how much concerns about accountability have motivated many of the theorists whose work has been explored. It can be pointed out, however, that if the arguments for institutional change in society are to move out from the texts of political philosophers and the pamphlets of forward-looking organisations, questions about how to inject them into the policy process will have to be confronted.

REFERENCES

Aberbach, J.D., R.D. Putman and B.A. Rockman (1981) *Bureaucrats and Politicians in Western Democracies*, Cambridge, Mass.: Harvard University Press.

Aglietta, M. (1987) *A Theory of Capitalist Regulation: The US experience*, London: Verso.

Albrow, M. (1970) *Bureaucracy*, London: Pall Mall.

Aldrich, H.E. (1976) 'Resource dependence and inter-organizational relations; local employment service offices and social services sector organizations', *Administration and Society*, **7**(4), pp. 419–54.

Alford, R. (1975) *Health Care Politics*, Chicago, Ill.: University of Chicago Press.

Allison, G.T. (1971) *Essence of Decision*, Boston, Mass.: Little Brown.

Argyris, C. (1964) *Integrating the Individual and the Organisation*, New York: Wiley.

Ashford, D.E. (1986) *The Emergence of the Welfare States*, Oxford: Blackwell.

Atkinson, M.M. and W.D. Coleman (1989) 'Strong states and weak states: sectoral policy networks in advanced capitalist economies', *British Journal of Political Science*, **19**, pp. 747–67.

Atkinson, P. (1985) *Language, Structure and Reproduction*, London: Methuen.

Audit Commission (1986) *Making a Reality of Community Care*, London: HMSO.

Auster, R.D. and M. Silver (1979) *The State as a Firm: Economic forces in political development*, The Hague: Martinus Nijhoff.

Bachrach, P. (1969) *The Theory of Democratic Elitism*, London: University of London Press.

Bachrach, P. and M.S. Baratz (1962) 'Two faces of power', *American Political Science Review*, **56**, pp. 641–51.

Bachrach, P. and M.S. Baratz (1963) 'Decisions and nondecisions: an analytical framework', *American Political Science Review*, **57**, pp. 1947–52.

Bachrach, P. and M.S. Baratz (1970) *Power and Poverty*, New York: Oxford University Press.

Baldwin, P. (1990) *The Politics of Social Solidarity*, Cambridge: Cambridge University Press.

Baldwin, R. (1995) *Rules and Government*, Oxford: Oxford University Press.

Ball, M., M. Harloe and M. Martens (1988) *Housing and Social Change in Europe and the USA*, London: Routledge.

Ball, S.J. (1990) *Politics and Policy Making in Education*, London: Routledge.

Barker, A. and B.G. Peters (eds) (1993) *The Politics of Expert Advice*, Edinburgh: Edinburgh University Press.

Barnard, C. (1938) *The Functions of the Executive*, Cambridge Mass.: Harvard University Press.

Barrett, M. (1980) *Women's Oppression Today*, London: Verso.

Barrett, S. and C. Fudge (eds) (1981) *Policy and Action*, London: Methuen.

Barrett, S. and M.J. Hill (1981) 'Report to the SSRC Central–Local Government Relations Panel on the "core" or theoretical component of the research on implementation', unpublished.

Baumgartner, M.P. (1992) 'The myth of discretion', in K. Hawkins (ed.), *The Uses of Discretion*, Oxford: Clarendon Press.

Becker, H.S. (ed.) (1966) *Social Problems: A modern approach*, New York: Free Press.

Beer, S.H. (1965) *Modern British Politics*, London: Faber and Faber.

Beetham, D. (1987) *Bureaucracy*, Milton Keynes: Open University Press.

Beetham, D. (1991) *The Legitimation of Power*, London: Macmillan.

Bell, D. (1960) *The End of Ideology*, New York: Free Press.

Benson, J.K. (1977) 'Organisations: a dialectical view', *Administrative Science Quarterly*, **22**(3), pp. 1–21.

Benson, J.K. (1983) 'Interorganizational networks and policy sectors', in D. Rogers and D. Whetten (eds), *Interorganizational Coordination*, Ames, Ia: Iowa State University Press.

Bentley, A.F. (1967) *The Process of Government*, Cambridge, Mass.: Belknap Press.

Berger, P.L. and T. Luckman (1975) *The Social Construction of Reality*, Harmondsworth: Penguin.

Bickel, A.M. (1970) *The Supreme Court and the Idea of Progress*, New York: Harper & Row.

Blau, P.M. (1955) *The Dynamics of Bureaucracy*, Chicago, Ill.: University of Chicago Press.

Blowers, A. (1984) *Something in the Air: Corporate power and the environment*, London: Harper & Row.

Boase, J.P. (1996) 'Institutions, institutionalized networks and policy choices: health policy in the US and Canada', *Governance*, **9**(3), pp. 287–310.

Bobbio, N. (1987) *The Future of Democracy*, Cambridge: Polity Press.

Booth, T. (1988) *Developing Policy Research*, Aldershot: Avebury.

Bottomore, T.B. (1966) *Elites and Society*, Harmondsworth: Penguin.

Bowe, R., S.J. Ball and A. Gold (1992) *Reforming Education and Changing Schools*, London: Routledge.

Braverman, H. (1974) *Labor and Monopoly Capital*, New York: Monthly Review Press.

Braybrooke, D. and C.E. Lindblom (1963) *A Strategy of Decision*, New York: Free Press.

Brittan, S. (1977) *The Economic Consequences of Democracy*, London: Temple Smith.

Brittan, S. (1990) *A Restatement of Economic Liberalism*, London: Social Market Foundation.

Brown, M.K. (1981) 'The allocation of justice and police–citizen encounters', in C.T. Goodsell (ed.), *The Public Encounter*, Bloomington: Indiana University Press.

Browne, A. and A. Wildavsky (1984) 'Should evaluation become implementation?', in J. Pressman and A. Wildavsky (eds), *Implementation* (revised edn), Berkley, Calif.: University of California Press.

Brugger, B. and S. Reglar (1994) *Politics, Economy and Society in Contemporary China*, Basingstoke: Macmillan.

Buchanan, J.M. and G. Tullock (1962) *The Calculus of Consent*, Ann Arbor, Mich.: University of Michigan Press.

Bull, D. (1980) 'The anti-discretion movement in Britain: fact or phantom?', *Journal of Social Welfare Law*, pp. 65–83.

Bulmer, M. (ed.) (1987) *Social Science Research and Government*, Cambridge: Cambridge University Press.

Burnham, J. (1942) *The Managerial Revolution*, London: Putnam.

Burns, T. and G.M. Stalker (1961) *The Management of Innovation*, London: Tavistock.

Butcher, T. (1995) *Delivering Welfare*, Buckingham: Open University Press.

Butler, D., A. Adonis and T. Travers (1994) *Failure in British Government: The politics of the poll tax*, Oxford: Oxford University Press.

Campbell, C. and G.K. Wilson (1995) *The End of Whitehall: Death of a paradigm?*, Oxford: Blackwell.

Castles, F.G. (1982) *The Impact of Parties*, London: Sage.

Castles, F. (1985) *The Working Class and Welfare*, Sydney: Allen and Unwin.

Castles, F. and D. Mitchell (1992) 'Identifying welfare state regimes: the links between politics, instruments and outcomes', *Governance*, 5(1), pp. 1–26.

Challis, L., S. Fuller, M. Henwood, R. Klein, W. Plowden, A. Webb, P. Whitingham and G. Wistow (1988) *Joint Approaches to Social Policy*, Cambridge: Cambridge University Press.

Chandler, A.D. (1977) *The Visible Hand: The managerial revolution in American business*, Cambridge, Mass.: Harvard University Press.

Chapman, R.A. (1970) *The Higher Civil Service in Britain*, London: Constable.

Child, J. (1972) 'Organization structure, environment and performance: the role of strategic choice', *Sociology*, **6**, pp. 1–22.

Clegg, S. (1979) *The Theory of Power and Organization*, London: Routledge and Kegan Paul.

Clegg, S. (1989) *Frameworks of Power*, London: Sage.

Clegg, S. (1990) *Modern Organizations*, London: Sage.

Clegg, S. and D. Dunkerley (1977) *Critical Issues in Organisations*, London: Routledge and Kegan Paul.

Clegg, S. and D. Dunkerley (1980) *Organisation, Class and Control*, London: Routledge and Kegan Paul.

Coase, R.H. (1937) 'The nature of the firm', *Economica*, **4**, pp. 386–405.

Cohen, J. and J. Rogers (1995) *Associations and Democracy*, London: Verso.

Cohen, M.D., J.G. March and J.P. Olsen (1972) 'A garbage can model of organizational choice', *Administrative Science Quarterly*, **17**, pp. 1–25.

Cohen, R. (1987) *The New Helots: Migrants in the international division of labour*, Aldershot: Avebury.

Colebatch, H. and P. Larmour (1993) *Market, Bureaucracy and Community*, London: Pluto.

Collier, R.B. and D. Collier (1991) *Shaping the Political Arena: Critical junctures, the labor movement and regime dynamics in Latin America*, Princeton, NJ: Princeton University Press.

Cox, R. (1987) *Production, Power and World Order*, New York: Columbia University Press.

Crenson, M.A. (1971) *The Unpolitics of Air Pollution*, Baltimore: Johns Hopkins Press.

Crozier, M. (1964) *The Bureaucratic Phenomenon*, Chicago, Ill.: University of Chicago Press.

Culyer, A.J. (1980) *The Political Economy of Social Policy*, Oxford: Martin Robertson.

Cunningham, G. (1963) 'Policy and practice', *Public Administration*, **41**, pp. 229–38.

Dahl, R.A. (1957) 'The concept of power', *Behavioural Science*, **2**, pp. 201–15.

Dahl, R.A. (1958) 'A critique of the ruling-élite model', *American Political Science Review*, **52**, pp. 463–9.

Dahl, R.A. (1961) *Who Governs?*, New Haven Conn.: Yale University Press.

Dahl, R.A. and C.E. Lindblom (1953) *Politics, Economics and Welfare* (2nd edn, 1976), Chicago, Ill.: Chicago University Press.

Davis, K.C. (1969) *Discretionary Justice*, Baton Rouge, La: Louisiana State University Press.

Deakin, N. and K. Walsh (1996) 'The enabling state: the role of markets and contracts', *Public Administration*, **74**, pp. 33–48.

Dearlove, J. and P. Saunders (1991) *Introduction to British Politics*, Cambridge: Polity Press.

Degeling, P. (1993) 'Policy as the accomplishment of an implementation structure: hospital restructuring in Australia', in M. Hill (ed.), *New Agendas in the Study of the Policy Process*, Hemel Hempstead: Harvester Wheatsheaf.

Degeling, P. and H.K. Colebatch (1984) 'Structure and action as constructs in the practice of public administration', *Australian Journal of Public Administration*, **43**(4), pp. 320–31.

Dell, E. (1991) *A Hard Pounding: Politics and the economic crisis*, Oxford: Oxford University Press.

Delphy, C. (1984) *Close to Home: A materialist analysis of women's oppression*, London: Hutchinson.

Dicey, A.V. (1905) *Lectures on the Relations between Law and Public Opinion*, London: Macmillan.

DiMaggio, P.J. and W. Powell (1983) 'The iron cage revisited: institutional isomorphism and collective rationality in organizational fields', *American Sociological Review*, **48**, pp. 147–60.

Donaldson, L. (1985) *In Defence of Organization Theory: A response to the critics*, Cambridge: Cambridge University Press.

Donnison, D.V. (1977) 'Against discretion', *New Society*, 15 September, pp. 534–6.

Downs, A. (1957) *An Economic Theory of Democracy*, New York: Harper and Row.

Dror, Y. (1964) 'Muddling through – "science" or inertia?', *Public Administration Review*, **24**, pp. 153–7.

Dror, Y. (1968) *Public Policymaking Re-examined*, San Francisco, Calif.: Chandler.

Dror, Y. (1986) *Policymaking under Adversity*, New Brunswick: Transaction Books.

Dunleavy, P. (1981) 'Professions and policy change: notes towards a model of ideological corporatism', *Public Administration Bulletin*, **36**, pp. 3–16.

Dunleavy, P. (1985) 'Bureaucrats, budgets and the growth of the state: reconstructing an instrumental model', *British Journal of Political Science*, **15**, pp. 299–328.

Dunleavy, P. (1986) 'Explaining the privatization boom: public choice versus radical approaches', *Public Administration*, **64**(1), pp. 13–34.

Dunleavy, P. (1991) *Democracy, Bureaucracy and Public Choice*, Hemel Hempstead: Harvester Wheatsheaf.

Dunleavy, P. (1995) 'Policy disasters: explaining the UK's record', *Public Policy and Administration*, **10**(2), pp. 52–69.

Dunleavy, P. and B. O'Leary (1987) *Theories of the State*, London: Macmillan.

Dunsire, A. (1978a) *Implementation in a Bureaucracy*, Oxford: Martin Robertson.

Dunsire, A. (1978b) *Control in a Bureaucracy*, Oxford: Martin Robertson.

Dworkin, R. (1977) *Taking Rights Seriously*, London: Duckworth.

Dye, T.R. (1976) *Policy Analysis*, Tuscaloosa, Ala.: University of Alabama Press.

Dyson, K. (1980) *The State Tradition in Western Europe*, Oxford: Martin Robertson.

Easton, D. (1953) *The Political System*, New York: Knopf.

Easton, D. (1965a) *A Systems Analysis of Political Life*, New York: Wiley.

Easton, D. (1965b) *A Framework for Political Analysis*, Englewood Cliffs, NJ: Prentice Hall.

Edelman, M. (1971) *Politics as Symbolic Action*, Chicago, Ill.: Markham.

Edelman, M. (1977) *Political Language: Words that succeed and policies that fail*, New York: Institute for the Study of Poverty.

Edelman, M. (1988) *Constructing the Political Spectacle*, Chicago: University of Chicago Press.

Elam, M.J. (1990) 'Puzzling out the post-Fordist debate: technology, markets and institutions', *Economic and Industrial Democracy*, **11**, pp. 9–38.

Elmore, R. (1978) 'Organisational models of social program implementation', *Public Policy*, **26**(2), pp. 185–228.

Elmore, R. (1980) 'Backward mapping: implementation research and policy decisions', *Political Science Quarterly*, **94**, pp. 601–16.

Elmore, R. (1981) 'Backward mapping and youth employment', unpublished paper prepared for the third meeting of the International Working Group on Policy Implementation.

Enthoven, A.C. (1985) *Reflections on the Management of the NHS*, London: Nuffield Provincial Hospitals Trust.

Esping-Andersen, G. (1990) *Three Worlds of Welfare Capitalism*, Cambridge: Polity Press.

Etzioni, A. (1961) *A Comparative Analysis of Complex Organisations*, New York: Free Press.

Etzioni, A. (1967) 'Mixed-scanning: a "third" approach to decision-making', *Public Administration Review*, **27**, pp. 385–92.

Evans, P.B., D. Rueschemeyer and T. Skocpol (eds) (1985) *Bringing the State Back In*, Cambridge: Cambridge University Press.

Fayol, H. (1916) *Administration Industrielle et Générale*, Paris.

Feldman, M. (1992) 'Social limits to discretion: an organizational perspective', in K. Hawkins (ed.), *The Uses of Discretion*, Oxford: Clarendon Press.

Fimister, G. and M. Hill (1993) 'Delegating implementation problems: social security, housing and community care in Britain', in M. Hill (ed.), *New Agendas in the Study of the Policy Process*, Hemel Hempstead: Harvester Wheatsheaf.

Firth, J. (1987) *Public Support for Residential Care*, London: DHSS.

Flynn, N. (1993) *Public Sector Management* (2nd edn), Hemel Hempstead: Harvester Wheatsheaf.

Flynn, R. (1991) 'Coping with cutbacks and managing retrenchment in health', *Journal of Social Policy*, **20**(2), pp. 215–36.

Follett, M.P. (1941) *Dynamic Administration*, London: Management Publications Trust.

Forrest, R. and A. Murie (1991) *Selling the Welfare State*, London: Routledge.

Fox, A. (1974) *Beyond Contract: Work, Power and Trust Relations*, London: Faber.

Friedrich, C.J. (1940) 'The nature of administrative responsibility', *Public Policy*, **1**, pp. 3–24.

Friedson, E. (1970) *Professional Dominance*, New York: Atherton.

Friend, J.K., J.M. Power and C.J.L Yewlett (1974) *Public Planning: The intercorporate dimension*, London: Tavistock.

Fukuyama, F. (1992) *The End of History and the Last Man*, New York: Free Press.

Galligan, D.J. (1986) *Discretionary Powers*, Oxford: Clarendon Press.

Gamble, A. (1994) *The Free Economy and the Strong State* (2nd edn), Basingstoke: Macmillan.

Gaventa, J. (1980) *Power and Powerlessness, Quiescence and Rebellion in an Appalachian Valley*, Oxford: Clarendon Press.

Gerth, H.H. and C.W. Mills (1948) *From Max Weber: Essays in sociology*, London: Routledge and Kegan Paul.

Gerth, H.H. and C.W. Mills. (1963) 'A Marx for the managers', in C.W. Mills, *Power, Politics and People*, Oxford: Oxford University Press.

Gibbins, J.R. (ed.)(1989) *Contemporary Political Culture*, London: Sage.

Giddens, A. (1976) *New Rules of Sociological Method*, London: Hutchinson.

Giddens, A. (1984) *The Constitution of Society*, Cambridge: Polity Press.

Giller, H. and A. Morris. (1981) 'What type of case is this? Social workers' decisions about children who offend', in M. Adler and S. Asquith (eds), *Discretion and Welfare*, London: Heinemann.

Ginsburg, N. (1992) *Divisions of Welfare*, London: Sage.

Glennerster, H., M. Matsaganis and P. Owens (1994) *Implementing Fundholding*, Buckingham: Open University Press.

Glennerster, H., A. Power and T. Travers (1991) 'A new era for social policy: a new enlightenment or a new leviathan?', *Journal of Social Policy*, **20**(3), pp. 389–414.

Goffman, E. (1971) *The Presentation of the Self in Everyday Life*, Harmondsworth: Penguin.

Goodin, R.E. (1982) *Political Theory and Public Policy*, Chicago, Ill.: University of Chicago Press.

Gordon, I., J. Lewis and K. Young (1977) 'Perspectives on policy analysis', *Public Administration Bulletin*, **25**, pp. 26–30.

Gough, I. (1979) *The Political Economy of the Welfare State*, London: Macmillan.

Gouldner, A.W. (1954) *Patterns of Industrial Bureaucracy*, Glencoe, Ill.: Free Press.

Gouldner, A.W. (1955) 'Metaphysical pathos and the theory of bureaucracy', *American Political Science Review*, **49**, pp. 496–507.

Gouldner, A.W. (1957–8) 'Cosmopolitans and locals: towards an analysis of latent social roles', *Administrative Science Quarterly*, **2**, pp. 281–306 and 444–80.

Grant, W.P. (1989) *Pressure Groups, Politics and Democracy in Britain*, London: Philip Allan.

Greenwood, E. (1957) 'Attributes of a profession', *Social Work*, **2**, pp. 45–55.

Greenwood, R., C.R. Hinings and S. Ranson (1975) 'Contingency theory and the organisation of local authorities. Part One: Differentiation and integration', *Public Administration*, **53**, pp. 1–24.

Gregory, R. (1989) 'Political rationality or incrementalism? Charles E. Lindblom's enduring contribution to public policy making', *Policy and Politics*, **17**(2), pp. 139–53.

Griffith, J.A.G. (1977) *The Politics of the Judiciary*, Glasgow: Fontana.

Griffiths Report (1988) *Community Care: Agenda for action*, London: HMSO.

Gunn, L. (1978) 'Why is implementation so difficult?', *Management Services in Government*, November, **33**, pp. 169–76.

Gustafsson, G. (1991) 'Swedish local government: reconsidering rationality and consensus', in J.J. Hesse (ed.), *Local Government and Urban Affairs in International Perspective*, Baden Baden: Nomos Verlagsgesellschaft.

Hall, P.A. (1986) *Governing the Economy: The politics of state intervention in Britain and France*, Cambridge: Polity Press.

Hall, S. and M. Jacques (1985) *The Politics of Thatcherism*, London: Lawrence and Wishart.

Ham, C. (1992) *Health Policy in Britain*, (3rd edn), London: Macmillan.

Hanf, K. (1993) 'Enforcing environmental laws: the social regulation of co-production', in M. Hill (ed.), *New Agendas in the Study of the Policy Process*, Hemel Hempstead: Harvester Wheatsheaf.

Hanf, K. and A.-I. Jensen (eds) (forthcoming) *Governance and Environmental Quality in Western Europe*, Hemel Hempstead: Harvester Wheatsheaf.

Hargrove, E.C. (1975) *The Missing Link*, Washington, DC: The Urban Institute.

Hargrove, E.C. (1983) 'The search for implementation theory', in R. Zeckhauser and D. Leebaert (eds), *What Role for Government? Lessons from policy research*, Durham, NC: Duke Press Policy Studies.

Harrison, S. and C. Pollitt (1994) *Controlling Health Professionals*, Buckingham: Open University Press.

Harrison, S., D.J. Hunter and C. Pollitt (1990) *The Dynamics of British Health Policy*, London: Unwin Hyman.

Harrop, M. (ed.) (1992) *Power and Policy in Liberal Democracies*, Cambridge: Cambridge University Press.

Hartmann, H. (1979) 'The unhappy marriage of Marxism and feminism', in L. Sargent (ed.), *Women and Revolution*, Boston, Mass.: South End Press.

Hasenfeld, Y. and D. Steinmetz. (1981) 'Client–official encounters in social service agencies', in C.T. Goodsell (ed.), *The Public Encounter*, Bloomington, Ind.: Indiana University Press.

Hawkins, K. (1984) *Environment and Enforcement*, Oxford: Clarendon Press.

Hayek, F.A. (1944) *The Road to Serfdom*, London: Routledge and Kegan Paul.

Hayek, F.A. (1960) *The Constitution of Liberty*, London: Routledge and Kegan Paul.

Heclo, H. (1972) 'Review article: policy analysis', *British Journal of Political Science*, **2**, pp. 83–108.

Heclo, H. (1978) 'Issue networks and the executive establishment', in A. King (ed.), *The New American Political System*, Washington, DC: American Enterprise Institute.

Heclo, H. and A. Wildavsky (1981) *The Private Government of Public Money*, London: Macmillan.

Hennessy, P. (1989) *Whitehall*, London: Secker and Warburg.

Hennessy, P. (1995) *The Hidden Wiring: Unearthing the British Constitution*, London: Gollancz.

Herzberg, F. (1966) *Work and the Nature of Man*, New York: Staples Press.

Hewart, Lord (1929) *The New Despotism*, London.

Hickson, D., C.R. Hinings, C.A. Lee, R.E. Schneck and J.M. Pennings (1971) 'A strategic contingencies theory of intra-organisational power', *Administrative Science Quarterly*, **16**(2), pp. 216–29.

Hill, M.J. (1969) 'The exercise of discretion in the National Assistance Board', *Public Administration*, **47**, pp. 75–90.

Hill, M. (1981) 'The policy-implementation distinction: a quest for rational control?', in S. Barrett and C. Fudge (eds), *Policy and Action*, London: Methuen.

Hill, M. (1983) 'The role of the British Alkali and Clean Air Inspectorate in air pollution control', in P.B. Downing and K. Hanf (eds), *International Comparisons in Implementing Pollution Laws*, Boston, Mass.: Kluwer Nijhoff.

Hill, M., S. Aaronovitch and D. Baldock (1989) 'Non-decision making in pollution control in Britain: nitrate pollution, the EEC Drinking Water Directive and agriculture', *Policy and Politics*, **17**(3), pp. 227–40.

Hirst, P. (1994) *Associative Democracy*, Cambridge: Polity Press.

Hirst, P. and G. Thompson (1992) 'The problem of "globalisation": international economic relations, national economic management and the formation of trading blocs', *Economy and Society*, **21**(4), pp. 355–96.

Hjern, B. and C. Hull (1982) 'Implementation research as empirical constitutionalism', in B. Hjern and C. Hull (eds), *Implementation Beyond Hierarchy*, special issue of *European Journal of Political Research*.

Hjern, B. and D.O. Porter (1981) 'Implementation structures: a new unit of administrative analysis', *Organisational Studies*, **2**, pp. 211–27.

Hofferbert, R. (1974) *The Study of Public Policy*, Indianapolis, Ind.: Bobbs Merrill.

Hoggett, P. (1991) 'A new management for the public sector?', *Policy and Politics*, **19**, pp. 143–56.

Hoggett, P. (1996) 'New modes of control in the public service', *Public Administration*, **74**, pp. 9–32.

Hogwood, B. (1987) *From Crisis to Complacency? Shaping public policy in Britain*, London: Oxford University Press.

Hogwood, B.W. and L.A. Gunn (1981) *The Policy Orientation*, University of Strathclyde: Centre for the Study of Public Policy.

Hogwood, B.W. and L. Gunn (1984) *Policy Analysis for the Real World*, London: Oxford University Press.

Hogwood, B.W. and B.G. Peters (1983) *Policy Dynamics*, Brighton: Harvester.

Hood, C.C. (1976) *The Limits of Administration*, Chichester: Wiley.

Hood, C. (1991) 'A public management for all seasons', *Public Administration*, **69**(1), pp. 3–19.

Hood, C. (1995) 'Contemporary public management: a new global paradigm?', *Public Policy and Administration*, **10**(2), pp. 104–17.

Howlett, M. and M. Ramesh (1995) *Studying Public Policy: Policy cycles and policy subsystems*, Toronto: Oxford University Press.

Hudson, B. (1987) 'Collaboration in social welfare: a framework for analysis', *Policy and Politics*, **15**(3), pp. 175–82.

Hudson, B. (1989) 'Michael Lipsky and street-level bureaucracy: a neglected perspective', in L. Barton (ed.), *Disability and Dependency*, Lewes: Falmer Press.

Hughes, E.C. (1958) *Men and their Work*, Glencoe, Ill.: Free Press.

Hunter, F. (1953) *Community Power Structure*, Chapel Hill, NC: University of North Carolina Press.

Hupe, P. (1990) 'Implementing a meta-policy: the case of decentralisation in the Netherlands', *Policy and Politics*, **18**(3), pp. 181–91.

Hupe, P. (1993) 'The politics of implementation: individual, organisational and political co-production in social services delivery', in M. Hill (ed.), *New Agendas in the Study of the Policy Process*, Hemel Hempstead: Harvester Wheatsheaf.

Hurrell, A. and B. Kinsbury (eds) (1992) *The International Politics of the Environment*, Oxford: Oxford University Press.

Huxham, C. and D. Macdonald (1992) 'Introducing collaborative advantage', *Management Decision*, **30**(3), pp. 50–6.

Hvinden, B. (1994) *Divided Against Itself: A study of integration in welfare bureaucracy*, Oslo: Universitetsforlaget.

Hwang, Yuan-shie (1995) 'Funding health care in Britain and Taiwan', Ph.D. thesis, University of Newcastle upon Tyne.

Illich, I. (1977) *Limits to Medicine*, Harmondsworth: Penguin.

Immergut, E.M. (1992) 'The rules of the game: the logic of health policy-making in France, Switzerland and Sweden', in S. Steinmo, K. Thelen and F. Longstreth (eds), *Structuring Politics: Historical institutionalism in comparative analysis*, Cambridge: Cambridge University Press.

Immergut, E.M. (1993) *Health Policy, Interests and Institutions in Western Europe*, Cambridge: Cambridge University Press.

Jacques, E. (1967) *Equitable Payment*, Harmondsworth: Penguin.

Jenkins, W.I. (1978) *Policy Analysis*, London: Martin Robertson.

Jessop, B. (1992) 'Fordism and post-Fordism: a critical reformulation', in A.J. Scott and M. Stormper (eds), *Pathways to Industrialisation and Regional Development*, London: Routledge.

Johnson, T.J. (1972) *Professions and Power*, London: Macmillan.

Jordan, A.G. (1986) 'Iron triangles, woolly corporatism and elastic nets: images of the policy process', *Journal of Public Policy*, **1**, pp. 95–123.

Jordan, A.G. and J.J. Richardson (1987) *British Politics and the Policy Process*, London: Unwin Hyman.

Jowell, J. (1973) 'The legal control of administrative discretion', *Public Law*, pp. 178–220.

Kemp, P. (1990) 'Income-related assistance with housing costs: a cross-national comparison', *Urban Studies*, **27**(6), pp. 795–808.

Kennedy, I. (1981) *The Unmasking of Medicine*, London: Allen and Unwin.

Kerr, C.A., J.T. Dunlop, F.H. Harbison and C.A. Myers (1973) *Industrialism and Industrial Man*, Harmondsworth: Penguin Books.

Kettunen, P. (1994) *Implementation in a Multi-Organizational Setting*, Turku: Turan Yliopisto.

Kickert, W.J.M. (1995) 'Steering at a distance: a new paradigm of public governance in Dutch higher education', *Governance*, **8**(1), pp. 135–57.

Kickert, W.J.M. and F.A. van Vucht (eds) (1995) *Public Policy and Administration Sciences in the Netherlands*, Hemel Hempstead: Harvester Wheatsheaf.

Kingdon, J.D. (1984) *Agendas, Alternatives and Public Policies*, Boston, Mass.: Little Brown.

Kingsley, J.D. (1944) *Representative Bureaucracy*, Yellow Springs Ohio: Antioch Press.

Knoepfel, P. and H. Weidner (1982) 'Formulation and implementation of air quality control programmes: patterns of interest consideration', *Policy and Politics*, **10**(1), pp. 85–109.

Knoke, D. (1990) *Policy Networks: The structural perspective*, Cambridge, Cambridge University Press.

Kochan, T.A. (1975) 'Determinants of power boundary units in an interorganizational bargaining relation', *Administrative Science Quarterly*, **20**, pp. 435–52.

Krasner, S.D. (1988) 'Sovereignty: an institutional perspective', *Comparative Political Studies*, **21**, pp. 66–94.

Kuhn, T. (1962) *The Structure of Scientific Revolutions*, Chicago, Ill.: Chicago University Press.

Laffin, M. (1986) 'Professional communities and policy communities in central–local relations', in M. Goldsmith (ed.), *New Research in Central–Local Relations*, Aldershot: Gower.

Lane, J.-E. (1987) 'Implementation, accountability and trust', *European Journal of Political Research*, **15**(5), pp. 527–46.

Laski, H.J. (1925) *A Grammar of Politics*, London: Allen and Unwin.

Lasswell, H. (1951) 'The policy orientation', in D. Lerner and H. Lasswell (eds), *The Policy Sciences*, Stanford, Calif.: Stanford University Press.

Lasswell, H.D. (1968) 'The policy sciences', in *Encyclopedia of the Social Sciences*, vol. 12, New York: Macmillan.

Lasswell, H.D. (1970) 'The emerging conception of the policy sciences', *Policy Sciences*, 1, pp. 3–14.

Latham, E. (1952) *The Group Basis of Politics*, Ithaca, NY: Cornell University Press.

Lau, L.J. (1986) *Models of Development: A comparative study of economic growth in South Korea and Taiwan*, San Francisco, Calif.: Institute for Contemporary Studies.

Lee, J.M. (1963) *Social Leaders and Public Persons*, London: Oxford University Press.

Lenin, V.I. (1917) *State and Revolution*, Moscow: Foreign Languages Publishing House.

Levine, S. and P. White (1961) 'Exchange as a conceptual framework for the study of interorganisational relationships', *Administrative Science Quarterly*, 5, pp. 583–601.

Lewis, B. (1995) *The Middle East*, London: Weidenfeld.

Lijphart, A. (1975) *The Politics of Accommodation: Pluralism and Democracy in the Netherlands*, Berkeley, Calif.: University of California Press.

Lindblom, C.E. (1959) 'The science of "muddling through"', *Public Administration Review*, 19, pp. 78–88.

Lindblom, C.E. (1965) *The Intelligence of Democracy*, New York: Free Press.

Lindblom, C.E. (1977) *Politics and Markets*, New York: Basic Books.

Lindblom C.E. (1979) 'Still muddling, not yet through', *Public Administration Review*, 39, pp. 517–25.

Lindblom, C.E. and E.J. Woodhouse (1993) *The Policy Making Process*, Englewood Cliffs, NJ: Prentice Hall.

Ling, T. (1994) 'The new managerialism and social security', in J. Clarke, A. Cochrane and E. McLaughlin (eds), *Managing Social Policy*, London: Sage.

Lipset, S.M. (1950) *Agrarian Socialism*, Berkeley, Calif.: University of California Press.

Lipsky, M. (1980) *Street-Level Bureaucracy*, New York: Russell Sage.

Littler, C.R. (1978) 'Understanding Taylorism', *British Journal of Sociology*, 29(2), pp. 185–202.

Long, S. (1981) 'Social control in the civil law: the case of income tax enforcement', in H.L. Ross (ed.), *Law and Deviance*, Beverley Hills, Calif.: Sage.

Lowe, P. (1986) *Countryside Conflicts*, Aldershot: Gower.

Lowi, T.A. (1972) 'Four systems of policy, politics and choice', *Public Administration Review*, 32, pp. 298–310.

Lukes, S. (1974) *Power: A radical view*, London: Macmillan.

McGregor, D. (1960) *The Human Side of Enterprise*, New York: McGraw-Hill.

Macintyre, S. (1985) *Winners and Losers*, Sydney: Unwin Hyman.

McLellan, D. (1971) *The Thought of Karl Marx*, London: Macmillan.

McLennan, G. (1989) *Marxism, Pluralism and Beyond*, Cambridge: Polity Press.

MacRae, C.D. (1977) 'A political model of the business cycle', *Journal of Political Economy*, **85**, pp. 239–64.

Majone, G. and A. Wildavsky (1978) 'Implementation as evolution', in H. Freeman (ed.), *Policy Studies Review Annual*, Beverley Hills, Calif.: Sage.

March, J.G. and J.P. Olsen (1984) 'The new institutionalism: organisational factors in political life', *American Political Science Review*, **78**, pp. 734–49.

March, J.G. and J.P. Olsen (1989) *Rediscovering Institutions*, New York: Free Press.

March, J.G. and J.P. Olsen (1996) 'Institutional perspectives on political institutions', *Governance*, **9**(3), pp. 248–64.

Marris, P. and M. Rein (1967) *Dilemmas of Social Reform*, London: Routledge and Kegan Paul.

Marsh, D. and R.A.W. Rhodes (1992a) *Policy Networks in British Government*, Oxford: Oxford University Press.

Marsh, D. and R.A.W. Rhodes (1992b) *Implementing Thatcherite Policies*, Buckingham: Open University Press.

Marshall, T.H. (1963) 'Citizenship and social class', in *Sociology at the Crossroads*, London: Heinemann.

Marx, F.M. (1957) *The Administrative State*, Chicago, Ill.: University of Chicago Press.

Marx, K. (1845) 'Theses on Feuerbach', reprinted in *Marx and Engels: Selected Works*, vol. II (1958), Moscow: Foreign Languages Publishing House.

Mashaw, J.L. (1983) *Bureaucratic Justice*, New Haven, Conn.: Yale University Press.

Merelman, R.M. (1968) 'On the neo-élitist critique of community power', *American Political Science Review*, **62**, pp. 451–60.

Merton, R.K. (1957) *Social Theory and Social Structure*, Glencoe, Ill.: Free Press.

Meynaud, J. (1965) *Technocracy*, London: Faber.

Michels, R. (1915) *Political Parties*, London: Constable.

Middlemas, K. (1979) *Politics in Industrial Society*, London: André Deutsch.

Middlemas, K. (1986) *Power, Competition and the State*, Oxford: Blackwell.

Miliband, R. (1969) *The State in Capitalist Society*, London: Weidenfeld and Nicolson.

Miliband, R. (1977) *Marxism and Politics*, Oxford: Oxford University Press.

Millett, K. (1970) *Sexual Politics*, New York: Avon Books.

Mills, C.W. (1956) *The Power Elite*, New York: Oxford University Press.

Mills, C.W. (1959) *The Sociological Imagination*, New York: Oxford University Press.

Mills, C.W. (1963) 'Culture and politics', in C.W. Mills, *Power, Politics and People*, New York: Oxford University Press.

Milward, H.B. and R.A. Francisco (1983) 'Subsystem politics and corporatism in the United States', *Policy and Politics*, **11**(3), pp. 273–93.

Minzberg, H. (1983) *Power in and Around Organizations*, Englewood Cliffs, NJ: Prentice Hall.

Mishra, R. (1984) *The Welfare State in Crisis*, Brighton: Wheatsheaf.

Moe, T.M. (1980) *The Organisation of Interests*, Chicago, Ill.: University of Chicago Press.

Moran, M. and T. Prosser (eds) (1994) *Privatisation and Regulatory Change in Europe*, Buckingham: Open University Press.

Moran, M. and B. Wood (1993) *States, Regulation and the Medical Profession*, Buckingham: Open University Press.

Mosca, C. (1939) *The Ruling Class*, trans. H.D. Kahn, London: McGraw-Hill.

Mosley, P. (1984) *The Making of Economic Policy*, Brighton: Wheatsheaf.

Mountjoy, R.S. and L.J. O'Toole (1979) 'Towards a theory of policy implementation: an organisational review', *Public Administration Review*, **39**, pp. 465–76.

Moynihan, D P. (1969) *Maximum Feasible Misunderstanding*, New York: Free Press.

Musgrave, R.A. (1959) *The Theory of Public Finance*, New York: McGraw-Hill.

Nelkin, D. (ed.) (1992) *Controversy: Politics of technical decisions* (3rd edn), London: Sage.

Niskanen, W.A. (1971) *Bureaucracy and Representative Government*, New York: Aldine-Atherton.

Nixon, J. (1980) 'The importance of communication in the implementation of government policy at the local level', *Policy and Politics*, **8**(2), pp. 127–46.

Nordhaus, W. (1975) 'The political business cycle', *Review of Economic Studies*, **42**, pp. 169–90.

Nordlinger, E.A. (1981) *On the Autonomy of the Democratic State*, Cambridge, Mass.: Harvard University Press.

O'Connor, J. (1973) *The Fiscal Crisis of the State*, New York: St Martin's Press.

Offe, C. (1974) 'Structural problems of the capitalist state', in K. von Beyme (ed.), *German Political Studies*, vol. 1, London: Sage.

Offe, C. (1976) 'Political authority and class structures', in P. Connerton (ed.), *Critical Sociology*, Harmondsworth: Penguin.

Olson, M. (1965) *The Logic of Collective Action*, Cambridge, Mass.: Harvard University Press.

Olson, M. (1982) *The Rise and Decline of Nations*, New Haven, Conn.: Yale University Press.

Osborne, D. and T. Gaebler (1992) *Reinventing Government*, Reading, Mass: Addison-Wesley.

Ouchi, W.G. (1980) 'Markets, bureaucracies and clans', *Administrative Science Quarterly*, **25**, pp. 129–41.

Panitch, L. (1980) 'Recent theorisations of corporatism: reflections on a growth industry', *British Journal of Sociology*, **31**(2), pp. 159–87.

Panitch, L. (1994) 'Globalisation and the state', in R. Miliband and L. Panitch (eds), *The Socialist Register 1994*, London: Merlin.

Pareto, V. (1966) *Sociological Writings*, ed. S.E. Finer, London: Pall Mall.

Parry, N. and Parry, J. (1976) *The Rise of the Medical Profession*, London: Croom Helm.

Parsons, W. (1995) *Public Policy*, Aldershot: Edward Elgar.

Peacock, A. (ed.) (1984) *The Regulation Game*, Oxford: Blackwell.

Perrow, C. (1972) *Complex Organizations: A critical essay*, Glenview, Ill.: Scott Foresman.

Peters, B.G. (1995) *The Politics of Bureaucracy* (5th edn), White Plains, NY: Longman.

Peters, T. and R.H. Waterman (1982) *In Search of Excellence*, New York: Harper and Row.

Piore, M. and C.F. Sabel (1984) *The Second Industrial Divide*, New York: Basic Books.

Pollitt, C. (1990) *Managerialism and the Public Services*, Oxford: Blackwell.

Polsby, N.W. (1963) *Community Power and Political Theory*, New Haven, Conn.: Yale University Press.

Popper, K.R. (1966) *The Open Society and its Enemies* (5th edn), London: Routledge and Kegan Paul.

Poulantzas, N. (1973) 'The problem of the capitalist state', in J. Urry and J. Wakeford (eds), *Power in Britain*, London: Heinemann. Poulantzas' article was originally published in *New Left Review*, **58** (1969).

Power, M. (1994) *The Audit Explosion*, London: Demos.

Pressman, J. and A. Wildavsky (1973) *Implementation*, Berkeley, Calif.: University of California Press.

Prosser, T. (1981) 'The politics of discretion: aspects of discretionary power in the supplementary benefits scheme', in M. Adler and S. Asquith (eds), *Discretion and Welfare*, London: Heinemann.

Prottas, J.M. (1978) 'The power of the street-level bureaucrat in public service bureaucracies', *Urban Affairs Quarterly*, **13**(3), pp. 285–312.

Prottas, J.M. (1979) *People Processing: The street-level bureaucrat in public service bureaucracies*, Lexington, Mass.: D.C. Heath.

Pusey, M. (1991) *Economic Rationalism in Canberra*, Cambridge: Cambridge University Press.

Pye, L.W. and S. Verba (1965) *Political Culture and Political Development*, Princeton, NJ: Princeton University Press.

Reissman, L. (1949) 'The study of role conceptions in bureaucracy', *Social Forces*, **27**, pp. 305–10.

Rendell, R. and C. Ward (1989) *Undermining the Central Line: Giving government back to the people*, London: Chatto and Windus.

Rex, J. (1986) *Race and Ethnicity*, Milton Keynes: Open University Press.

Rhodes, R.A.W. (1981) *Control and Power in Central–Local Government Relations*, Farnborough: Saxon House.

Rhodes, R.A.W. (1988) *Beyond Westminster and Whitehall*, London: Unwin Hyman.

Rhodes, R.A.W. (1995) 'From prime ministerial power to core executive', in R.A.W. Rhodes and P. Dunleavy (eds), *Prime Minister, Cabinet and Core Executive*, Basingstoke: Macmillan.

Richardson, J. (ed.)(1982) *Policy Styles in Western Europe*, London: Allen and Unwin.

Richardson, J.J. and A.G. Jordan (1979) *Governing under Pressure*, Oxford: Martin Robertson.

Roethlisberger, F.J. and W.J. Dickson (1939) *Management and the Worker*, Cambridge, Mass.: Harvard University Press.

Rothstein, B. (1992) 'Labor-market institutions and working-class strength', in S. Steinmo, K. Thelen and F. Longstreth (eds), *Structuring Politics: Historical institutionalism in comparative analysis*, Cambridge: Cambridge University Press.

Sabatier, P. (1986) 'Top-down and bottom-up approaches to implementation research: a critical analysis and suggested synthesis', *Journal of Public Policy*, **6**(1), pp. 21–48.

Sabatier, P. and H. Jenkins-Smith (eds) (1993) *Policy Change and Learning: An advocacy coalition approach*, Boulder, Colo.: Westview Press.

Sabatier, P. and D. Mazmanian (1979) 'The conditions of effective implementation: a guide to accomplishing policy objectives, *Policy Analysis*, **5** (Fall), pp. 481–504.

Sabel, C.F. (1982) *Work and Politics*, Cambridge: Cambridge University Press.

Sainsbury, R. (1992) 'Administrative justice: discretion and procedure in social security decision-making', in K. Hawkins (ed.), *The Uses of Discretion*, Oxford: Clarendon Press.

Salaman, G. (1979) *Work Organisations*, London: Longman.

Salisbury, R.H. (1979) 'Why no corporatism in the United States?', in P.C. Schmitter and G. Lembruch (eds), *Trends Towards Corporatist Intermediation*, London: Sage.

Sandhu, K.S. and P. Wheatley (1990) *The Management of Success: The moulding of modern Singapore*, Boulder, Colo.: Westview Press.

Satyamurti, C. (1981) *Occupational Survival*, Oxford: Blackwell.

Saunders, P. (1981) *Social Theory and the Urban Question*, London: Hutchinson.

Schattschneider, E.E. (1960) *The Semi-Sovereign People*, New York: Holt, Rinehart and Winston.

Scheingold, S.A. (1974) *The Politics of Rights*, New Haven, Conn.: Yale University Press.

Schmitter, P. (1974) 'Still the century of corporatism?', *Review of Politics*, **36**, pp. 85–131.

Schultze, C.L. (1968) *The Politics and Economics of Public Spending*, Washington, DC: Brookings.

Schumpeter, J. (1947) *Capitalism, Socialism and Democracy* (2nd revised edn), London: Allen and Unwin.

Schwarzmantel, J. (1994) *The State in Contemporary Society*, Hemel Hempstead: Harvester Whcatshcaf.

Scott Report (1996) *Inquiry into the Export of Defence Equipment and Dual-use Goods to Iraq and Related Prosecutions*, vol. 1, House of Commons Papers 1995–96, London: HMSO.

Self, P. (1985) *Political Theories of Modern Government*, London: Allen and Unwin.

Self, P. (1993) *Government by the Market?*, Basingstoke: Macmillan.

Selznick, P. (1949) *TVA and the Grass Roots*, Berkeley, Calif.: University of California Press.

Selznick, P. (1957) *Leadership in Administration*, New York: Harper and Row.

Selznick, P. (1996) 'Institutionalism "old" and "new"', *Administrative Science Quarterly*, **41**, pp. 270–7.

Shambaugh, D. (1995) *Deng Xiaoping*, Oxford: Clarendon Press.

Sharpe, L.J. and Newton, K. (1984) *Does Politics Matter? The determinants of public policy*, Oxford: Oxford University Press.

Sieber, S. (1981) *Fatal Remedies: The ironies of social intervention*, New York: Plenum.

Simon, H.A. (1957) *Administrative Behaviour* (2nd edn), New York: Macmillan.

Skocpol, T. (1995) *Social Policy in the United States*, Princeton, NJ: Princeton University Press.

Skocpol, T. and K. Finegold (1982) 'State capacity and economic intervention in the early New Deal', *Political Science Quarterly*, **97**, pp. 255–78.

Skok, J.E. (1995) 'Policy issue networks and the public policy cycle: a structural-functional framework for public administration', *Public Administration Review*, **55**(4), pp. 325–32.

Smith, B.C. (1976) *Policy Making in British Government*, London: Martin Robertson.

Smith, B.C. (1988) *Bureaucracy and Political Power*, Brighton: Harvester.

Smith, G. (1981) 'Discretionary decision-making in social work', in M. Adler and S. Asquith (eds), *Discretion and Welfare*, London: Heinemann.

Smith, G. and D. May (1980) 'The artificial debate between rationalist and incrementalist models of decision-making', *Policy and Politics*, **8**(2), pp. 147–61.

Smith, M.J. (1993) *Pressure, Power and Policy*, Hemel Hempstead: Harvester Wheatsheaf.

Solomos, J., B. Findlay, S. Jones and P. Gilroy (1982) 'The organic crisis of British capitalism and race: the experience of the seventies', in Centre for Contemporary Cultural Studies, *The Empire Strikes Back*, London: Hutchinson.

Stephens, P. (1996) *Politics and the Pound*, London: Macmillan.

Stewart, J. and M. Clarke (1987) 'The public services orientation: issues and dilemmas', *Public Administration*, **65**, pp. 161–77.

Taylor, F.W. (1911) *The Principles of Scientific Management*, New York: Harper.

Thelen, K. and S. Steinmo (1992) 'Historical institutionalism in comparative politics', in S. Steinmo, K. Thelen and F. Longstreth (eds), *Structuring Politics: Historical institutionalism in comparative analysis*, Cambridge: Cambridge University Press.

Thompson, H. (1995) 'Joining the ERM: analysing a core executive policy disaster', in R.A.W. Rhodes and P. Dunleavy (eds), *Prime Minister, Cabinet and Core Executive*, Basingstoke: Macmillan

Thompson, J.B. (1989) 'The theory of structuration', in D. Held and J.B. Thompson (eds), *Social Theory of Modern Societies: Anthony Giddens and his critics*, Cambridge: Cambridge University Press.

Thurber, J.A. (1991) 'Dynamics of policy subsystems in American politics', in A.J. Cigler and A. Loomis (eds), *Interest Group Politics* (3rd edn), Washington, DC: Congressional Quarterly.

Titmuss, R.M. (1971) 'Welfare rights, law and discretion', *Political Quarterly*, **42**(2), pp. 113–32.

Truman, D. (1958) *The Governmental Process*, New York: Alfred Knopf.

Tullock, G. (1967) *The Politics of Bureaucracy*, New York: Public Affairs Press.

Tullock, G. (1976) *The Vote Motive*, London: Institute of Economic Affairs.

Urwick, L.F. (1943) *The Elements of Administration*, London: Pitman.

Van Meter, D. and C.E. Van Horn (1975) 'The policy implementation process: a conceptual framework', *Administration and Society*, **6**(4), pp. 445–88.

Wade, H. (1967) *Administrative Law*, Oxford: Clarendon Press.

Wallas, G. (1948) *Human Nature in Politics*, London: Constable.

Wallerstein, I. (1979) *The Capitalist World Economy*, Cambridge: Cambridge University Press.

Walsh, K. (1995) *Public Services and Market Mechanisms*, Basingstoke: Macmillan.

Walter, A. (1993) *World Power and World Money*, Hemel Hempstead: Harvester Wheatsheaf.

Weatherley, R. (1979) *Reforming Special Education: Policy implementation from state level to street level*, Cambridge, Mass.: MIT Press.

Weatherley, R. (1980) 'Implementing social programs: the view from the front line' (paper delivered at the annual meeting of the American Political Science Association, Washington, DC).

Weatherley, R. (1992) *From Entitlement to Contract: Reshaping the welfare state in Australia*, Working Paper No. 7, Administration, Compliance and Governability Program, Canberra: Australian National University.

Weatherley, R. and M. Lipsky (1977) 'Street-level bureaucrats and institutional innovation: implementing special education reform', *Harvard Educational Review*, **47**(2), pp. 171–97.

Webb, A. and G. Wistow (1982) *Whither State Welfare*, London: RIPA.

Weber, M. (1947) *The Theory of Social and Economic Organization*, trans. A.M. Henderson and T. Parsons, Glencoe, Ill.: Free Press.

Weir, M., S. Orloff and T. Skocpol (eds) (1988) *The Politics of Social Policy in the United States*, Princeton, NJ: Princeton University Press.

Westergaard, J. (1977) 'Class, inequality and "corporatism"', in A. Hunt (ed.), *Class and Class Structure*, London: Lawrence and Wishart.

Whitmore, R. (1984) 'Modelling the policy/implementation distinction', *Policy and Politics*, **12**(3), pp. 241–68.

Wilding, P. (1982) *Professional Power and Social Welfare*, London: Routledge.

Wilenski, P. (1986) *Public Power and Public Administration*, Sydney: RAIPA.

Wilensky, H.L. (1964) 'The professionalisation of everyone', *American Journal of Sociology*, **70**, pp. 137–58.

Wilensky, H.L. (1975) *The Welfare State and Equality*, Berkeley, Calif.: University of California Press.

Williamson, O. (1975) *Markets and Hierarchies*, New York: Free Press.

Williamson, O. (1985) *The Economic Institutions of Capitalism*, New York: Free Press.

Wilson, J.Q. (1973) *Political Organizations*, Beverley Hills, Calif.: Sage.

Wilson, W. (1887) 'The study of administration', *Political Science Quarterly*, **2**, pp. 197–222.

Winkler, J. (1976) 'Corporatism', *Archives Européennes de Sociologie*, XVII(1), pp. 100–36.

Wittfogel, K.A. (1963) *Oriental Despotism*, New Haven, Conn.: Yale University Press.

Wolfe, A. (1977) *The Limits of Legitimacy*, New York: Free Press.

Wolfinger, R.E. (1971) 'Nondecisions and the study of local politics', *American Political Science Review*, **65**, pp. 1063–80.

Woodward, J. (1965) *Industrial Organisation: Theory and practice*, London: Oxford University Press.

Yergin, D. (1991) *The Prize: The epic quest for oil, money and power*, London: Simon & Schuster.

Young, H. (1989) *One of Us: A biography of Mrs Thatcher*, London: Macmillan.

Young, K. (1977) 'Values in the policy process', *Policy and Politics*, **5**(2), pp. 1–22.

Zimmerman, D.H. (1971) 'The practicalities of rule use', in J.D. Douglas (ed.), *Understanding Everyday Life*, London: Routledge and Kegan Paul.

INDEX